Jack Drescher, MD
Kenneth J. Zucker, PhD
Editors

Ex-Gay Research
Analyzing the Spitzer Study and Its Relation to Science, Religion, Politics, and Culture

Pre-publication
REVIEWS,
COMMENTARIES,
EVALUATIONS . . .

"This is a must-read book for anyone who wants to understand the implications of ex-gay research on society, politics, religion, science, and culture. It is a smart book with unusual depth and knowledge and adroitly tackles one of the most controversial topics of our times. I thoroughly enjoyed reading it and highly recommend it to anyone interested in the explosive subject."

Wayne R. Besen
Author, *Anything But Straight: Unmasking the Scandals and Lies Behind the Ex-Gay Myth*

"At last, a single publication about attempts to change sexual orientation—a book that has the current research, evaluation, and commentary on one of the most decisive issues facing gay and lesbian people and the therapists working with them. The book attempts a balanced analysis—as balanced as one can be when so much pseudoscience is used by proponents of 'conversion' or 'reparative' therapy. This book is a must-have for all people concerned about and working with gay and lesbian people."

Robert Paul Cabaj, MD
Director,
San Francisco Community
Behavioral Health Services

HPP

Harrington Park Press®
An Imprint of The Haworth Press, Inc.
New York • London • Oxford

Ex-Gay Research
Analyzing the Spitzer Study and Its Relation to Science, Religion, Politics, and Culture

HARRINGTON PARK PRESS®
Titles of Related Interest

Ex-Gay Research

Analyzing the Spitzer Study and Its Relation to Science, Religion, Politics, and Culture

Jack Drescher, MD
Kenneth J. Zucker, PhD
Editors

HPP

Harrington Park Press®
An Imprint of The Haworth Press, Inc.
New York • London • Oxford

For more information on this book or to order, visit
http://www.haworthpress.com/store/product.asp?sku=5503

or call 1-800-HAWORTH (800-429-6784) in the United States and Canada
or (607) 722-5857 outside the United States and Canada

or contact orders@HaworthPress.com

Published by

Harrington Park Press®, an imprint of The Haworth Press, Inc., 10 Alice Street, Binghamton, NY
13904-1580.

PUBLISHER'S NOTE
The development, preparation, and publication of this work has been undertaken with great care.
However, the Publisher, employees, editors, and agents of The Haworth Press are not responsible
for any errors contained herein or for consequences that may ensue from use of materials or
information contained in this work. The Haworth Press is committed to the dissemination of ideas
and information according to the highest standards of intellectual freedom and the free exchange of
ideas. Statements made and opinions expressed in this publication do not necessarily reflect the
views of the Publisher, Directors, management, or staff of The Haworth Press, Inc., or an
endorsement by them.

Cover design by Marylouise E. Doyle.

Library of Congress Cataloging-in-Publication Data

Ex-gay research : analyzing the Spitzer study and its relation to science, religion, politics, and
culture / Jack Drescher, Kenneth J. Zucker, editors.
    p. cm.
    Includes bibliographical references and index.
    ISBN-13: 978-1-56023-556-9 (hard : alk. paper)
    ISBN-10: 1-56023-556-X (hard : alk. paper)
    ISBN-13: 978-1-56023-557-6 (soft : alk. paper)
    ISBN-10: 1-56023-557-8 (soft : alk. paper)
    1. Homosexuality—Treatment—Social aspects. 2. Gays—Mental health. 3. Gays—Mental
health services. 4. Psychotherapy. I. Drescher, Jack, 1951- II. Zucker, Kenneth J.

RC558.E98 2006
  362.196'8583—dc22

2005029380

CONTENTS

ABOUT THE EDITORS

Jack Drescher, MD, is a fellow and a training and supervising analyst at the William Alanson White Institute of Psychiatry, Psychoanalysis and Psychology and a clinical assistant professor of psychiatry at SUNY–Downstate. A distinguished fellow of the American Psychiatric Association, he chairs the APA's Committee on Lesbian, Gay and Bisexual Issues. Dr. Drescher is a founding member of the Committee on Sexual Minorities of the Group for the Advancement of Psychiatry (GAP) and former chair of its Committee on Human Sexuality. He is author of *Psychoanalytic Therapy and the Gay Man* (1998, The Analytic Press), co-editor, with Ariel Shidlo and Michael Schroeder, of *Sexual Conversion Therapy: Ethical, Clinical, and Research Perspectives* (2001, The Haworth Medical Press), and edits The Analytic Press's Bending Psychoanalysis book series. Dr. Drescher is in full-time private practice in New York City.

Kenneth J. Zucker, PhD, is professor of psychology and psychiatry at the University of Toronto. He is the head of the Gender Identity Service in the Child, Youth, and Family Program at the Centre for Addiction and Mental Health. He has served on the DSM-III-R, DSM-IV, and DSM-IV-TR Subcommittees on Gender Identity Disorders. He co-authored with Susan J. Bradley *Gender Identity Disorder and Psychosexual Problems in Children and Adolescents* (Guilford Press, 1995). Since 2002, he has been the editor of *Archives of Sexual Behavior* and is currently president-elect of the International Academy of Sex Research.

doi:10.1300/5503_a

CONTRIBUTORS

John Bancroft, MD, was director of the Kinsey Institute for Research in Sex, Gender, and Reproduction at Indiana University from 1995 until 2004, and has now retired to live near Oxford, England. He has been involved in various aspects of sex research throughout his career. A psychiatrist by training, he worked at the Medical Research Council's Reproductive Sciences Unit in Edinburgh, Scotland, for nearly twenty years before joining the Kinsey Institute. He is the author of *Human Sexuality and Its Problems.* From 1990 to 1995, he was editor of the *Annual Review of Sex Research* and has twice served as president of the International Academy of Sex Research.

A. Lee Beckstead, PhD, is a psychologist working full-time in private practice in Salt Lake City, Utah. His research and clinical interests have focused on understanding how to resolve sexual, social, and religious conflicts.

Wayne Besen is the author of *Anything But Straight: Unmasking the Scandals and Lies Behind the Ex-Gay Myth.* He is a former spokesperson for the Human Rights Campaign, America's largest GLBT advocacy group. He has appeared in media such as *USA Today, The Washington Post, Rolling Stone, CNN, NBC Nightly News,* and Fox's *The O'Reilly Factor.*

A. Dean Byrd, PhD, MBA, MPH, is president of Thrasher Research Fund and clinical professor at the University of Utah School of Medicine, with appointments in the Department of Family and Preventive Medicine and in the Department of Psychiatry. He also has an adjunct appointment in the Department of Family and Consumer Studies at the University of Utah.

Helena M. Carlson, PhD, is professor emerita of Psychology at Lewis and Clark College in Portland, Oregon. A fellow of the Society for the Psychological Study of Social Issues and of the American Psychological Association, her past research is cross-cultural and di-

doi:10.1300/5503_b

verse, covering such groups as police, women, blacks, gays, the un-
employed, Irish nomadic people (the Travellers), sexual victimization, Northern Ireland police, and the homeless. The common theme
running through this research centers on her interest in the social control of deviancy.

Kenneth M. Cohen, PhD, is a licensed clinical psychologist working at Cornell University's Counseling and Psychological Services in
Ithaca, New York. He provides individual and group psychotherapy,
specializing in lesbian, gay, and bisexual issues. Dr. Cohen is a lecturer in Cornell's Feminist, Gender, and Sexuality Studies program
for which he teaches the course Gender and Sexual Minorities. He
co-authored the textbook, *The Lives of Lesbians, Gays, and Bisexuals*
(Harcourt Brace) and writes about gay youth development and the
etiology of sexual orientation.

Lisa M. Diamond, PhD, is assistant professor of psychology and
gender studies at the University of Utah. Her research focuses on the
nature and development of same-sex sexuality and affectional bonding. She has been particularly interested in the longitudinal course of
sexual identity development and in the multiple environmental and
psychosocial factors that influence the emergence and expression of
sexual and affectional feelings for same-sex and other-sex partners at
different stages of life. Dr. Diamond also studies how attachment relationships help adolescents and adults regulate negative emotions
and physiological stress, and whether romantic relationships are
uniquely beneficial in this regard. Dr. Diamond's research has been
supported by grants from the National Institute of Mental Health
(NIMH), the John Templeton Foundation, the Society for the Psychological Study of Social Issues, and the William T. Grant Foundation.

Jeannie D. DiClementi, PsyD, is assistant professor in the Department of Psychology at Indiana University–Purdue University Fort
Wayne, and is currently a regional trainer for the American Psychological Association's HIV Office for Psychology Education (HOPE),
a member of the Purdue University Institutional Review Board, and
advisory board member of the Behavioral Health and Family Studies
Institute in northeast Indiana.

Richard C. Friedman, MD, is clinical professor of psychiatry at
Weill Medical School, Cornell University, and an attending psychia-
trist at Payne Whitney Psychiatric Clinic, New York Presbyterian
Hospital. He has published widely in the area of sexual orientation

and has edited four books. He is the author of *Male Homosexuality: A Contemporary Psychoanalytic Perspective* and co-author with Jennifer I. Downey of *Sexual Orientation and Psychoanalysis: Sexual Science and Clinical Practice.*

John H. Gagnon, PhD, is Distinguished Professor of Sociology Emeritus at the State University of New York at Stony Brook. He is the author or co-author of *Sex Offenders: An Analysis of Types, Sexual Conduct, Human Sexualities, The Social Organization of Sexuality: Sexual Practices in the United States,* and *Sex in America.* A recent volume of essays was published titled *An Interpretation of Desire.* These days he lives in Nice, France.

Lawrence Hartmann, MD, practices child, adolescent, and adult psychiatry in Cambridge, Massachusetts, and has taught at Harvard Medical School for thirty-five years. He is past president of the American Psychiatric Association.

Gregory M. Herek, PhD, is professor of psychology at the University of California–Davis. He has published more than eighty scholarly articles on prejudice against lesbians and gay men, antigay violence, AIDS-related stigma, and related topics. A fellow of the American Psychological Association (APA) and the American Psychological Society, he received the 1996 APA Award for Distinguished Contributions to Psychology in the Public Interest. He has provided congressional testimony at hearings on antigay violence and on military personnel policy and has assisted the APA in preparing amicus briefs for numerous court cases related to sexual orientation. He is currently writing a book on sexual prejudice.

Scott L. Hershberger, PhD, is professor of psychology at the California State University–Long Beach. He has published more than eighty scientific papers concerned with such topics as psychometric theory, multivariate analysis, behavior genetics, and sexual behavior. He is the co-author of *Multivariate Statistical Methods,* and co-editor of *Modeling Intraindividual Variability with Repeated Measures Data* and *The New Rules of Measurement.* He is also a fellow of the Royal Statistical Society; is a member of the International Academy of Sex Research, the International Statistical Institute, and the Society for Multivariate Experimental Psychology; and sits on the editorial board of three journals.

Craig A. Hill, PhD, is associate professor of psychology at Indiana University–Purdue University Fort Wayne. His areas of research include dispositional sexual motivation, sexual coercion, and romantic relationships and sexuality.

Donald F. Klein, MD, is professor of psychiatry at the College of Physicians and Surgeons of Columbia University, attending psychiatrist at New York Presbyterian Hospital, and director of Psychiatric Research and of the Department of Therapeutics at New York State Psychiatric Institute. In the 1960s, he discovered the antipanic effectiveness of imipramine. His scientific work has been in the evaluation of psychiatric therapies, both psychotherapeutic and pharmacotherapeutic. He served on the DSM-III Task Force for Nomenclature and Statistics, which resulted in the publication of the DSM-III.

Richard B. Krueger, MD, is a psychiatrist and medical director of the Sexual Behavior Clinic at New York State Psychiatric Institute. He is an associate clinical professor of psychiatry in the Department of Psychiatry, Columbia University, College of Physicians and Surgeons. He consults on sex offenders for the New York State Office of Mental Health, and his research interests include the psychopharmacological treatment of compulsive and aggressive sexual behavior.

Sean Lund is national news media coordinator for the Gay and Lesbian Alliance Against Defamation (GLAAD).

Nathaniel McConaghy, DSc, began studying psychiatry in Melbourne in 1951 and continued the study in Vancouver and London. He was associate professor in the School of Psychiatry, University of New South Wales, Australia, from 1970 until retirement in 1992. During that time, his major research was into the use of penile volume plethysmography, sexual orientation, cognitive behavioral therapy, compulsive behavior, and cognitive aspects of schizophrenia. He was awarded the degree of doctor of science in 1990. Following retirement, he treated patients with sexual disorders until the end of 2003. He continues to work as a member of the New South Wales Mental Health Review Tribunal.

Joseph Nicolosi, PhD, is a graduate of the New School for Social Research in New York and the California School of Professional Psychology in Los Angeles. He is licensed as a psychologist in California. He is the founder and director of the Thomas Aquinas Psychological Clinic in Encino, California, and specializes in the treatment of homosexual men who are dissatisfied with their sexual orientation. Dr. Nicolosi is president and principal research investigator of the National Association for Research and Therapy of Homosexuality

(NARTH), the only U.S. professional group organized to protect the right of homosexual patients to receive treatment to modify unwanted attractions. Dr. Nicolosi is the author of *Reparative Therapy of Male Homosexuality* and *Healing Homosexuality: Case Stories of Reparative Therapy,* and co-author with Linda Ames Nicolosi of *A Parent's Guide to Preventing Homosexuality.*

Jussi Nissinen, MSc, is a psychotherapist and is secretary general of the Finnish Organization for Sexual Equality (SETA), a board member of the Finnish Organization for Lesbian, Gay and Bisexual Professionals within Health Care and Social Work (STEAM), and co-editor of *FinnQueer* Web magazine (www.finnqueer.net).

Drew Rendall, PhD, is associate professor in the Department of Psychology and Neuroscience at the University of Lethbridge, Lethbridge, Alberta, Canada. His interests are in the form, function, and evolution of natural patterns of social behavior, communication, and cognition. He does comparative research on baboons in South Africa, on humans in contemporary Western cultures, and on a variety of small mammals and birds.

Cathy Renna was formerly the news media director for the Gay and Lesbian Alliance Against Defamation (GLAAD). She is presently the director of media relations for Fenton Communications.

Bruce Rind, PhD, is adjunct professor in the Department of Psychology at Temple University. He is a social psychologist, teaching psychology and statistics and researching in the areas of persuasion compliance and human sexuality.

Paula C. Rodríguez Rust, PhD, is a sociologist and survey researcher specializing in the study of sexual identity and its correlation with sexual behaviors and attractions. She has published two books, including *Bisexuality in the United States: A Social Science Reader,* and conducted the International Bisexual Identities, Communities, Ideologies, and Politics (IBICIP) study. She is a scholar-in-residence at Hamilton College and lives in New Jersey.

Theodorus G. M. Sandfort, PhD, is associate professor at the HIV Center at the New York State Psychiatric Institute and the Department of Sociomedical Sciences of the Mailman School of Public Health at Columbia University. His research interests center around sexual health, homosexuality, and sexual development. He was president of the Dutch Society for Sexology and of the International Academy of Sex Research.

Ritch C. Savin-Williams, PhD, is professor of clinical and developmental psychology and chair of the Department of Human Development at Cornell University. Dr. Savin-Williams has written seven books on adolescent development. The latest, tentatively titled *The "New" Gay Teen: Post-Gay and Gayishness Among Contemporary Teenagers,* is in press. Dr. Savin-Williams is also a licensed clinical psychologist with a private practice specializing in identity, relationship, and family issues among young adults. He has served as an expert witness on same-sex marriage, gay adoption, and Boy Scout court cases and is on numerous professional review boards. Dr. Savin-Williams received the 2001 Award for Distinguished Scientific Contribution from Division 44 (The Society for the Psychological Study of Lesbian, Gay, and Bisexual Concerns) of the American Psychological Association. He has written a junior high school curriculum for the Unitarian Universalist Association, *Beyond Pink and Blue: Exploring Our Stereotypes of Sexuality and Gender.*

Charles Silverstein, PhD, made a presentation before the American Psychiatric Association's Committee on Nomenclature that ultimately led to the 1973 removal of homosexuality as a psychiatric disorder from the DSM. He is currently a clinical instructor at New York University Medical School and a supervisor of therapists at the Institute for Human Identity. He is the author of six books, including *The Joy of Gay Sex* and *Gays, Lesbians and Their Therapists: Studies in Psychotherapy.*

Robert L. Spitzer, MD, is professor of psychiatry at Columbia University and is chief of the Biometrics Research Department at the New York State Psychiatric Institute. In 1974, the American Psychiatric Association appointed Dr. Spitzer to chair its Task Force on Nomenclature and Statistics, and in this capacity he assumed the leadership role in the development of DSM-III, published in 1980, which became the authoritative classification of mental disorders for the mental health professions. In 1983, Dr. Spitzer was appointed to chair the American Psychiatric Association's Work Group to Revise DSM-III and coordinated that effort, resulting in the publication of DSM-III-R in 1987. He was active in the development of DSM-IV, which was published in 1994, as special advisor to the American Psychiatric Association's Task Force on DSM-IV. In 1994, Dr. Spitzer received the American Psychiatric Association's award for psychiatric research for his contributions to psychiatric assessment and diagnosis. In 2000, he was the Thomas William Salmon Medal recipient from the New York Academy of Medicine. He has pioneered the development of several widely used diagnostic assessment procedures, including the Research Diagnostic Criteria, the Schedule for Affective Disorders and Schizophrenia (SADS), and the Structured Clinical Interview for DSM-IV (SCID).

Olli Stålström, PhD, is former lecturer of sociology at the University of Kuopio, Finland. He is a board member of the Finnish Organization for Lesbian, Gay and Bisexual Professionals within Health Care and Social Work (STEAM) and co-editor of *FinnQueer* Web magazine (www.finqueer.net).

Donald S. Strassberg, PhD, is professor in the Department of Psychology, University of Utah, where he has been a faculty member for twenty-eight years. His primary areas of research are human sexual function, dysfunction, and deviation. He currently serves on the editorial boards of *Archives of Sexual Behavior, Journal of Sex and Marital Therapy,* and *Sexual Abuse: A Journal of Research and Treatment.* He maintains a part-time private practice as a clinical psychologist, specializing in sexual and other relationship problems, and is Diplomate in Clinical Psychology (American Board of Professional Psychology) and fellow of the Albert Ellis Institute.

Marcus C. Tye, PhD, is associate professor of psychology at Dowling College in Oakdale, New York, and a clinical psychologist whose research interests and clinical work have included privileged communication in psychotherapy, fair custody evaluations with LGBT parents, and credibility assessment.

Paul L. Vasey, PhD, is assistant professor in the Deparment of Psychology and Neuroscience at the University of Lethbridge, Lethbridge, Alberta. He studies the development and evolution of female homosexual behavior in free-ranging Japanese macaques at Arashiyama, Japan. He also conducts research in Western Samoa on the development and well-being of transgendered males known as fa'afafine.

Milton L. Wainberg, MD, is assistant professor of clinical psychiatry at Columbia University and adjunct assistant professor at the Mount Sinai School of Medicine in New York. He is currently the director of medical education of the Columbia University HIV Mental Health Training Project at the New York State Psychiatric Institute. He has been working in clinical as well as academic and research activities in sexuality, homosexuality, HIV, and substance abuse care and prevention for thirteen years in the United States and internationally. He has a National Institute of Mental Health (NIMH) funded grant to develop an HIV-prevention intervention for psychiatric patients in Brazil. He has collaborated in similar activities in South Africa. He is involved in other national-HIV prevention studies funded by National Institute on Alcohol Abuse and Alcoholism (NIAAA), National Institute on Drug Abuse (NIDA), and Centers for Disease Control (CDC). He is a member of the Committee on AIDS of the American Psychiatric Association and serves as the chair of the Health Work Group of the New York City HIV Planning Council.

Jerome C. Wakefield, DSW, PhD, is university professor and professor in the School of Social Work at New York University and lecturer in Psychiatry at Columbia University College of Physicians and Surgeons. He is also an affiliate faculty at the Institute for Health, Health Care Policy, and Aging Research and the Center for Cognitive Science, both at Rutgers. He is the author of more than 100 publications focusing on the conceptual foundations of the mental health professions, especially the concept of mental disorder and the validity of diagnostic criteria.

Roger L. Worthington, PhD, is associate professor in the Department of Educational, School, and Counseling Psychology and faculty diversity fellow in the Office of the Vice Provost for Minority Affairs, International Programs, and Faculty Development at the University of Missouri–Columbia. He is the author of numerous articles and chapters on sexual identity and LGB issues and the recipient of awards for teaching and advocacy. His research, teaching, consultation, and practice interests focus broadly on underserved and underrepresented groups, with particular emphasis on issues of sexual identity, LGB affirmativeness, multicultural counseling competencies, vocational psychology, ethics, training, and supervision. He has served on the editorial boards of the *Journal of Counseling Psychology* and *The Counseling Psychologist* and served as a guest co-editor of a special issue of *Career Development Quarterly.*

Mark A. Yarhouse, PsyD, is a licensed clinical psychologist and associate professor of psychology at Regent University in Virginia Beach, Virginia. He is director of the Institute for the Study of Sexual Identity and co-author of the book *Sexual Identity Synthesis: Attributions, Meaning-Making, and the Search for Congruence.*

Preface

This volume is a collection of articles and essays originally published in *Archives of Sexual Behavior,* Volume 32, Number 5, 2003 (edited by Ken Zucker) and the *Journal of Gay & Lesbian Psychotherapy,* Volume 7, Number 3, 2003 (edited by Jack Drescher).* The central focus of both journal issues was Robert Spitzer's (2003) "ex-gay study," first presented at the American Psychiatric Association (APA) meeting in New Orleans in May 2001 and later published in *Archives* (reprinted in this volume).

One impetus for Dr. Spitzer's decision to do the study was the 2000 position statement of the American Psychiatric Association cautioning *against* clinical efforts to change same-sex attractions (APA, 2000, and also reprinted in this volume). Citing a paucity of definitive research, the APA position paper called for further study into the risks and benefits of sexual-conversion therapies. Spitzer's response was to ask and try to answer a narrow, scientific question: Is changing one's sexual orientation at all possible? As the essays in this collection reveal, significant disagreement exists on how to interpret his study's methods as well as its findings.

Due to wider cultural debates about homosexuality, the ongoing interest in this study continues beyond the predictable groups of sexology scholars and clinical practitioners. For example, the 2001 APA presentation of the study by Dr. Spitzer was widely taken up by the international media (Lund and Renna, 2003, and reprinted in this volume) and by politicians in the United States and abroad (Stålström and Nissinen, 2003, and reprinted in this volume). Consequently, collecting these essays in one volume will increase the study's access to a general audience. Finally, given the "spin" surrounding the relative merits and deficiencies of the study, placing this study in its wider

---

*Some changes to the original text include updating source references and altering chapter cross-references to conform with the layout of this publication; any such changes are indicated using brackets.

doi:10.1300/5503_c

context—scientific, religious, political, and cultural—might help interested readers reach their own conclusions.

REFERENCES

American Psychiatric Association (2000), Commission on Psychotherapy by Psychiatrists (COPP): Position statement on therapies focused on attempts to change sexual orientation (reparative or conversion therapies). *American J. Psychiatry,* 157:1719-1721.

Lund, S. and Renna, C. (2003), An analysis of the media response to the Spitzer study. *J. Gay & Lesbian Psychotherapy,* 7(3):55-67.

Spitzer, R. L. (2003), Can some gay men and lesbians change their sexual orientation? 200 participants reporting a change from homosexual to heterosexual orientation. *Archives Sexual Behavior,* 32(5):403-417.

Stålström, O. and Nissinen, J. (2003), The Spitzer study and the Finnish parliament. *J. Gay & Lesbian Psychotherapy,* 7(3):83-95.

Section I:
Editors' Introduction

The Politics and Science
of "Reparative Therapy"

Kenneth J. Zucker

It is now 30 years since the American Psychiatric Association deleted homosexuality per se as a mental disorder from the second edition of the *Diagnostic and Statistical Manual of Mental Disorders* (American Psychiatric Association, 1968), and the history of this remarkable transformative event has been well-described elsewhere (Bayer, 1981; Bayer and Spitzer, 1982; Spitzer, 1981; see also Nakajima, 2003). Prior to this diagnostic migration from abnormality to normality, the literature was replete with various treatment approaches designed to alter a person's same-sex sexual orientation. Although the DSM-III (American Psychiatric Association, 1980) contained the diagnosis of Ego-Dystonic Homosexuality (which was subsequently deleted from the DSM-III-R) (American Psychiatric Association, 1987), reports of sexual orientation change treatments began to wane (see, e.g., Adams and Sturgis, 1977; Byrd and Nicolosi, 2002; MacIntosh, 1994) and gradually replaced by various therapeutic approaches designed to be more "affirmative" in helping an individual adapt to a same-sex sexual orientation and to address an array of identified unique needs of gay and lesbian clients (e.g., Bernstein and Miller, 1996; Cabaj and Stein, 1996;Campos and Goldfried, 2001; Chernin and Johnson, 2003; Cohler and Galatzer-Levy, 2000; Division 44/Committee on Lesbian, Gay, and Bisexual Concerns Joint Task Force on Guidelines for Psychotherapy with

This chapter appeared originally as "Editorial: The Politics and Science of 'Reparative Therapy'" in *Archives of Sexual Behavior* 32(5):399-402. Copyright 2003 Kluwer Academic/Plenum Publishers. Reprinted with permission.

Lesbian, Gay, and Bisexual Clients, 2000; Drescher, 1998; Friedman, 1988; Friedman and Downey, 1999, 2002; Galatzer-Levy, 2001; Garnets, Hancock, Cochran, Goodchilds, and Peplau, 1991; Isay, 1997; Lewes, 1988; Magee and Miller, 1997; Paul, Barrett, Crosby, and Stall, 1996; Perez, DeBord, and Bieschke, 2000; Phillips, Bartlett, and King, 2001; Ritter and Terndrup, 2002; Roughton, 2001; Ruiz, Lile, and Matorin, 2002; Winer, Anderson, Cohler, and Shelby, 2002).

Although it is well-known that not all mental health professionals agreed with the decision to remove homosexuality from the DSM (see, e.g., Nicolosi, Byrd, and Potts, 2000a), it is clear that only a small minority of contemporary practitioners still regard homosexuality per se as pathological. Matters of diagnostics aside, it is also clear that, similar to their heterosexual counterparts, gays and lesbians seek out therapy for all kinds of reasons (Jones and Gabriel, 1999). Indeed, even one scholarly journal, *Journal of Gay & Lesbian Psychotherapy*, is devoted specifically to gay and lesbian therapeutics.

In the early 1990s, a "movement" of clinical dissenters appeared on the scene. They argued that some clients with a homosexual sexual orientation wished, for various reasons, to change their sexual orientation and it was argued, also for various reasons, that this desire should not only be respected, but treated. Led by Socarides, a psychoanalyst who, it is well-known, always disagreed with the decision to remove homosexuality from the DSM (see, e.g., Socarides, 1995), and Nicolosi, a psychologist, the dissenters have described a technique known as "reparative therapy" to treat both gay men and lesbians (e.g., Nicolosi, 1991; Socarides and Kaufman, 1994). An organization, the National Association for Research and Therapy of Homosexuality (NARTH), was founded in 1992, and it has a newsletter, the *NARTH Bulletin,* a Web site, and an annual conference. For readers interested in learning about the intellectual and ideological positions of NARTH, a subscription to the *NARTH Bulletin* is worth the few dollars it costs.

Of course, the concept of "change" in itself is a complex parameter. Interestingly enough, the question of sexual orientation change has, over the past couple of decades, been approached from two theoretical and ideological camps that are as far apart as one can imagine. On the one hand is the reparative therapy movement, which is both politically and ideologically conservative and "rightist." On the other hand is the social constructionist movement, which is both politically and ideologically liberal and "leftist," and the constructionists, just as the reparativists, have often argued that sexual orientation is more fluid than it is fixed (see, e.g., Bem, 1995; Brookey, 2002; Epstein, 1991; Kauth, 2000; Kitzinger and Wilkinson, 1995; Kitzinger, Wilkinson, and Perkins, 1992; Peplau, Spalding, Conley, and Veniegas, 1999; Richardson and Seidman, 2002; Rothblum, 2000; Stein, 1999; Weeks, 1985, 1995, 2000; Young-Bruehl, 2001). At times, there really is something to the expression that science and politics make strange bedfellows!

Not surprisingly, the discourse between NARTH and its critics has been extremely heated. The rhetoric about reparative therapy has far exceeded any empirical evidence about its effectiveness and efficacy, or lack thereof, and has largely focused on ethics and sexual politics (Brookey, 2000; Davison, 1978, 2001; Drescher, 2002; Green, 2003; Haldeman, 1991, 1994; Halpert, 2000; Hicks, 1999; Kemena, 2000; Murphy, 1991, 1992a, 1992b, 1997; Rosik, 2003; Saunes, 2002; Selle, 2003; Shidlo, Schroeder, and Drescher, 2001; Silverstein, 1977; Sturgis and Adams, 1978; Tozer and McLanahan, 1999). As this debate moved into formal resolutions by professional organizations critiquing "reparative therapy" (American Psychiatric Association, 1998, 2000; American Psychological Association, 1998), it is rather disconcerting, from a (narrow) empirical perspective, that so little information is available about the outcome of this form of treatment. Such resolutions raise complex ethical issues in their own right, including matters of individual autonomy in arranging a "contractual" agreement between client and therapist (see, e.g., Szasz, 1965).

Of course, the absence of empirical information is all too common for many psychological treatments for many "problems in living" and/or disorders (see, e.g., Heiman and Meston's [1997] thoughtful appraisal of the psychological treatment literature on sexual dysfunctions). In this respect, the absence of such data for "reparative therapy" is not that surprising (indeed, one might also note that, despite the multiplicity of published works on affirmative psychotherapies for gays and lesbians, they, too, lack any clear empirical foundation, at least if one uses standard guidelines for empirically validated treatments (see, e.g., American Psychological Association, 1995; Streiner, 2002).

It is really only in the last couple of years that we are beginning to see the semblance of some research about who exactly are the types of clients who seek out this form of treatment and some data on out-come (Beckstead, 1999, 2001; Beckstead and Morrow, 2003; Nico-losi, Byrd, and Potts, 2000b; Shidlo and Schroeder, 2002). From a scientific standpoint, however, the empirical database remains rather primitive, and any decisive claim about benefits or harms really must be taken with a rather substantial grain of salt. Without such data it is difficult to understand how professional societies can issue any clear statement that is not contaminated by rhetorical fervor. Sexual science should encourage the establishment of a methodologically sound data-base from which more reasoned and nuanced conclusions might be drawn.

[The] issue of *Archives of Sexual Behavior* [in which many of the book's chapters were published] contain[ed] an invited target article by Spitzer that examined a sample of 200 reparative therapy clients who sought treatment to change their sexual orientation. Because of the nature of the study, the [journal's] editor was of the view that it should be published only with the opportunity for detailed peer com-mentary, along with a reply by the author. Accordingly, after the arti-cle went through several revisions, a call was issued for commentar-ies with announcements sent to four electronic list serves: SEXNET, an Internet research discussion group (sexnet@listserv.acns.nwu.edu), the International Academy of Sex Research (www.iasr.org), the Society for Sex Therapy and Research (sstargazemaurice@interchange.ubc.ca), and Division 44 (div44@lists.apa.org) of the American Psy-chological Association. Of approximately 40 individuals who ex-pressed an interest in writing a commentary, 26 commentaries were received and these immediately follow the target article, followed by a reply from Spitzer.

It [was] the editor's view that a scholarly journal is a legitimate fo-rum to address controversial scientific and ethical issues rather than leaving the complexity of the attendant discourse to "the street."

REFERENCES

Adams, H.E. & Sturgis, E.T. (1977), Status of behavioral reorientation techniques in the modification of homosexuality: A review. *Psychological Bulletin*, 84: 1171-1188.

American Psychiatric Association (1968), *Diagnostic and Statistical Manual of Mental Disorders*, 2nd edition. Washington, DC: American Psychiatric Press.

American Psychiatric Association (1980), *Diagnostic and Statistical Manual of Mental Disorders*, 3rd edition. Washington, DC: American Psychiatric Press.

American Psychiatric Association (1987), *Diagnostic and Statistical Manual of Mental Disorders*, 3rd edition–Revised. Washington, DC: American Psychiatric Press.

American Psychiatric Association (1998), Position statement on psychiatric treatment and sexual orientation. *Amer. J. Psychiat.*, 156:1131.

American Psychiatric Association (2000), Commission on Psychotherapy by Psychiatrists (COPP): Position statement on therapies focused on attempts to change sexual orientation (Reparative or conversion therapies). *Amer. J. Psychiat.*, 157:1719-1721.

American Psychological Association (1995), Training in and dissemination of empirically-validated psychological treatments: Report and recommendations. *The Clinical Psychologist*, 48:3-24.

American Psychological Association (1998), Proceedings of the American Psychological Association, Incorporated, for the Legislative Year 1997. Minutes of the annual meeting of the Council of Representatives August 14 and 17, 1997, Chicago, IL, and Minutes of the June, August, and December 1997 meetings of the Board of Directors. *American Psychologist*, 53:882-939.

Bayer, R. (1981), *Homosexuality and American Psychiatry: The Politics of Diagnosis*. New York: Basic Books.

Bayer, R. & Spitzer, R.L. (1982), Edited correspondence on the status of homosexuality in DSM-III. *J. History of the Behavioral Sciences*, 18:32-52.

Beckstead, A.L. (1999), "Gay is not me": Seeking congruence through sexual reorientation therapy. Unpublished master's thesis, University of Utah, Salt Lake City, UT.

Beckstead, A.L. (2001), The process toward self-acceptance and self identity of individuals who underwent sexual reorientation therapy. Unpublished doctoral dissertation, University of Utah, Salt Lake City, UT.

Beckstead, A.L. & Morrow, S.L. (2003), Clients' experiences of conversion therapy: The need for a new treatment model. Manuscript submitted for publication.

Bem, S.L. (1995), Dismantling gender polarization and compulsory heterosexuality: Should we turn the volume up or down? *J. Sex Research*, 32:329-334.

Bernstein, G.S. & Miller, M.E. (1996), Behavior therapy with lesbian and gay individuals. *Progress in Behavior Modification*, 30:123-136.

Brookey, R.A. (2000), Saints or sinners: Sociobiological theories of male homosexuality. *International J. Sexuality & Gender Studies*, 5:37-58.

Brookey, R.A. (2002), *Reinventing the Male Homosexual: The Rhetoric and Power of the Gay Gene*. Bloomington: Indiana University Press.

Byrd, A.D. & Nicolosi, J. (2002), A meta-analytic review of treatment of homosexuality. *Psychological Reports*, 90:1139-1152.

Cabaj, R.P. & Stein, T.S., eds. (1996), *Textbook of Homosexuality and Mental Health*. Washington, DC: American Psychiatric Press.

Campos, P.E. & Goldfried, M.R. (2001), Introduction: Perspectives on therapy with gay, lesbian, and bisexual clients. *J. Clinical Psychology*, 57:609-613.

Chernin, J.N. & Johnson, M.R. (2003), *Affirmative Psychotherapy and Counseling for Lesbians and Gay Men*. Thousand Oaks, CA: Sage.

Cohler, B.J. & Galatzer-Levy, R.M. (2000), *The Course of Gay and Lesbian Lives: Social and Psychoanalytic Perspectives*. Chicago: University of Chicago Press.

Davison, G.C. (1978), Not can but ought: The treatment of homosexuality. *J. Consulting & Clinical Psychology*, 46:170-172.

Davison, G.C. (2001), Conceptual and ethical issues in therapy for the psychological problems of gay men, lesbians, and bisexuals. *J. Clinical Psychology*, 57:695-704.

Division 44/Committee on Lesbian, Gay, and Bisexual Concerns Joint Task Force on Guidelines for Psychotherapy With Lesbian, Gay, and Bisexual Clients (2000), Guidelines for psychotherapy with lesbian, gay, and bisexual clients. *American Psychologist*, 55:1440-1451.

Drescher, J. (1998), *Psychoanalytic Therapy and the Gay Man*. Hillsdale, NJ: The Analytic Press.

Drescher, J. (2002), Ethical issues in treating gay and lesbian patients. *Psychiatric Clinics of North America*, 25(3):605-621.

Epstein, S. (1991), Sexuality and identity: The contribution of object relations theory to a constructionist sociology. *Theory & Society*, 20:825-873.

Friedman, R.C. (1988), *Male Homosexuality: A Contemporary Psychoanalytic Perspective*. New Haven, CT: Yale University Press.

Friedman, R.C. & Downey, J.I. (1999), Internalized homophobia and gender-valued self-esteem in the psychoanalysis of gay patients. *Psychoanalytic Review*, 86:325-347.

Friedman, R.C. & Downey, J.I. (2002), *Sexual Orientation and Psychoanalysis: Sexual Science and Clinical Practice*. New York: Columbia University Press.

Galatzer-Levy, R.M. (2001), Finding our way in perplexity: The meanings of sex in the analysis of a gay man. *J. American Psychoanalytic Association*, 49:1219-1234.

Garnets, L., Hancock, K.A., Cochran, S.D., Goodchilds, J., & Peplau, L.A. (1991), Issues in psychotherapy with lesbians and gay men. *American Psychologist*, 46:964-972.

Green, R.-J. (2003), When therapists do not want their clients to be homosexual: A response to Rosik's article. *J. Marital & Family Therapy*, 29:29-38.

Haldeman, D. (1991), Sexual orientation conversion therapy for gay men and lesbians: A scientific examination. In: *Homosexuality: Research Implications for Public Policy*, eds. J.C. Gonsiorek & J.D. Weinrich. Newbury Park, CA: Sage Publications, pp. 149-161.

Haldeman, D. (1994), The practice and ethics of sexual orientation conversion therapy. *J. Consulting & Clinical Psychology,* 62(2):221-227.

Halpert, S.C. (2000), "If it ain't broke, don't fix it": Ethical considerations regarding conversion therapies. *International J. Sexuality & Gender Studies,* 5:19-35.

Heiman, J.R. & Meston, C.M. (1997), Empirically validated treatment for sexual dysfunction. *Annual Review of Sex Research,* 8:148-194.

Hicks, K. (1999), Reparative therapy: Whether parental attempts to change a child's sexual orientation can legally constitute child abuse. *American University Law Review,* 49:505-547.

Isay, R. (1996), *Becoming Gay: The Journey to Self-Acceptance.* New York: Pantheon.

Jones, M.A. & Gabriel, M.A. (1999), Utilization of psychotherapy by lesbians, gay men, and bisexuals: Findings from a nationwide survey. *American J. Orthopsychiatry,* 69:209-219.

Kauth, M.R. (2000), *True Nature: A Theory of Sexual Attraction.* New York: Kluwer Academic/Plenum.

Kemena, B. (2000), Changing homosexual orientation? Considering the evolving activities of change programs in the United States. *J. Gay & Lesbian Medical Association,* 4:85-93.

Kitzinger, C. & Wilkinson, S. (1995), Transitions from heterosexuality to lesbianism: The discursive production of lesbian identities. *Developmental Psychology,* 31:95-104.

Kitzinger, C., Wilkinson, S., & Perkins, R. (1992), Theorizing heterosexuality. *Feminism & Psychology,* 2:293-324.

Lewes, K. (1988), *The Psychoanalytic Theory of Male Homosexuality.* New York: Simon and Schuster.

MacIntosh, H. (1994), Attitudes and experiences of psychoanalysts in analyzing homosexual patients. *J. American Psychoanalytic Association,* 42:1183-1207.

Magee, M. & Miller, D. (1997), *Lesbian Lives: Psychoanalytic Narratives Old and New.* Hillsdale, NJ: The Analytic Press.

Murphy, T.F. (1991), The ethics of conversion therapy. *Bioethics,* 5:123-138.

Murphy, T.F. (1992a), Freud and sexual reorientation therapy. *J. Homosexuality,* 23(3):21-38.

Murphy, T.F. (1992b), Redirecting sexual orientation: Techniques and justifications. *J. Sex Research,* 29:501-523.

Murphy, T.F. (1997), *Gay Science: The Ethics of Sexual Orientation Research.* New York: Columbia University Press.

Nakajima, G.A. (2003), The emergence of an international lesbian, gay, and bisexual psychiatric movement. *J. Gay & Lesbian Psychotherapy,* 7(1/2):165-188. Reprinted in: *The Mental Health Professions and Homosexuality: International Perspectives,* eds. V. Lingiardi & J. Drescher. Binghamton, NY: The Haworth Press, pp. 165-188.

Nicolosi, J. (1991), *Reparative Therapy of Male Homosexuality: A New Clinical Approach.* Northvale, NJ: Aronson.

Nicolosi, J., Byrd, A.D., & Potts, R.W. (2000a), Beliefs and practices of therapists who practice sexual reorientation psychotherapy. *Psychological Reports,* 86: 689-702.

Nicolosi, J., Byrd, A.D., & Potts, R.W. (2000b), Retrospective self reports of changes in homosexual orientation: A consumer survey of conversion therapy clients. *Psychological Reports,* 86:1071-1088.

Paul, J.P., Barrett, D.C., Crosby, G.M., & Stall, R.D. (1996), Longitudinal changes in alcohol and drug use among men seen at a gay-specific substance abuse treatment agency. *J. Studies on Alcohol,* 57:475-485.

Peplau, L.A., Spalding, L.R., Conley, T.D., & Veniegas, R.C. (1999), The development of sexual orientation in women. *Annual Review of Sex Research,* 10:70-99.

Perez, R.M., DeBord, K.A., & Bieschke, K.J., eds. (2000), *Handbook of Counseling and Psychotherapy with Lesbian, Gay, and Bisexual Clients.* Washington, DC: American Psychological Association.

Phillips, P., Bartlett, A., & King, M. (2001), Psychotherapists' approaches to gay and lesbian patients/clients: A qualitative study. *British J. Medical Psychology,* 74:73-84.

Richardson, D. & Seidman, S., eds. (2002), *Handbook of Lesbian and Gay Studies.* London: Sage.

Ritter, K. & Terndrup, A., eds. (2002), *Handbook of Affirmative Psychotherapy with Lesbians and Gay Men.* New York: Guilford.

Rosik, C.H. (2003), When therapists do not acknowledge their moral values: Green's response as a case study. *J. Marital & Family Therapy,* 29:39-45.

Rothblum, E.D. (2000), Sexual orientation and sex in women's lives: Conceptual and methodological issues. *J. Social Issues,* 56:193-204.

Roughton, R.E. (2001), Four men in treatment: An evolving perspective on homosexuality and bisexuality, 1965 to 2000. *J. American Psychoanalytic Association,* 49:1187-1217.

Ruiz, P., Lile, B., & Matorin, A.A. (2002), Treatment of a dually diagnosed gay male patient: A psychotherapy perspective. *American J. Psychiatry,* 159:209-215.

Saunes, G. (2002), Reorientation therapy: Ethically inexcusable? [Letter]. *Tidsskrift for den Norske Laegeforening,* 122:2656-2657.

Selle, M.S. (2003), Reorientation therapy is professionally and ethically inexcusable. *Tidsskrift for den Norske Laegeforening,* 123:83-84.

Shidlo, A. & Schroeder, M. (2002), Changing sexual orientation: A consumers' report. *Professional Psychology: Research & Practice,* 33(3):249-259.

Shidlo, A., Schroeder, M., & Drescher, J., eds. (2001), *Sexual Conversion Therapy: Ethical, Clinical and Research Perspectives.* Binghamton, NY: The Haworth Press.

Silverstein, C. (1977), Homosexuality and the ethics of behavioral intervention. *J. Homosexuality,* 2:205-211.

Socarides, C. (1995), *Homosexuality: A Freedom Too Far.* Phoenix, AZ: Adam Margrave Books.

Socarides, C.W. & Kaufman, B. (1994), Reparative therapy [Letter]. *American J. Psychiatry,* 151:157-159.

Spitzer, R.L. (1981), The diagnostic status of homosexuality in DSM III: A reformulation of the issues. *American J. Psychiatry,* 138:210-215.

Stein, E. (1999), The Mismeasure of Desire: *The Science, Theory, and Ethics of Sexual Orientation.* New York: Oxford University Press.

Streiner, D.L. (2002), The 2 "Es" of research: Efficacy and effectiveness trials. *Canadian J. Psychiatry,* 47:552-556.

Sturgis, E.T. & Adams, H.E. (1978), The right to treatment: Issues in the treatment of homosexuality. *J. Consulting & Clinical Psychology,* 46:165-169.

Szasz, T.S. (1965), *The Ethics of Psychoanalysis: The Theory and Method of Autonomous Psychotherapy.* New York: Dell.

Tozer, E. & McLanahan, M. (1999), Treating the purple menace: Ethical considerations of conversion therapy and affirmative alternatives. *The Counseling Psychologist,* 27:722-742.

Weeks, J. (1985), *Sexuality and Its Discontents: Meanings, Myths and Modern Sexualities.* Boston: Routledge and Kegan Paul.

Weeks, J. (1995), *Invented Moralities: Sexual Values in an Age of Uncertainty.* New York: Columbia University Press.

Weeks, J. (2000), *Making Sexual History.* Cambridge, England: Polity Press.

Winer, J.A., Anderson, J.W., Cohler, B.J., & Shelby, R.D., eds. (2002), *Rethinking Psychoanalysis and the Homosexualities.* Hillsdale, NJ: Analytic Press.

Young-Bruehl, E. (2001), Are human beings "by nature" bisexual? *Studies in Gender and Sexuality,* 2:179-213.

2

Gold or Lead?
Introductory Remarks on Conversions

Jack Drescher

On May 9, 2001, Robert L. Spitzer, MD, presented an unpublished paper at an American Psychiatric Association (APA) scientific symposium in New Orleans. Although APA symposia are generally staid affairs, this presentation, "Can Some Gay Men and Lesbians Change Their Sexual Orientation?,"[1] caused a media sensation and swiftly became the focus of talk shows and international headlines.

Why so much attention to this paper? Why so much press and public interest in the question of whether people can change their sexual orientation? In part, this has to do with the way media outlets tell news stories (see Lund and Renna, 2003). Another reason for this interest stems from events in which Dr. Spitzer participated thirty years ago when a related question was being debated: "Is homosexuality a mental disorder?"

At that time, APA's *Diagnostic and Statistical Manual of Mental Disorders* (DSM) regarded "homosexuality" as a mental illness, just as it did schizophrenia, personality disorders, and substance abuse. APA meetings of that era routinely featured presentations by psychiatrists on how to "treat" and "cure" homosexuality.

Homosexuality's diagnostic status had always been taken for granted as a matter to be decided by mental health practitioners. So who raised the question of whether homosexuality is a mental disorder? And how was the question decided? Following the 1969 Stonewall riots, energized gay and lesbian activists accused psychiatry of perpet-

This chapter appeared originally under the same title in the *Journal of Gay & Lesbian Psychotherapy* 7(3):1-11. Copyright 2003 The Haworth Press, Inc.

Published by The Haworth Press, Inc., 2006. All rights reserved.
doi:10.1300/5503_02

uating social prejudices against homosexuality in the language of science and medicine. They accused psychiatrists of ignoring a body of nonpsychiatric research which indicated that nonpathological expressions of homosexuality were common.[2] Even some psychiatrists of that time agreed with this research (Bayer, 1981; Scasta, 2002; Rosario, 2003), although they were a minority voice and not in any position to effect a diagnostic change. Furthermore, as a conservative medical organization, the APA was not initially receptive to studying the validity of scientific research done in other fields, particularly since those nonpsychiatric studies had concluded that psychiatric pathologizing was misguided.

In an effort to get the APA to consider this other body of research, gay and lesbian activists disrupted the 1970 and 1971 annual conventions. This strategy succeeded in getting the APA's attention. In the next few years, there were formal meetings between the activists and APA officials. This ultimately led to a historical chain of events: the first gay-affirmative presentations at an APA meeting (1971, 1972); intense deliberations by and debates within APA's scientific committees on the question of what constituted a psychiatric illness; and, finally, the 1973 removal of homosexuality from the DSM-II by the APA Board of Trustees (BOT). In a dramatic coda to those events, psychiatrists who opposed homosexuality's removal petitioned for an APA membership referendum to overturn the findings of the BOT. Their efforts were thwarted when, in 1974, the APA membership voted to uphold the Board's decision (Bayer, 1981; Hire, 2002; Scasta, 2002; Drescher, 2003a; Rosario, 2003).

So, is homosexuality a mental illness? Can some gay men and lesbians change their sexual orientation? If these were purely scientific questions, the APA's 1973 decision to remove homosexuality might have settled the matter there. The straightforward answers would be, "No, psychiatry and the scientific research say that homosexuality is not an illness. There is no reason to try and change it."[3] However, beneath the surface of such scientific questions lurk morality tales (Drescher, 1998a): In this case, the questions which underlie the moral concerns are, "Is homosexuality normal? Is homosexuality a good thing or a bad thing?"

In 1973, both gay activists and their antihomosexual psychiatric opponents were keenly aware of the subtext. The latter understood that changing homosexuality's status as an illness would remove the impetus for gay patients to seek psychiatric treatment.[4] The former believed that if psychiatrists said gay people were not ill, this could lead toward greater social acceptance of them and their relationship. In fact, there was one immediate consequence of removing homosexuality from the DSM. In 1974, APA issued a trailblazing position statement, deploring antigay discrimination and supporting "homosexuals'" civil rights (American Psychiatric Association, 1974).[5] Other mental health professionals soon followed suit.

Despite its statements of support, organized psychiatry was still not publicly prepared to say that homosexuality was a normal variant of human sexuality. In fact, Ronald Bayer, in his definitive account of those events, thought the gay activists calculations were wrong. He doubted that psychiatry could change attitudes toward homosexuality, arguing that

> the psychiatric mainstream must ultimately affirm the standards of health and disease of the society within which it works. It cannot hold to discordant views regarding the normal and abnormal, the desirable and undesirable, and continue to perform its socially sanctioned function. (Bayer, 1981, p. 194)

This prediction turned out to be both right *and* wrong.

After the 1973 APA decision, cultural attitudes about homosexuality shifted very slowly in the United States and elsewhere. Those who accepted scientific authority on such matters, gradually came to accept the position supported by the nonpsychiatric research and advocated by those early gay activists. A new perspective emerged in Western societies: if homosexuality is not an illness, and if one does not literally accept biblical prohibitions against homosexuality, and if gay people are able and prepared to function as productive citizens, then what is wrong with being gay?

This perspective proved persuasive and gathered momentum. Consider that in 1973, "homosexual behavior" was illegal in most of the fifty United States. By 2003, three-quarters of the states had repealed their sodomy laws. Then, on June 26, 2003, the U.S. Supreme Court made a 6-3 historic ruling in *Lawrence and Garner v. Texas* to overturn the country's remaining sodomy laws. Similar shifts gradually took place in the international mental health community as well. In 1992, the World Health Organization accepted American psychiatry's view and removed the diagnosis of homosexuality *per se* from the tenth edition of *International Classification of Diseases* (ICD-10) (Nakajima, 2003).[6]

Increasingly, the secular view of homosexuality as pathological was gradually replaced by the belief that it was a normal variant of human sexuality. Based upon this conclusion, same-sex marriage—or some form of recognized civil union—is now an option for gay men and lesbians in Belgium, The Netherlands, France, Germany, Finland, Sweden, Norway, Denmark, Iceland, Switzerland, the U.S. state of Vermont,[7] and the Canadian provinces of British Columbia, Ontario, and Quebec.[8] In addition, numerous municipalities and corporations throughout the United States, Europe, Australia, South Africa, South America, and Canada offer some form of domestic partnership rights and benefits for same-sex couples. National and state governments are increasingly addressing the rights of same-sex couples to adopt and to act as foster parents to children. Even the Episcopal Church is seriously considering adopting rituals to bless same-sex relationships.

None of these changes would have been possible without the 1973 APA decision.

Nevertheless, Bayer's aforementioned assessment of the consequences of psychiatry's taking a normalizing view of homosexuality was not entirely wrong. Since its removal from the DSM, some segments of society have rejected and fought against the increasingly open acceptance of homosexuality. They have become vociferous political opponents of gay men and lesbians' struggle for equal rights and of their efforts to form legal, committed relationships and families. Where the mental health mainstream has depathologized homosexuality, sexual conversion therapists and so called ex-gays have attacked psychiatry and the other mental health professions for their normalizing claims. They have further attempted to resurrect the argument that homosexuality *is* a mental disorder (Drescher, 1998b; Besen, 2003; Stålström and Nissinen, 2003). Finally, despite the mental health mainstream warnings of the potentially harmful consequences of trying to change one's sexual orientation (American Psychiatric Association, 2000; Drescher, 2002a,b; Shidlo and Schroeder, 2002), religious and social conservatives aggressively market sexual conversion therapies as both a miracle cure and an alternative to being gay.

In other words, the seemingly scientific question of whether people can change their sexual orientation has been subsumed within the political debates known as the *culture wars*.

Painted in broad strokes, two major positions on homosexuality are held in the culture wars. The *normal/identity model* regards homosexuality as a normal variation of human sexual expression. This position holds that to be gay or lesbian is to be a member of a sexual minority. In general, proponents of this model either believe that homosexuality is biologically inborn or that gay people are "made that way" by their creator. This position holds that for most people, homosexuality is fixed and immutable; that similar to race, one's sexual orientation is intrinsic to one's identity. It follows that one should not be subject to discrimination for being gay, lesbian, or bisexual (GLB).[9] It also follows, if one accepts this model, that GLB individuals facing societal antihomosexual attitudes should have legal protections that allow them to work in any job setting (including the armed forces and the public schools), to form legally recognized, committed relationships (with all the benefits that accrue from such recognition), to have the right to raise children, and to live wherever they choose. In *Lawrence and Gardner v. Texas,* the Supreme Court majority edged the United States closer toward acceptance of a *normal/identity model* in its nod to the category of "homosexual persons":

> When sexuality finds overt expression in intimate conduct with another person, the conduct can be but one element in a personal bond that is more enduring. The liberty protected by the Constitution allows homosexual persons the right to make this choice. . . . When homosexual conduct is made criminal by the law of the State, that declaration in and of itself is an invitation to subject homosexual persons to discrimination both in the public and in the private spheres.[10]

The opposing side in the culture wars favors an *illness/behavior model.* It defines any open expressions of homosexuality as behavioral symptoms of a psychiatric illness, a moral failing, or a spiritual illness. This position maintains that homosexuality is harmful since neither psychiatric or spiritual illness can provide a foundation for creating a normal identity, a normal family life, or a stable society. Proponents of this model further argue that homosexual feelings and behaviors are not innate, that they are a learned behavior that can be changed, either through some kind of psychotherapy or through faith healing. Because this model holds that homosexuality is just a behavior, no such thing as a gay or lesbian person or identity can exist: no one is "born gay." Every time a sufficiently motivated individual changes his or her sexual behavior, it "proves" that homosexuality is not intrinsic to a person's identity. It then follows, from this belief, that there is no substantive basis for enacting any laws intended to protect individuals on the basis of a sexual orientation.

In the 1973 APA debate, the psychiatrists who supported the removal of homosexuality defended the decision as a reasoned interpretation of scientific data. Insofar as their deliberations ultimately turned out to be favorable to the gay and lesbian civil rights movement, the experience provided important lessons about science's impact on politics and culture. Both sides in today's culture wars now evoke scientific authority to support their political positions, although each offers alternative interpretations of the existing data. Although there is often room in scientific discussions for reasonable disagreement, even antihomosexual, religious groups have adopted a scientific argument strategy as well. Drawing upon techniques developed by the faux scientific discipline of "creationism" (Tiffen, 1994), antihomosexual religious beliefs are also packaged in pseudoscientific language. All this makes it increasingly difficult to disentangle any scientific discussion of the degree to which a sexual orientation is fixed or mutable from moral questions about the extent to which individuals choose their sexual desire, behavior, and identity or from the contemporary political issues surrounding GLB civil rights (Drescher, Byne, and Stein, 2004).

This mixture of science, religion, sexual morality, cultural warfare, and identity politics is embodied in a recently published study, "Can Some Gay Men and Lesbians Change Their Sexual Orientation?: 200 Participants Reporting a Change from Homosexual to Heterosexual Orientation" (Spitzer, 2003).[11] Regardless of what one thinks of the study's scientific merit (Sandfort, 2003; Silverstein, 2003), its 2001 APA presentation, the numerous reactions it has evoked since then, and now its final publication delineate the shape and contours of the culture wars.

For example, Spitzer's own story resonates with the conversion narratives told by his study's ex-gay subjects. His first transformation took place in the 1970s, when he served on the APA's Task Force on Nomenclature and Statistics, the scientific committee that eventually recommended removing homosexuality to the APA Board. According to Bayer's (1981) chronicle of those events:

> Though Henry Brill had titular authority over the committee, Robert Spitzer, who was committed to an expeditious resolution of the controversy, zealously assumed a central role in directing its considerations, suggesting appropriate clinical and research literature to his colleagues for study. The intensity of his involvement, however, was not linked initially to any strong allegiance to a substantive position. *Certainly he was not at first a supporter of the effort to delete homosexuality from the nomenclature.* Indeed, when paired with Paul Wilson, a psychiatrist from Washington DC, to draft a discussion paper for the committee, Spitzer could not accept Wilson's version because of its support for declassification. What is remarkable is that because of his sense of mission he was, despite his unformed views, able to dominate both the pace and the direction of the committee's work. *In fact, it was Spitzer's own conceptual struggle with the issue of homosexuality that framed the committee's considerations.* (pp. 123-124, emphasis added)

The story of Spitzer changing his beliefs is one of the more compelling narratives to emerge from the historical account of the 1973 APA decision: A heterosexual scientist, taught to believe that homosexuality was an illness, became convinced by the objective scientific evidence that it was not. The story of this metamorphosis buttressed the position of the nascent GLB civil rights movement, although it led those who disagreed to challenge Spitzer's objectivity. One disgruntled psychiatric opponent called Spitzer "someone who crosses far over the line, from science to open advocacy of a political position" (Socarides, 1995, p. 166). By the year 1999, however, Spitzer had become intrigued by the question of whether individuals could change their sexual orientation, and just as he had once sympathized with the fearfully closeted homosexual psychiatrists of the Gay-P-A (Ashley, 2002; Scasta, 2002; Drescher, 2003a), now he took up the cause of the professionally marginalized sexual conversion therapists and of members of the ex-gay movement.

Other parallels to the events of thirty years ago exist in Spitzer's recent conversion. As media accounts of his support for sexual conversion therapies proliferated, Spitzer was again subjected to attacks, albeit from the other side of the cultural divide. At times, his demonization by members of the GLB community began to equal, if not surpass, the earlier personal attacks he had endured from his antihomosexual psychiatric opponents. In part, personal attacks were inevitable since *it was Spitzer's personal story of conversion* rather than the scientific merit of his study that was garnering all the headlines. In part, however, attacks from the GLB community were provoked by Spitzer, allowing antihomosexual conservatives to harness his impressive scientific credentials for their own political purposes. For example, he let Focus on the Family and several ex-gay groups use his name in a May 2000 paid newspaper ad in *USA Today*. Together they attacked the APA for taking a position against reparative therapy (see Figure 2.1).

With Spitzer's conversion to this new cause, those who once reviled him for his role in the 1973 APA decision are now staking their own claims of credibility upon his earlier reputation for scientific objectivity (Nicolosi, 2001). Sexual conversion therapists have used the

FIGURE 2.1. Focus on the Family ad in *USA Today,* May 2000.

media attention he and his study attracted to burnish their own tarnished images within the profession and to legitimize their claims of effecting "cures" (Drescher, 2003b). One result has been their promotion of a consumer-oriented, ex-gay advertising campaign that is similar to this: Spitzer's study says sexual conversion therapy has been scientifically proven to work! Don't listen to what the gay competition tells you. Try it!

To which the *Journal of Gay & Lesbian Psychotherapy* [in which this chapter was first published] can only respond: let the buyer beware.

In an effort to move the discussion beyond sound bites, attacks, and hucksterism, the contributors to [the] issue of the *JGLP* [and this book] address the scientific merit of Spitzer's study; the psychological, cultural, and personal meanings of sexual conversion; and some of the social consequences of the publicity surrounding this study.

Theodorus Sandfort's "Studying Sexual Orientation Change: A Methodological Review of the Spitzer Study" [Chapter 32] offers a straightforward criticism of the methodological inadequacies of Spitzer's study. He goes on to suggest how Spitzer could have done a better study, and then concludes with suggestions about what Spitzer should have done but did not.

"The Religious Conversion of Homosexuals: Subject Selection is the Voir Dire of Psychological Research" [Chapter 33] is by Charles Silverstein. Dr. Silverstein was one of the original gay activists who met with Dr. Spitzer thirty years ago and helped convince his committee to recommend removing homosexuality from the DSM (Bayer, 1981; Sbordone, 2003). In addition to a critical analysis of Spitzer's methodology, Silverstein's [chapter] further examines the ethical issues involved in sexual orientation change, the question of efficacy, and some deficiencies in the methodology of this research. He concludes by suggesting some strategies for countering the potentially harmful effects ensuing from publication of Spitzer's study.[12]

Explaining the "spin" surrounding Spitzer's study is Sean Lund and Cathy Renna's "An Analysis of the Media Response to the Spitzer Study" [Chapter 34]. Lund and Renna both monitor and respond to media reports on GLBT (gay, lesbian, bisexual, and transgender) issues for the Gay and Lesbian Alliance Against Defamation (GLAAD). Their original contribution to the *JGLP* is a case study of how the media covered Spitzer's 2001 APA presentation and of the public response to that coverage. They explain how "media routines" dictate that coverage of scientific issues that intersect with political or cultural ones tend to minimize the science and focus instead on the political or cultural conflict. They explain how this media approach marginalizes legitimate scientific insights and promotes simplistic, misrepresentative interpretations of complex issues.

"*Political* Science" [Chapter 35] is a chapter excerpted from Wayne Besen's (2003) recently published book, *Anything But Straight: Unmasking the Scandals and Lies Behind the Ex-Gay Myth*. Besen presents an account of his own communications with Dr. Spitzer around the time of the study's presentation in 2001 as well as his analysis of what the study means and how it can be used to hurt GLB people. Although written in a polemical manner, Besen's chapter is included in this collection as a representative sample of the political reception Spitzer's study received in the GLB community.

In "The Spitzer Study and the Finnish Parliament" [Chapter 36] Olli Stålström and Jussi Nissinen offer a rather startling account of the study's social impact in the wider world. They detail how Spitzer's 2001 APA presentation was drawn into the Finnish parliamentary debate on same-sex civil unions. When Spitzer was contacted by supporters of civil unions, he wrote a letter to the Finnish parliament criticizing the misuse of his study by opponents of civil unions. The author's acknowledge Spitzer's unique role in helping the passage of same-sex civil unions in Finland.[13]

This issue's [and this book's] conclusion is an interview with Dr. Spitzer. A self-described supporter of GLB civil rights, Spitzer recognizes that his study has given "aid and comfort to the enemy." Nevertheless, he thinks "the study does provide some information that is of value which was not there before the study. I think that as a scientist you are entitled to study what you decide is of scientific interest."

NOTES

1. The presentation was one of five papers presented at a Scientific Symposium sponsored by the *JGLP*'s parent organization, the Association of Gay and Lesbian Psychiatrists (AGLP), titled "Clinical Issues and Ethical Concerns Regarding Attempts to Change Sexual Orientation: An Update."

2. See Kinsey, Pomeroy, and Martin, 1948; Ford and Beach, 1951; Kinsey et al., 1953; Hooker, 1957; Szasz, 1965.

3. In 2000, the APA's Commission on Psychotherapy by Psychiatrists issued a position statement on sexual conversion therapies. Its recommendations included the following statement:

> Psychotherapeutic modalities to convert or "repair" homosexuality are based on developmental theories whose scientific validity is questionable. Furthermore, anecdotal reports of "cures" are counterbalanced by anecdotal claims of psychological harm. In the past four decades, "reparative" therapists have not produced any rigorous scientific research to substantiate their claims of cure. Until there is such research available, APA recommends that ethical practitioners refrain from attempts to change individuals' sexual orientation, keeping in mind the medical dictum to First, do no harm. (American Psychiatric Association, 1974)

4. Spitzer actually offered a political settlement to these opponents. In 1973, he suggested the DSM-II substitute the diagnosis of "homosexuality" with an alternative, "sexual orientation disturbance" (SOD). According to SOD criteria, only those "bothered by," "in conflict with," or who "wished to change" their sexual orientation had a mental disorder. SOD, however, had several conceptual problems. For example, the diagnosis could also apply to heterosexuals, although no cases of unhappy heterosexuals seeking psychiatric treatment to become gay were reported. In 1980, with Spitzer eventually chairing the Task Force on Nomenclature and Statistics, SOD was modified in the DSM-III to "ego-dystonic homosexuality" (EDH). EDH did not resolve the thorny issue of making patients' subjective distress about homosexuality the determining factor in making a diagnosis. In 1987, EDH was removed from the DSM-III-R (Krajeski, 1996).

5. The APA statement reads:

> Whereas, homosexuality *per se* implies no impairment in judgment, stability, reliability, or general social or vocational capabilities, therefore, be it resolved that the APA deplores all public and private discrimination against homosexuals in such areas as employment, housing, public accommodation, and licensing, and declares that no burden of proof of such judgment, capacity, or reliability shall be placed upon homosexuals greater than that imposed on other persons. Further the [APA] supports and urges the enactment of civil rights legislation at the local, state, and federal level that would offer homosexual citizens the same protection now guaranteed to others on the basis of race, creed, color, etc. Further the [APA] supports and urges the repeal of all discriminatory legislation singling out homosexual acts by consenting adults in private.

6. Even before 1992, in countries in which psychiatric organizations independently followed the American example, the pace of homosexuality's social acceptance also accelerated; in some cases, change occurred more rapidly than in the United States (Lingiardi and Drescher, 2003). In countries such as Japan and China it was the diagnostic change of the ICD-10 that eventually led them, in turn, to revise their earlier diagnostic assessment of homosexuality per se as an illness (Nakajima, 2003; Wu, 2003).

7. At the time of this writing [2003], court challenges to legalize same-sex marriage were taking place in both New Jersey and Massachusetts. The New Jersey case is now on appeal and the Massachusetts Court has just ruled that the state must institute same-sex marriage.

8. In June 2003, Canada's highest court ordered the Canadian Parliament to draft legislation legalizing same-sex marriage for all of Canada.

9. Transsexual and transgender issues are closely related to GLB issues. However, to avoid going too far afield in this discussion, I have chosen to focus on GLB issues alone. For a thoughtful assessment of the linkages between GLB and trans issues, see Devor, 2002.

10. See http://caselaw.lp.findlaw.com/scripts/getcase.pl?court=US&vol=000& invol=02-102&friend=nytimes.

11. The *JGLP* [and this book's editors] thanks Ken Zucker, PhD, editor of *Archives of Sexual Behavior*, as well as Dr. Spitzer for making the study available before its publication so that some of this issue's [and this book's] contributors could have the opportunity to respond to its publication in a timely manner.

12. The general question has been raised whether researchers should consider any potential social harm that might arise from their scientific research (Byne, Schuklenk, Lasco, and Drescher, 2002). In particular, questions about the potential harm of Spitzer's study to the GLB community have been raised by numerous mental health professionals as well (Wainberg et al., 2003). For reports of harm done by sexual conversion therapies, see Shidlo, Schroeder, and Drescher (2001) and Shidlo and Schroeder (2002).

13. Also see Hausman, 2001.

REFERENCES

American Psychiatric Association (1974), Position statement on homosexuality and civil rights. *Amer. J. Psychiat.*, 131:497.

American Psychiatric Association (2000), Commission on Psychotherapy by Psychiatrists (COPP): Position statement on therapies focused on attempts to change sexual orientation (Reparative or conversion therapies). *Amer. J. Psychiat.*, 157:1719-1721.

Ashley, K. (2002), An interview with Stuart E. Nichols, Jr., MD. *J. Gay & Lesbian Psychotherapy*, 6(4):55-71.

Bayer, R. (1981), *Homosexuality and American Psychiatry: The Politics of Diagnosis*. New York: Basic Books.

Besen, W. R. (2003), *Anything But Straight: Unmasking the Scandals and Lies Behind the Ex-Gay Myth*. Binghamton, NY: Harrington Park Press.

Byne, W., Schuklenk, U., Lasco, M. & Drescher, J. (2002), The origins of sexual orientation: No genetic link to social change. In: *The Double-Edged Helix: Social Implications of Genetics in a Diverse Society*, eds. J. S. Alper, C. Ard, A. Asch, J. Beckwith, P. Conrad, & L. N. Geller. Baltimore: Johns Hopkins University Press, pp. 197-214.

Devor, H. (2002), Who are "we"? Where sexual orientation meets gender identity. *J. Gay & Lesbian Psychotherapy*, 6(2):5-21.

Drescher, J. (1998a), *Psychoanalytic Therapy and the Gay Man*. Hillsdale, NJ: The Analytic Press.

Drescher, J. (1998b), I'm your handyman: A history of reparative therapies. *J. Homosexual.*, 36(1):19-42. Reprinted in: *Sexual Conversion Therapy: Ethical, Clinical and Research Perspectives,* eds. A. Shidlo, M. Schroeder, & J. Drescher. Binghamton, NY: The Haworth Press, 2001, pp. 5-24.

Drescher, J. (2001), Ethical concerns raised when patients seek to change same-sex attractions. *J. Gay & Lesbian Psychotherapy,* 5(3/4):181-210. Reprinted in: *Sexual Conversion Therapy: Ethical, Clinical and Research Perspectives,* eds. A. Shidlo, M. Schroeder, & J. Drescher. Binghamton, NY: The Haworth Press, 2001, pp. 181-210.

Drescher, J. (2002a), Sexual conversion ("reparative") therapies: A history and update. In: *Mental Health Issues in Lesbian, Gay, Bisexual, and Transgender Communities (Review of Psychiatry,* 21:4), eds. B. E. Jones & M. J. Hill. Washington, DC: American Psychiatric Press, pp. 71-91.

Drescher, J. (2002b), Ethical issues in treating gay and lesbian patients. *Psychiatric Clinics of North America,* 25(3):605-621.

Drescher, J. (2003a), An interview with Robert L. Spitzer, MD. *J. Gay & Lesbian Psychotherapy,* 7(3):97-111.

Drescher, J. (2003b), The Spitzer study and the culture wars. *Arch. Sexual Behavior,* 32(5):431-432.

Drescher, J., Byne, W., & Stein, T.S. (2004), Homosexuality, gay and lesbian identities, and homosexual behavior. In: *Kaplan and Sadock's Comprehensive Textbook of Psychiatry,* 8th Edition, eds. B. Sadock & V. Sadock. Baltimore, MD: Williams and Wilkins.

Hausman, K. (2001), Finland's Parliament assesses U.S. reparative-therapy study. *Psychiatric News,* December 21, 36(24):11.

Hire, R.O. (2002), An interview with Robert Jean Campbell III, MD. *J. Gay & Lesbian Psychotherapy,* 6(3):81-96.

Hooker, E. (1957), The adjustment of the male overt homosexual. *J. Proj. Tech,* 21:18-31.

Kinsey, A., Pomeroy, W., & Martin, C. (1948), *Sexual Behavior in the Human Male.* Philadelphia, PA: Saunders.

Kinsey, A., Pomeroy, W., Martin, C., & Gebhard, P. (1953), *Sexual Behavior in the Human Female.* Philadelphia, PA: Saunders.

Krajeski, J. (1996), Homosexuality and the mental health professions. In: *Textbook of Homosexuality and Mental Health,* eds. R.P. Cabaj & T.S. Stein. Washington, DC: American Psychiatric Press, pp. 17-31.

Lingiardi, V. & Drescher, J., eds. (2003), *The Mental Health Professions and Homosexuality: International Perspectives.* Binghamton, NY: The Haworth Press.

Lund, S. & Renna, C. (2003), An analysis of the media response to the Spitzer study. *J. Gay & Lesbian Psychotherapy,* 7(3):55-67.

Nakajima, G.A. (2003), The emergence of an international lesbian, gay, and bisexual psychiatric movement. *J. Gay & Lesbian Psychotherapy,* 7(1/2):165-188. Reprinted in: *The Mental Health Professions and Homosexuality: International*

Perspectives, eds. V. Lingiardi & J. Drescher. Binghamton, NY: The Haworth Press, pp. 165-188.

Nicolosi, L.A. (2001), Historic gay advocate now believes change is possible. Available online at: http://www.narth.com/docs/spitzer3.html.

Rosario, V.A. (2003), An interview with Judd Marmor, MD. *J. Gay & Lesbian Psychotherapy,* 7(4):23-34.

Sandfort, T.G.M. (2003), Studying sexual orientation change: A methodological review of the Spitzer study, "Can some gay men and lesbians change their sexual orientation?" *J. Gay & Lesbian Psychotherapy,* 7(3):15-29.

Sbordone, A.J. (2003), An interview with Charles Silverstein, PhD. *J. Gay & Lesbian Psychotherapy,* 7(4):49-61.

Scasta, D. (2002), John E. Fryer, MD, and the Dr. H. Anonymous episode. *J. Gay & Lesbian Psychotherapy,* 6(4):73-84.

Shidlo, A. & Schroeder, M. (2002), Changing sexual orientation: A consumers' report. *Professional Psychology: Research & Practice,* 33(3):249-259.

Shidlo, A., Schroeder, M., & Drescher, J., eds. (2001), *Sexual Conversion Therapies: Ethical, Clinical and Research Perspectives.* Binghamton, NY: The Haworth Medical Press.

Silverstein, C. (2003), The religious conversion of homosexuals: Subject selection is the *voir dire* of psychological research. *J. Gay & Lesbian Psychotherapy,* 7(3): 31-53.

Socarides, C. (1995), *Homosexuality: A Freedom Too Far.* Phoenix, AZ: Adam Margrave Books.

Spitzer, R. L. (2003), Can some gay men and lesbians change their sexual orientation? 200 participants reporting a change from homosexual to heterosexual orientation. *Archives of Sexual Behavior,* 32(5):403-417.

Stålström, O. & Nissinen, J. (2003), The Spitzer study and the Finnish parliament. *J. Gay & Lesbian Psychotherapy,* 7(3):83-95.

Szasz, T. (1965), Legal and moral aspects of homosexuality. In: *Sexual Inversion: The Multiple Roots of Homosexuality,* ed. J. Marmor. New York: Basic Books, pp. 124-139.

Tiffen, L. (1994), *Creationism's Upside-Down Pyramid: How Science Refutes Fundamentalism.* Amherst, NY: Prometheus Books.

Wainberg, M.L, Bux, D., Carballo-Dieguez, A., Dowsett, G.W., Dugan, T., Forstein, M., Goodkin, K., Hunter, J., Irwin, T., Mattos, P., McKinnon, K., O'Leary, A., Parson, J., & Stein, E. (2003), Science and the Nuremberg Code: A question of ethics and harm. *Arch. Sexual Behavior,* 32(5):455-457.

Wu, J. (2003), From *"long yang"* and *"dui shi"* to *tongzhi:* Homosexuality in China. *J. Gay & Lesbian Psychotherapy,* 7(1/2):117-143. Reprinted in: *The Mental Health Professions and Homosexuality: International Perspectives,* eds. V. Lingiardi & J. Drescher. Binghamton, NY: The Haworth Press, pp. 117-143.

Section II:
Perspectives on Changing
Sexual Orientation

3

Position Statement on Therapies Focused on Attempts to Change Sexual Orientation (Reparative or Conversion Therapies)

Commission on Psychotherapy by Psychiatrists (COPP)
American Psychiatric Association

PREAMBLE

In December of 1998, the Board of Trustees issued a position statement that the American Psychiatric Association opposes any psychiatric treatment, such as "reparative" or conversion therapy, which is based upon the assumption that homosexuality per se is a mental disorder or based upon the a priori assumption that a patient should change his or her sexual homosexual orientation. In doing so, the APA joined many other professional organizations that either oppose or are critical of "reparative" therapies, including the American Academy of Pediatrics, the American Medical Association, the American Psychological Association, The American Counseling Association, and the National Association of Social Workers.[1]

The following Position Statement expands and elaborates upon the statement issued by the Board of Trustees in order to further address public and professional concerns about therapies designed to change a patient's sexual orientation or sexual identity. It augments rather than replaces the 1998 statement.

This chapter appeared originally under the same title in the *American Journal of Psychiatry* 157:1719-1721. Copyright 2000 American Psychiatric Association.

Published by The Haworth Press, Inc., 2006. All rights reserved.
doi:10.1300/5503_03

POSITION STATEMENT

In the past, defining homosexuality as an illness buttressed society's moral opprobrium of same-sex relationships.[2] In the current social climate, claiming homosexuality is a mental disorder stems from efforts to discredit the growing social acceptance of homosexuality as a normal variant of human sexuality. Consequently, the issue of changing sexual orientation has become highly politicized. The integration of gays and lesbians into the mainstream of American society is opposed by those who fear that such an integration is morally wrong and harmful to the social fabric. The political and moral debates surrounding this issue have obscured the scientific data by calling into question the motives and even the character of individuals on both sides of the issue. This document attempts to shed some light on this heated issue.

The validity, efficacy, and ethics of clinical attempts to change an individual's sexual orientation have been challenged.[3-6] To date, there are no scientifically rigorous outcome studies to determine either the actual efficacy or harm of reparative treatments. There is sparse scientific data about selection criteria, risks versus benefits of the treatment, and long-term outcomes of reparative therapies. The literature consists of anecdotal reports of individuals who have claimed to change, people who claim that attempts to change were harmful to them, and others who claimed to have changed and then later recanted those claims.[7-9]

With little data about patients, it is possible to evaluate the theories that rationalize the conduct of "reparative" or conversion therapies. First, they are at odds with the scientific position of the American Psychiatric Association, which has maintained, since 1973, that homosexuality per se is not a mental disorder. The theories of "reparative" therapists define homosexuality as either a developmental arrest, a severe form of psychopathology, or some combination of both.[10-15] In recent years, noted practitioners of "reparative therapy" have openly integrated older psychoanalytic theories that pathologize homosexuality with traditional religious beliefs condemning homosexuality.[16-18]

The earliest scientific criticisms of the early theories and religious beliefs informing "reparative" or conversion therapies came primarily from sexology researchers.[19-27] Later, criticisms emerged from psychoanalytic sources as well.[28-39] There has also been an increasing body of religious thought arguing against traditional, biblical interpretations that condemn homosexuality and that underlie religious types of "reparative" therapy.[40-46]

RECOMMENDATIONS

1. APA affirms its 1973 position that homosexuality per se is not a diagnosable mental disorder. Recent publicized efforts to repathologize homosexuality by claiming that it can be cured are often guided not by rigorous scientific or psychiatric research, but sometimes by religious and political forces opposed to a full civil rights for gay men and lesbians. APA recommends that the APA respond quickly and appropriately as a scientific organization when claims that homosexuality is a curable illness are made by political or religious groups.

2. As a general principle, a therapist should not determine the goal of treatment either coercively or through subtle influence. Psychotherapeutic modalities to convert or "repair" homosexuality are based on developmental theories whose scientific validity is questionable. Furthermore, anecdotal reports of "cures" are counterbalanced by anecdotal claims of psychological harm. In the past four decades, "reparative" therapists have not produced any rigorous scientific research to substantiate their claims of cure. Until there is such research available, APA recommends that ethical practitioners refrain from attempts to change individuals' sexual orientation, keeping in mind the medical dictum to First, do no harm.

3. The "reparative" therapy literature uses theories that make it difficult to formulate scientific selection criteria for their treatment modality. This literature not only ignores the impact of social stigma in motivating efforts to cure homosexuality, it is a literature that actively stigmatizes homosexuality as well. "Reparative" therapy literature also tends to overstate the treatment's accomplishments while neglecting any potential risks to patients. APA encourages and supports research in the National Institute of Mental Health (NIMH) and the academic research community to further determine "reparative" therapy's risks versus its benefits.

NOTES

1. National Association for Research and Treatment of Homosexuality (1999), American counseling association passes resolution to oppose reparative therapy. NARTH Website (http://www.narth.com/docs/acaresolution.html).

2. Bayer, R. (1981), *Homosexuality and American Psychiatry: The Politics of Diagnosis.* New York: Basic Books.

3. Haldeman, D. (1991), Sexual orientation conversion therapy for gay men and lesbians: A scientific examination. In: *Homosexuality: Research Implications for Public Policy,* eds. J.C. Gonsiorek & J.D. Weinrich. Newbury Park, CA: Sage Publications, pp. 149-161.

4. Haldeman, D. (1994), The practice and ethics of sexual orientation conversion therapy. *J. Consulting & Clinical Psychology,* 62(2):221-227.

5. Brown, L. S. (1996), Ethical concerns with sexual minority patients. In: *Textbook of Homosexuality and Mental Health,* eds. R.P. Cabaj & T.S. Stein. Washington, DC: American Psychiatric Press, pp. 897-916.

6. Drescher, J. (1997), What needs changing? Some questions raised by reparative therapy practices. *New York State Psychiatric Society Bulletin,* 40(1):8-10.

7. Duberman, M. (1991), *Cures: A Gay Man's Odyssey.* New York: Dutton.

8. White, M. (1994), *Stranger at the Gate: To be Gay and Christian in America.* New York: Simon & Schuster.

9. Isay, R. (1996), *Becoming Gay: The Journey to Self-Acceptance.* New York: Pantheon.

10. Freud, S. (1905), Three essays on the theory of sexuality. *Standard Edition of the Complete Psychological Works of Sigmund Freud,* 7:123-246. London: Hogarth Press, 1953.

11. Rado, S. (1940), A critical examination of the concept of bisexuality. *Psychosomatic Medicine,* 2:459-467. Reprinted in: *Sexual Inversion: The Multiple Roots of Homosexuality,* ed. J. Marmor. New York: Basic Books, 1965, pp. 175-189.

12. Bieber, I., Dain, H., Dince, P., Drellich, M., Grand, H., Gundlach, R., Kremer, M., Rifkin, A., Wilbur, C., & Bieber T. (1962), *Homosexuality: A Psychoanalytic Study.* New York: Basic Books.

13. Socarides, C. (1968), *The Overt Homosexual.* New York: Grune & Stratton.

14. Ovesey, L. (1969), *Homosexuality and Pseudohomosexuality.* New York: Science House.

15. Hatterer, L. (1970), *Changing Homosexuality in the Male.* New York: McGraw-Hill.

16. Moberly, E. (1983), *Homosexuality: A New Christian Ethic.* Cambridge, UK: James Clarke & Co.

17. Harvey, J. (1987), *The Homosexual Person: New Thinking in Pastoral Care.* San Francisco, CA: Ignatius.

18. Nicolosi, J. (1991), *Reparative Therapy of Male Homosexuality: A New Clinical Approach.* Northvale, NJ: Aronson.

19. Kinsey, A., Pomeroy, W., & Martin, C. (1948), *Sexual Behavior in the Human Male.* Philadelphia, PA: Saunders.

20. Kinsey, A., Pomeroy, W., Martin, C., & Gebhard, P. (1953), *Sexual Behavior in the Human Female.* Philadelphia, PA: Saunders.

21. Ford, C. & Beach, F. (1951), *Patterns of Sexual Behavior.* New York: Harper.

22. Hooker, E. (1957), The adjustment of the male overt homosexual. *J. Projective Technique,* 21:18-31.

23. Bell, A & Weinberg, M. (1978), *Homosexualities: A Study of Diversity Among Men & Women.* New York: Simon and Schuster.

24. Bell, A., Weinberg, M., & Hammersmith S. (1981), *Sexual Preference: Its Development in Men and Women.* Bloomington, IN: Indiana University Press.

25. LeVay, S. (1991), A difference in hypothalamic structure between heterosexual and homosexual men. *Science,* 253:1034-1037.

26. Hamer, D., Hu, S., Magnuson, V., Hu, N., & Pattatucci, A. (1993), A linkage between DNA markers on the X-chromosome and male sexual orientation. *Science,* 261:321-327.

27. Bem, D. (1996), Exotic becomes erotic: A developmental theory of sexual orientation. *Psychol. Review,* 103(2):320-335.

28. Marmor, J., ed. (1965), *Sexual Inversion: The Multiple Roots of Homosexuality.* New York: Basic Books.

29. Mitchell, S. (1978), Psychodynamics, homosexuality, and the question of pathology. *Psychiatry,* 41:254-263.

30. Marmor, J., ed. (1980), *Homosexual Behavior: A Modern Reappraisal.* New York: Basic Books.

31. Mitchell, S. (1981), The psychoanalytic treatment of homosexuality: Some technical considerations. *Int. Rev. Psycho-Anal.,* 8:63-80.

32. Morgenthaler, F. (1984), *Homosexuality Heterosexuality Perversion,* trans. A. Aebi. Hillsdale, NJ: The Analytic Press, 1988.

33. Lewes, K. (1988), *The Psychoanalytic Theory of Male Homosexuality.* New York: Simon and Schuster. Reissued as *Psychoanalysis and Male Homosexuality* (1995), Northvale, NJ: Aronson.

34. Friedman, R.C. (1988), *Male Homosexuality: A Contemporary Psychoanalytic Perspective.* New Haven, CT: Yale University Press.

35. Isay, R. (1989), *Being Homosexual: Gay Men and Their Development.* New York: Farrar, Straus & Giroux.

36. O'Connor, N. & Ryan, J. (1993), *Wild Desires and Mistaken Identities: Lesbianism & Psychoanalysis.* New York: Columbia University.

37. Domenici, T. & Lesser, R.C., eds. (1995), *Disorienting Sexuality: Psychoanalytic Reappraisals of Sexual Identities.* New York: Routledge.

38. Magee, M. & Miller, D. (1997), *Lesbian Lives: Psychoanalytic Narratives Old and New.* Hillsdale, NJ: The Analytic Press.

39. Drescher, J. (1998), *Psychoanalytic Therapy and The Gay Man.* Hillsdale, NJ: The Analytic Press.

40. Boswell, J. (1980), *Christianity, Social Tolerance and Homosexuality.* Chicago, IL: University of Chicago Press.

41. McNeil, J. (1993), *The Church and the Homosexual,* Fourth Edition. Boston, MA: Beacon.

42. Pronk, P. (1993), *Against Nature: Types of Moral Argumentation Regarding Homosexuality.* Grand Rapids, MI: William B. Eerdmans.

43. Boswell, J. (1994), *Same-Sex Unions in Premodern Europe.* New York: Villard Books.

44. Helminiak, D. (1994), *What the Bible Really Says About Homosexuality.* San Francisco, CA: Alamo Press.

45. Gomes, P. J. (1996), *The Good Book: Reading the Bible with Mind and Heart.* New York: Avon.

46. Carrol, W. (1997), On being gay and an American Baptist minister. *The InSpiriter,* Spring, pp. 6-7,11.

Can Some Gay Men and Lesbians Change Their Sexual Orientation? 200 Participants Reporting a Change from Homosexual to Heterosexual Orientation

Robert L. Spitzer

INTRODUCTION

In recent years, there has been a marked change about both the desirability and feasibility of attempts to alter a homosexual sexual orientation. In the past, such change was generally considered both desirable and possible (Bieber et al., 1962; Hatterer, 1970; Socarides, 1978). An increasing number of clinicians believe that such change rarely, if ever, occurs and that psychotherapy with this goal often is harmful by increasing self-loathing, lowered self-esteem, hopelessness, and depression (American Psychiatric Association, 2000; Friedman and Downey, 2002; Haldeman, 2001). Several authors have argued that clinicians who attempt to help their clients change their homosexual orientation are violating professional ethical codes by providing a "treatment" that is ineffective, often harmful, and reinforces in their clients the false belief that homosexuality is a disorder and needs treatment (Drescher, 2001; Forstein, 2001; Isay, 1996; Murphy, 1992; Shidlo and Schroeder, 2002).

This chapter appeared originally under the same title in *Archives of Sexual Behavior* 32(5):403-417. Copyright 2003 Kluwer Academic/Plenum Publishers. Reprinted with permission.

A preliminary report of the results of this study was presented at the annual meeting of the American Psychiatric Association, May 9, 2001, in New Orleans, Louisiana.

doi:10.1300/5503_04

At the present time, only a very small number of mental health professionals (primarily psychologists, social workers, mental health counselors, and pastoral ministers) provide therapy with the goal of helping their clients change their sexual orientation from homosexual to heterosexual. Therapy with this goal is often referred to as "reparative therapy." There are also religious "ex-gay" ministries that offer individual counseling and group support to gay men and lesbians who wish to change their sexual orientation. An example is Exodus International, an interdenominational Christian organization that promotes the message of "Freedom from homosexuality through the power of Jesus Christ" (Exodus International Web site, retrieved October 15, 2002, from http://www.exodusinternational.org). Finally, there are a small number of 12-step programs, such as Sexual Addicts Anonymous.

Many individuals receiving reparative therapy from a mental health professional also get support or counseling from an ex-gay ministry. In this article, any help from a mental health professional or an ex-gay ministry for the purpose of changing sexual orientation will be referred to as "reparative therapy" or simply as "therapy." Reparative therapists believe that same-sex attractions reflect a developmental disorder and can be significantly diminished through development of stronger and more confident gender identification. Reparative therapists say that their gay male patients (who comprise the majority of their caseload) suffer from a lifelong feeling of "being on the outside" of male activities and "not feeling like one of the guys." When therapy succeeds in demystifying males and maleness, their romantic and erotic attractions to men diminish and opposite-sex attractions may gradually develop. A prominent reorientation therapist estimates that only about a third of the male clients that pursue a course of reparative therapy actually develop heterosexual attractions, another third diminish their unwanted male attractions and decrease their unwanted same-sex behaviors but do not develop heterosexual attractions; the remaining third remain essentially unchanged (J. Nicolosi, personal communication, November 13, 2000).

"The Surgeon General" (2001), the American Academy of Pediatrics (1983), and all of the major mental health associations in the United States, representing psychiatry (American Psychiatric Association, 2000), psychology (American Psychological Association, 1997), social work (National Association of Social Work, 1997), and counseling (American Counseling Association, 1998) have each issued position statements warning of possible harm from such therapy and asserting that there is no evidence that such therapy can change one's sexual orientation. For example, the 1998 American Psychiatric Association Position Statement on Psychiatric Treatment and Sexual Orientation (see American Psychiatric Association, 1999, p. 1131) states:

> . . . there is no published scientific evidence supporting the efficacy of reparative therapy as a treatment to change one's sexual orientation. . . . The potential risks of reparative therapy are great, including depression, anxiety, and self-destructive behavior.

Is this seemingly authoritative position statement true, that there is "no published scientific evidence" supporting the efficacy of reparative therapy to change sexual orientation? The answer depends on what is meant by "scientific evidence." If scientific evidence requires a study with randomized assignment of individuals to a treatment condition, reliable and valid assessment of target symptoms before treatment, when treatment is concluded, and at follow-up, then it is certainly true that there are no such studies of reparative therapy. However, the same can be said about many widely used types of psychotherapy, including gay affirmative therapy, whose efficacy has never been subjected to a rigorous study (Bieschke et al., 2000). There is, however, a large literature relevant to the issue of the possibility of changing sexual orientation. Adams and Sturgis (1977) critically reviewed 37 studies of behavior therapy to change sexual orientation and concluded that, "Although sexual orientation techniques have achieved moderately positive results, research is needed to improve the efficacy of the procedures" (p. 1186). More recently, Goetze (2001) identified 84 articles or books having some relevance to the possibility of sexual orientation change, searching PsychLit and MedLine databases as well as bibliographies of relevant papers or books. Thirty-one of the 84 studies reported some quantitative outcome, not just general discussion and claims about the possibility of changing sexual orientation. Twelve of the 31 studies, however, did not provide enough outcome data to evaluate the effect of the treatment.

Two well-known examples of such studies are Bieber et al. (1962) and Socarides (1978). Bieber et al. (1962) reported a study in which 58 psychoanalysts filled out questionnaires on 106 gay males who had been in psychoanalytic treatment. Bieber and his associates studied the results of these questionnaires, which focused on sexual behavior, not attraction and fantasy. Seventy-two of the men were exclusively homosexual before treatment. At a 5-year follow-up, 13 percent ($n = 14$) of these men exhibited exclusively heterosexual behavior and 13 percent ($n = 14$) bisexual behavior. Socarides (1978) reported that 44 percent ($n = 20$) of 45 of his patients who were in long-term psychoanalytic therapy developed "full heterosexual functioning"—a term that he did not define. He did not distinguish between overt sexual behavior and sexual attraction. Furthermore, he provided no data on sexual history.

Of the 84 studies cited by Goetze (2001), the remaining 19 provided some data suggesting that in some participants a homosexual orientation can be changed to varying degrees by a variety of interventions (Barlow and Agras, 1973; Berger, 1994; Callahan, 1976; Ellis, 1959; Freeman and Meyer, 1975; Golwyn and Sevlie, 1993; Hadden, 1966; Hadfield, 1958; Hatterer, 1970; Liss and Welner, 1973; MacIntosh, 1994; Masters and Johnson, 1979; McCrady, 1973; Mintz, 1966; Pattison and Pattison, 1980; Poe, 1952; Shechter, 1992; van den Aardweg, 1986; Wolpe, 1969).

Of these 19 studies, the one by van den Aardweg (1986) is perhaps the most informative regarding change from a homosexual or bisexual orientation to an exclusively heterosexual orientation. His study comprised a follow-up of 101 of his former clients, several years after having been treated in a form of psychoanalysis that he called "anti-complaining therapy." Eleven (11 percent) of the patients had experienced a "radical change," defined as "no homosexual interests except for occasional and weak homosexual 'flashes' at most and the restoration of full heterosexuality."

Although providing some evidence for the efficacy of reparative therapy, all of these 19 studies have one or more serious methodological shortcomings, including no assessment of specific changes in sexual orientation (e.g., changes in masturbatory fantasies), no detailed sexual history, no follow-up assessment, no informants, no consecutive series, no objective measures, and possible bias in that the researcher conducted the therapy.

The 2000 American Psychiatric Association "Position Statement on Therapies Focused on Attempts to Change Sexual Orientation" (American Psychiatric Association, 2000) noted that "there have been no scientifically rigorous outcome studies to determine either the actual efficacy or harm of 'reparative' treatments. . . . APA encourages and supports research . . . to further determine 'reparative' therapy's risks versus its benefits" (p. 1719). This study attempts to contribute to that research by studying whether some individuals receiving reparative therapy do, in fact, change their sexual orientation from homosexual to heterosexual.

Critics of reparative therapy acknowledge that the therapy can change homosexual behavior by the individual resisting acting on homosexual feelings and can also succeed in getting the individual to relabel his or her homosexual orientation as heterosexual. They claim, however, that homosexual orientation itself remains unchanged. For the purposes of this study, homosexual orientation is operationalized by multiple measures of same-sex attraction, arousal, fantasy, and yearning as well as overt behavior.

This study tests the following hypothesis: Some individuals whose sexual orientation is predominantly homosexual can become predominantly heterosexual following some form of reparative therapy (which can take the form of psychotherapy, counseling, or participation in an ex-gay ministry program).

This study involves systematically interviewing a large group of individuals who report that their sexual orientation had been predominantly homosexual, but who now report that because of some kind of therapy they have sustained for at least 5 years some change to a heterosexual orientation. If such individuals are found, the specific changes in components of sexual orientation and their magnitude are examined as well as changes in overt homosexual behavior, self-identity, and how bothered the individuals are by homosexual feelings. In addition, because sexuality in gay men and lesbians may be experienced and expressed differently, as is the case with heterosexual individuals, gender differences in the reported changes are also examined.

METHOD

Participant Recruitment and Entry Criteria

Announcements aimed at recruiting participants requested individuals who had sustained some change in homosexual orientation for at least 5 years. To be accepted into the study, however, it was necessary for an individual to satisfy two criteria: (1) predominantly homosexual attraction for many years, and in the year before starting therapy, at least 60 on a scale of sexual attraction (where 0 = *exclusively heterosexual* and 100 = *exclusively homosexual*); and (2) after therapy, a change of at least 10 points, lasting at least 5 years, toward the heterosexual end of the scale of sexual attraction. These criteria were designed to identify individuals who reported at least some minimal change in sexual attraction, not merely a change in overt homosexual behavior or self-identity as "gay" or "straight." It should be noted that individuals who satisfied these criteria were not excluded from the study if they had had homosexual sex during or following therapy.

Over a 16-month period (January 2000 to April 2001), 274 individuals were recruited who wanted to participate in the study. Of these, 200 (143 males, 57 females) satisfied the entry criteria and constitute the study sample. The 74 excluded individuals did not meet the entry criteria for a variety of reasons: the change was for less than 5 years ($n = 27$), there was a change in behavior and self-identity but no change in sexual attraction ($n = 18$), the individual had never been predominantly homosexual ($n = 12$), and other, miscellaneous reasons ($n = 17$; e.g., three priests who did not want to function heterosexually).

Forty-three percent of the 200 participants learned about the study from ex-gay religious ministries and 23 percent from the National Association for Research and Therapy of Homosexuality, a group of mental health professionals and lay people who defend the right of gay men and lesbians to receive sexual reorientation therapy. In all but a few cases, these individuals were not chosen by these organizations; the individuals decided on their own to participate after reading repeated notices of the study that these two organizations had sent to their members. Nine percent of the participants were recruited from their former therapists who had heard about the study. The remaining

25 percent of the participants were largely referred by therapists who provide sexual reorientation therapy or by other individuals that were participating in the study. All of the participants, not the referral source, called the author to arrange for an interview.

The New York State Psychiatric Institute Institutional Review Board approved the study protocol and waived the requirement of written informed consent.

Sample Description

The mean age of the 143 male participants was 42 years ($SD = 8.0$) and for the 57 females it was 44 years ($SD = 8.5$). Seventy-six percent of the men and 47 percent of the women were married at the time of the interview $\chi^2(1) = 14.2$, $p < .001$). Twenty-one percent of the males and 18 percent of the females were married before beginning therapy. Almost all were Caucasian (95 percent). Most had completed college (76 percent). Participants lived mainly in the United States (East 14 percent, West 35 percent, Midwest 15 percent, South 25 percent), with the remaining 16 percent mostly in Europe.

Most participants were Christian (protestant 81 percent, Catholic 8 percent, Mormon 7 percent). Three percent were Jewish. The vast majority (93 percent) of the participants reported that religion was "extremely" or "very" important in their lives. Nineteen percent of the participants were mental health professionals or directors of ex-gay ministries.

Almost half of the participants (41 percent) reported that they had at some time prior to the therapy been "openly gay." Over a third of the participants (males 37 percent, females 35 percent) reported that they had had serious thoughts of suicide, related to their homosexuality. The majority of participants (78 percent) had publicly spoken in favor of efforts to change homosexual orientation, often at their church.

Description of Structured Interview and Interview Measures

A structured telephone interview was developed with 114 closed-ended questions. The responses were either dichotomous ("yes" or "no") or a number on a defined numeric scale (e.g., 0 to 100 or 1 to 10). Sixty of these questions addressed sexual feelings, fantasy, and behavior. There were also several open-ended questions (e.g., "What were the most important things you talked about in your therapy?"). Almost all questions focused on two time periods: the year before starting therapy (called PRE) and the year before the interview (called POST).

There were 10 self-report measures used to assess different aspects of sexual orientation: (1) Sexual Attraction Scale that ranged from 0 *(only to opposite sex)* to 100 *(only to same sex)*; (2) Sexual Orientation Self-Identity Scale that ranged from 0 (views own sexual orientation as *exclusively heterosexual*) to 100 (views own sexual orientation as *exclusively homosexual*); (3) severity of being bothered by homosexual feelings on a response scale of 1 *(not at all)* to 5 *(extremely)*; (4) frequency of homosexual sex on a scale that ranged from 1 *(never)* to 5 *(nearly every day)*; (5) frequency of yearning for romantic emotional intimacy with a person of the same sex on a response scale that ranged from 1 *(never)* to 5 *(nearly every day)*; (6) frequency of looking with lust or daydreaming about having sex with a person of the same sex (as earlier); (7) percentage of masturbation occasions with homosexual fantasies on a response scale that ranged from 0 to 100; (8) percentage of masturbation occasions with heterosexual fantasies (as earlier); (9) percentage of heterosexual sex occasions with homosexual fantasies (as earlier); (10) use of gay pornography on a response scale that ranged from 1 *(never)* to 5 *(nearly every day)*.

There were three measures for participants having heterosexual sex: (1) frequency of sex on a response scale of 1 *(never)* to 5 *(nearly every day)*; (2) emotional satisfaction with heterosexual relationship on a response scale of 1 *(about as bad as it can be)* and 10 *(about as good as it can be)*; (3) physical satisfaction with heterosexual sex (as earlier). See the Appendix for exact wording of the questions for the 13 measures.

Participants wanted to not only change their sexual orientation, but to function well heterosexually. For the purpose of this study, a variable called "Good Heterosexual Functioning" was created, defined as requiring all five of the following criteria: (1) during the past year, the participant was in a heterosexual relationship and regarded it as "loving"; (2) overall satisfaction in the emotional relationship with their partner (at least 7 on a 1 to 10 scale where 10 is *as good as it can be* and 1 is *as bad as it can be*); (3) heterosexual sex with partner at least a few times a month; (4) physical satisfaction from heterosexual sex at least 7 (the same 1 to 10 scale); (5) during no more than 15 percent of heterosexual sex occasions thinks of homosexual sex.

Participants were asked about 11 possible reasons they had for wanting to change their sexual orientation (list of possible reasons developed during a pilot study). For each reason, participants in the study were asked how important the reason was for them with response categories of "not at all" to "extremely important."

The interview, which the author administered by telephone, took about 45 minutes. A research assistant independently rated audio recordings of the interviews of a sample of 43 participants (chosen on the basis of when the research assistant was available). Complete agreement between the author's coding and the independent coding of variables was calculated as 1; less than complete agreement as 0. The mean agreement across 50 key variables for the 43 participants was .98, indicating very high interrater reliability for the coding of the subject's answers. The audio recordings and the entire study data set are available on request.

Assessment of Marital Relationship

To assess the quality of marital relationships, after the interview the participants were mailed two copies of the Dyadic Adjustment Scale (Spanier, 1976), a validated instrument. Participants and their spouses were instructed to complete the forms independently and mail them to the author.

RESULTS

Motivation to Change

Most participants noted more than one of the 11 reasons asked about. The most commonly reported reasons were that the individual did not find life as a gay man or lesbian emotionally satisfying (males, 85 percent; females, 70 percent; $\chi^2(1) = 4.5, p < .05$), conflict between their same-sex feelings and behavior and the tenets of their religion (79 percent), and desire to get married or stay married (males, 67 percent; females, 35 percent; $\chi^2(1) = 15.8, p < .001$).

Brief Description of Therapy

The great majority (90 percent) of the participants reported using more than one type of therapy. Almost half (47 percent) reported that seeing a mental health professional was the only or most helpful kind of therapy. Most commonly, this was a psychologist (48 percent) or a pastoral counselor (25 percent). Only rarely (5 percent) was it a psychiatrist. About a third (34 percent) of the participants reported that the only or most helpful type of therapy involved attending an ex-gay or other religious support group. The remainder of the participants (19 percent) reported that the only or most helpful type of therapy included such things as repeated meetings with a heterosexual role model, bibliotherapy, or rarely, on their own, changing their relationship to God.

To learn something about the focus of the therapy, individuals were asked, "What were the most important things you talked about in your (therapy)?" Topics often mentioned were dysfunctional family relationships and traumatic childhood experiences, and a variety of other psychological issues (e.g., underlying motivations for same-sex attraction). Only 5 percent of the participants mentioned a topic with a religious content (e.g., relationship with God, what God expects).

Participants were also asked, "How did you translate what you learned into actually changing your feelings?" Often mentioned were linking childhood or family experiences to the development of their sexual feelings, having nonsexual relationships with individuals of the same sex (often in the context of an ex-gay support group), thought stopping (e.g., "When I got such thoughts, I didn't go down that route"), avoiding "tempting" situations, and gradually falling in love with a member of the opposite sex.

Temporal Sequence of Sexual Arousal

The mean age at onset of sexual arousal to the same sex was 12 years ($SD = 2.9$). About 18 years ($SD = 7.8$) later, at age 30, was the beginning of the therapy that they found helpful. The mean duration from the onset of the therapy to the participant beginning to feel a change in their sexual orientation was 1.9 ($SD = 1.9$) years. At the time of the interview, 21 percent ($n = 42$) reported that they were still involved in some form of reparative therapy, usually referring to continuing to attend an ex-gay support group or, on their own, having a lifelong struggle with the underlying issues that they believed were related to their becoming homosexual. For these participants, the mean duration of therapy up until the interview was 15.0 (SD = 7.7) years. For the 79 percent (n = 158) of the participants who were no longer involved in any type of reparative therapy, the mean duration of the therapy was 4.7 (SD = 3.5) years.

Homosexual–Heterosexual Measures Prior to Therapy

Most of the participants reported that they "often" or "very often" had same-sex attraction as teenagers (males, 85 percent; females, 61 percent; $\chi^2(1)$ = 11.5, p < .001). In contrast, many participants as teenagers "never" or "only rarely" had opposite-sex attraction (males, 62 percent; females, 42 percent; $\chi^2(1)$ = 5.9, p < .025).

Although all of the participants had been sexually attracted to members of the same sex, a small proportion had never engaged in consensual homosexual sex (males, 13 percent; females, 4 percent; $\chi^2(1)$ = 3.2, p < .10). Significantly more males than females had engaged in consensual homosexual sex with more than 50 different sexual partners during their lifetime (males, 34 percent; females, 2 percent; $\chi^2(1)$ = 20.6, p < .001). Significantly more males than females had not experienced consensual heterosexual sex before the therapy effort (males, 53 percent; females, 33 percent; $\chi^2(1)$ = 5.6, p < .025).

Measures at PRE and POST

The mean of the Sexual Attraction Scale for both males and females at PRE was in the very high homosexual range: males, 91 (SD = 19.8); females, 88 (SD = 13.8), $t(198)$ = 1.3, *ns*. The mean of the Sexual Orientation Self-Identity Scale for both males and females at PRE was also in the very high homosexual range: males, 77 (SD = 24.5); females, 76.5 (SD = 26.7), $t(183)$ < 1.[1] The mean of the Sexual Attraction Scale for both males and females at POST was in the very high heterosexual range, with females significantly more heterosexual than the males: males, 23 (SD = 21.4); females, 8; (SD = 14.5); $t(198)$ = 4.82, p < .001. The mean of the Sexual Orientation Self-Identity Scale for females (n = 57) and males (n = 139) at POST was also in the high heterosexual range, with the females significantly more heterosexual than the males: males, 8.5 (SD = 14.5); females, 3.0 (SD = 8.1); $t(194) = 3.0, p < .005$.[2]

To compare the amount of change from PRE to POST, the PRE values were subtracted from the POST values. On the Sexual Attraction Scale, the mean change in females was 80 ($n = 57$; $SD = 20$), significantly more than that in males, 67.8 ($n = 143$; $SD = 20$; $t(198) = -3.6, p < .001$). On the Sexual Orientation Self-Identity Scale, the mean change in males was 68.1 ($n = 131$; $SD = 28.3$), not significantly different from the change in females, 73.4, ($n = 52$; $SD = 29.3$; $t(181) = -1.1$.

Figure 4.1 shows the percentage of participants falling within five 20-point intervals on the Sexual Attraction Scale at PRE and at POST. Figure 4.2 shows the same for the Sexual Orientation Self-Identity Scale. At PRE, 46 percent of the males and 42 percent of the females reported exclusively same sex attraction. At POST, 17 percent of the males and significantly more of the females, 54 percent, reported exclusively opposite sex attraction ($\chi^2(1) = 27.0, p < .001$).

How successful was the therapy in decreasing overt homosexual behavior? Figure 4.3 shows the frequency of overt homosexual behavior at PRE and at POST. Of the 158 participants who were no lon-

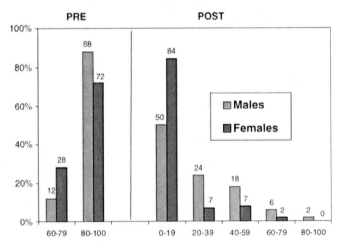

Sexual Attraction Scale (20-Point Intervals)

100 = only same sex, 0 = only opposite sex

FIGURE 4.1. PRE and POST frequency of 20-point intervals of the Sexual Attraction Scale.

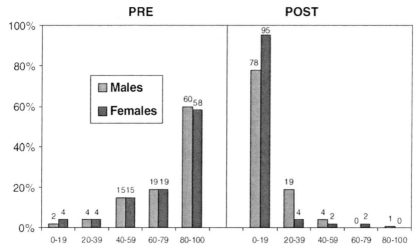

FIGURE 4.2. PRE and POST frequency of 20-point intervals of the Sexual Orientation Self-Identity Scale.

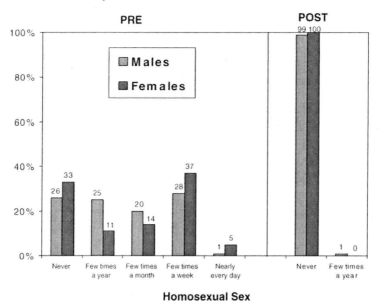

FIGURE 4.3. PRE and POST frequency of homosexual sex.

ger in therapy at the time of the interview, 13 percent of the males and 10 percent of the females reported a brief recurrence (usually just a few days) of overt homosexual behavior since last being in therapy. Only two participants (both males) reported any overt homosexual behavior at POST.

What percentage of participants at POST reported virtually complete change in all of the nine key measures (sexual orientation, sexual orientation identity, and severity of being bothered by unwanted homosexual feelings)? This was defined as follows: "0" on Sexual Attraction Scale, "0 percent" on the same-sex fantasies scale during masturbation, and "never" on the scales assessing lustful thoughts, yearning for romantic emotional intimacy, gay pornography, bothered by homosexual feelings, and overt homosexual behavior with excitement. (*Note:* Defined this way, it would even exclude a man who reported that once or twice a year, when he sees the kind of man he was previously attracted to, he had a mild and fleeting lustful thought). Defined this way, complete change was the case for only 11 percent of the males but a larger percentage of the females, 37 percent $(\chi^2 2(1) = 17.4, p < .001)$.

A slightly less stringent criterion identified participants who at POST had no more than very low values on measures of homosexual orientation, defined as scores of 0 to 10 on 0 to 100 scales or a frequency not greater than "a few times a year" on frequency scales. Twenty-nine percent of the males and 63 percent of the females $(\chi^2(1) / 18.1, p < .001)$ met this criterion at POST.

Figure 4.4 shows how much the individual was bothered by unwanted homosexual feelings. At PRE, 76 percent ($n = 108$) of the males and 65 percent ($n = 37$) of the females reported being "markedly" or "extremely" bothered by unwanted homosexual feelings. At POST, only 1 male and no female reported being "markedly" or "extremely" bothered by unwanted homosexual feelings. At POST, 26 percent ($n = 37$) of the males and 49 percent ($n = 28$) of the females reported being bothered "not at all" by unwanted homosexual feelings, $(\chi^2(1) = 9.0, p < .01)$.

To summarize the results on all 10 measures assessing homosexuality, they have been dichotomized at a point that the author regarded as indicating more than a slight level of homosexuality. Table 4.1 shows the percentage of male and female participants at PRE and POST for the 10 dichotomized variables. It can be seen that there was

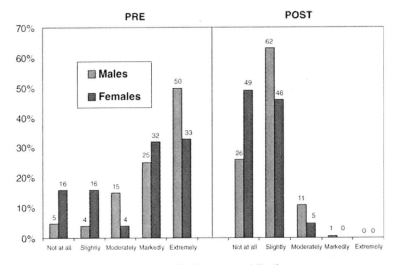

Bothered by Homosexual Feelings

FIGURE 4.4. PRE and POST severity of being bothered by homosexual feelings.

a marked reduction on all change measures. This was not only on the three measures of overt behavior and sexual orientation self-identity, as critics of reparative therapy might expect, but also on the seven variables assessing sexual orientation itself. On 5 of the 10 measures at PRE and at POST, females showed significantly less homosexuality and more heterosexuality than males.

Good Heterosexual Functioning

At PRE, none of the females and only 2.1 percent ($n = 3$) of the males satisfied the criteria for Good Heterosexual Functioning. Sixty-six percent ($n = 94$) of the males and 44 percent ($n = 25$) of the females ($\chi^2(1) = 6.7$, $p = .01$) satisfied the criteria for Good Heterosexual Functioning at POST.

Was Good Heterosexual Functioning at POST less frequent, as one would expect, in those individuals who had been extreme on homosexual measures? A small proportion of the participants (16 percent, 27 males and 6 females) before therapy were extreme on reported homosexual measures in that they had no heterosexual attraction as a

TABLE 4.1. Percentage of Male and Female Participants at PRE and POST on 10 Dichotomized Homosexual Measures.[a]

Homosexual measure	Males (percent)		Females (percent)	
	PRE	POST	PRE	POST
20 or higher on the Sexual Attraction Scale (0 = exclusively heterosexual, 100 = exclusively homosexual)	100 (n = 143)	53 (n = 143)*	100 (n = 57)	16 (n = 57)*
20 or higher on the Sexual Orientation Self-Identity Scale (0 = exclusively heterosexual, 100 = exclusively homosexual)	98 (n = 133)	22 (n = 139)*	96 (n = 52)	5 (n = 57)*
Homosexual sex at least a few times a month	50 (n = 143)	1 (n = 143)	56 (n = 57)	0 (n = 57)
At least moderately bothered by homosexual feelings	91 (n = 143)*	11 (n = 143)	68 (n = 57)*	5 (n = 57)
Yearning for romantic emotional involvement with same sex at least a few times a month	78 (n = 143)	8 (n = 143)	88 (n = 57)	4 (n = 57)
Looking with lust at same sex or daydreaming about having sex with same sex at least a few times a month	99 (n = 143)	31 (n = 143)*	98 (n = 57)	5 (n = 57)*
Same-sex fantasies on 20 percent or more masturbatory occasions among participants who masturbated	94 (n = 138)	45 (n = 112)	92 (n = 50)	18 (n = 39)
Opposite-sex fantasies (without trying) on 20 percent or more of masturbatory occasions among participants who masturbated	9 (n = 138)*	69 (n = 112)	26 (n = 50)*	72 (n = 39)
Same-sex fantasies during 20 percent or more of heterosexual sex occasions among participants who had heterosexual sex	51 (n = 51)	6 (n = 111)	54 (n = 24)	13 (n = 31)
Use of gay pornography at least a few times a month	38 (n = 143)*	1 (n = 143)	11 (n = 57)*	2 (n = 57)

[a]All measures have been dichotomized at point that the author would regard as indicating more than a slight level of homosexuality.

*Male versus female rates that are significantly different, two-tailed, at $p < .01$.

teenager or in the year before the change effort, never had heterosexual sex with excitement, and in the year before the change effort had no opposite sex fantasies during masturbation. The expected result was not obtained: 20 of these 33 participants (61 percent, 17 males and 3 females) satisfied these criteria for Good Heterosexual Functioning at POST, a prevalence similar to that of the entire sample.

Fifty-six participants (28 percent) had regular heterosexual sex both at PRE and at POST (in all but one case with the same person, their spouse). As would be expected, very few of these 56 participants reported Good Heterosexual Functioning at PRE (5 percent, $n = 3$). In contrast, 84 percent ($n = 47$) of these participants reported Good Heterosexual Functioning at POST.

Table 4.2 shows at POST a marked increase in the frequency of heterosexual sex, more satisfaction in the emotional relationship with their spouse, and more physical satisfaction with heterosexual sex.

Ninety-four (72 percent) of the 130 couples sent the Dyadic Adjustment Scale returned completed forms. Mean scores for the instrument's Overall Adjustment Scale for the 94 participants or their spouses were not significantly different from the instrument's normative group of 218 married couples (power = .81 to detect an effect size of .35 or larger with $p < .05$). Thus, on average, participants reported the same degree of marital adjustment as the instrument's normative reference group.

Depression has been reported to be a common side effect of unsuccessful attempts to change sexual orientation. This was not the case for our participants, who often reported that they were "markedly" or

TABLE 4.2. Heterosexual Sex and Relationship PRE and POST for 56 Participants Who Had Heterosexual Sex Both at PRE and at POST.

Measure	PRE (percent)	POST (percent)
Heterosexual sex at least a few times a month	52	95
Emotional satisfaction with heterosexual relationship at least 8 on a 1 to 10 scale (1 = *about as bad as it can be*, 10 = *about as good as it can be*)	14	80
Physical satisfaction with heterosexual sex at least 8 on a 1 to 10 scale (same as above)	25	89

Note: To summarize the results, the three measures have been dichotomized.

"extremely" depressed at PRE (males 43 percent, females 47 percent), but rarely that depressed at POST (males 1 percent, females 4 percent). To the contrary, at POST the vast majority reported that they were "not at all" or only "slightly" depressed (males 91 percent, females 88 percent).

Participants were presented with a list of several ways that the therapy might have been "very helpful" (apart from change in sexual orientation). Notable were feeling more masculine (males) or more feminine (females) (87 percent) and developing intimate nonsexual relations with the same sex (93 percent).

DISCUSSION

This study had a number of advantages over previous studies of attempts to measure change in sexual orientation. The assessment of the participants was far more detailed than the assessment in previous studies, which were usually limited to one or two global measures of sexual orientation. The sample size was larger than any previous study of sexual orientation change in which the participant himself or herself was directly assessed. The use of a structured interview makes it possible for others to know exactly how the participants were evaluated. The near perfect interrater reliability of the coding of the participants' responses indicates no bias in interviewer coding of the participant responses. An important feature of the study is that the entire data set and the audiotapes are available for review.

There are several limitations to the study. Ideally, the research interviewer in a study is blind to the research hypothesis and has no vested interest in the results. Because the author conducted the interviews, this was not the case in this study. Although initially skeptical, in the course of the study, the author became convinced of the possibility of change in some gay men and lesbians. The fact that the study results are based on a structured interview reduces, but does not eliminate, the possibility that interviewer bias influenced the participants' responses.

The study relied exclusively on self-report, as is almost always the case in psychotherapy treatment efficacy studies. The study would have greatly benefited by also using objective measures of sexual orientation, such as penile or vaginal photoplethysmography. This was judged to be not feasible as funds were not available for the high cost of regional testing and of having a large number of individuals travel long distances to the testing sites.

Given the fallibility of memory for past events, it is impossible to be sure how accurate individuals were in answering questions about how they felt during the year before starting the therapy, which on average was about 12 years before the interview. Using a prospective design, in which participants were evaluated before entering therapy and then many years later, would provide much more information than the design that was used. However, such a study was not feasible. It would be extremely expensive, would require outside funding, and the results would not be available for at least 6 years (assuming a year to enter participants and a follow-up period of 5 years).

Are the participants' self-reports of change, by-and-large, credible or are they biased because of self-deception, exaggeration, or even lying? This critical issue deserves careful examination in light of the participants' and their spouses' high motivation to provide data supporting the value of efforts to change sexual orientation. Again, it is impossible to be sure, but comparing the actual results to the results that might be expected if such systematic bias were present suggests (at least to the author) that, by and large, this is not the case. Several such comparisons follow.

If there was significant bias, one might expect that many participants would report complete or near complete change in all sexual orientation measures at POST. Only 11 percent of the males and 37 percent of the females did so. One might also expect that many participants would report a rapid onset of change in sexual feelings after starting therapy. In fact, participants reported that it took, on average, a full 2 years before they noticed a change in sexual feelings. If there was bias, one would expect that participants would be reluctant to admit any use of gay pornography. In fact, 24 percent of the males and 4 percent of the females acknowledged that at POST they had used gay pornography.

If systematic bias was present, one would expect that the magnitude of the bias for females would be similar to that for males. However, marked gender differences were found. On the 10 change measures, females at PRE and at POST never had values closer to the homosexual end of the respective scale than did the males. In 4 of the 10 measures at either PRE or POST, females reported values significantly closer to the heterosexual end of the respective scale than did the males. These gender differences are consistent with the literature suggesting greater female plasticity in sexual orientation (Baumeister, 2000; Diamond, 2003; Friedman and Downey, 2002; Kitzinger and Wilkinson, 1995).

The married participants, as were all participants, were motivated to provide evidence for the benefits of reparative therapy. If their reports of marital adjustment were biased to show how helpful the therapy was for their marriage, one would expect that the married participants would report a level of marital adjustment higher than that of the normative reference group of the Dyadic Adjustment Scale. Most participants who were married before starting therapy did report significant improvement in marital adjustment. However, they did not report a current level of adjustment higher than that of the normative reference group for this instrument.

Finally, real change in sexual orientation seems plausible (again, at least to the author) as the participants used change strategies commonly effective in psychotherapy (Mahoney, 1991). For example, participants often developed a narrative linking childhood or family experiences to current problems, received support from a group or individual, used thought stopping, and avoided situations that triggered homosexual feelings.

It is unclear how many gays and lesbians in the general population would want to change their sexual orientation or how representative the study sample is of those who would be interested in therapy with that goal. Obviously, this study cannot address the question of how often sexual reorientation therapy actually results in the substantial changes reported by most of the participants in this study. To recruit the 200 participants, it was necessary to repeatedly send notices of the study over a 16-month period to a large number of participants who had undergone some form of reparative therapy. This suggests that the marked change in sexual orientation reported by almost all of the study subjects may be a rare or uncommon outcome of reparative therapy. However, there may be other reasons for the difficulty in recruiting subjects, such as reluctance of ex-gays to be interviewed and reluctance of therapists to contact former clients.

The participants in the study all believed that the changes they experienced were due primarily to their therapy. However, the lack of a control group leaves the issue of causality open. It is logically possible that a small proportion of gay men and lesbians change their sexual orientation without therapy and that the changes experienced by the participants were causally unrelated to their therapy. The issue of causality can only be answered by a study with random assignment of gay men and lesbians wishing to change their sexual orientation to either a treatment group (some form of reparative therapy) or a control group. The difficulties in conducting such a study are almost certainly insurmountable. For example, potential participants wishing to change their sexual orientation are unlikely to agree to being assigned to the control group, which would not provide therapy for several years.

This study indicates that some gay men and lesbians, following reparative therapy, report that they have made major changes from a predominantly homosexual orientation to a predominantly heterosexual orientation. The changes following reparative therapy were not limited to sexual behavior and sexual orientation self-identity. The changes encompassed sexual attraction, arousal, fantasy, yearning, and being bothered by homosexual feelings. The changes encompassed the core aspects of sexual orientation. Even participants who only made a limited change nevertheless regarded the therapy as extremely beneficial. Participants reported benefit from nonsexual changes, such as decreased depression, a greater sense of masculinity in males, and femininity in females, and developing intimate nonsexual relations with members of the same sex.

There is no doubt about what the participants in the study reported. The key question is judging the credibility of their self-reports. One possibility is that some of the participants actually changed their predominantly homosexual orientation to a predominantly heterosexual orientation. Another possibility is that all of the individuals constructed elaborate self-deceptive narratives (or even lied) when they claimed to have changed, at least to some extent, their sexual orientation. For the reasons already noted, the author believes that the participants' self-reports in this study are by-and-large credible and that probably few, if any, elaborated self-deceptive narratives or lied. If this is the case, it supports the study hypothesis that change in sexual orientation following some kind of therapy does occur in some gay men and lesbians. This is contrary to the conventional view that homosexual behavior can be resisted or relabeled, but that true change in well established sexual orientation (arousal, fantasy, feelings of lust) does not occur.

The findings in this study are in marked contrast to the conclusions of another study (Beckstead, 2001). Beckstead studied 18 men and 2 women who claimed to have benefited from sexual reorientation therapy. A major motivation to change sexual orientation, as in many of the participants in this study, was conflict between their same-sex feelings and behavior and the tenets of their religion. Beckstead did not report exactly how he applied his "qualitative" methodology to assess change in sexual orientation; he did not use a structured interview. His conclusion:

> Participants reported that their sense of peace and contentment did not indicate a change in sexual orientation but a change in self-acceptance, self-identity, focus, and behavioral patterns. No substantial or generalized heterosexual arousal was reported, and participants were not able to modify their tendency to be attracted to their same sex. (p. 103)

Because Beckstead's sample and the sample in this study appear to be quite similar, the contrasting findings of the two studies regarding change in sexual orientation from reparative therapy are puzzling, to say the least.

The answer to the puzzle (at least to the author's satisfaction) has been provided by Beckstead (L. Beckstead, personal communication, October 21, 2002). Apparently, many of his participants did report increased heterosexual attraction following reparative therapy. However, after listening to how they described their heterosexual arousal, Beckstead concluded that it was not "generalized heterosexual arousal" for two main reasons: either because the arousal was limited to one person (e.g., only the subject's spouse), whereas typically heterosexuals are attracted to more than one person of the opposite sex; or because the opposite sex arousal in his participants didn't have the "intensity" that is typically present in heterosexuals. In the article itself, Beckstead does not explain to the reader the justification for his arbitrary definition of what constitutes a significant increase in heterosexual arousal.

It is true that many of the participants in this study did report that their heterosexual arousal was limited to one person, but most reported that it was not (males, 72 percent; females, 76 percent). Beckstead would apparently consider reparative therapy as a failure for the many participants in this study who, prior to reparative therapy, had been unable to become sexually aroused by the opposite sex, but following the therapy were, but only to their spouse.

What about Beckstead's reporting that his participants "were not able to modify their tendency to be attracted to their same sex?" Consider the many cases in this study who made substantial changes in sexual attraction and fantasy, and were now for the first time enjoying heterosexual sex but the change in sexual attraction was not complete. For example, there may occasionally be lustful fantasies of low intensity seeing someone of the same sex who reminded the participant of a previous same-sex partner. Because such a change is not complete, strictly speaking such a participant continues to have a "tendency to same-sex attraction." It makes no clinical sense to ignore such a change and this would never be done in the case of evaluating the efficacy of any psychosocial or pharmacological therapy.

It probably is the case that reparative therapy rarely, if ever, results in heterosexual arousal that is as intense as a person who never had same sex attractions. However, advocates of reparative therapy do not make that claim. One would not judge a psychosocial treatment for a sexual dysfunction as a failure if it did not result in sexual function indistinguishable from that of individuals who never had experienced such a disorder.

Critics of reparative therapy assert that the claims of success in changing sexual orientation are limited to anecdotal reports of individuals who have had the reparative therapy, or of therapists who provide such therapy. This study, with the database available to other researchers, clearly goes beyond anecdotal information and provides evidence that reparative therapy is sometimes successful. For the participants in our study, there was no evidence of harm. To the contrary, they reported that it was helpful in a variety of ways beyond changing sexual orientation itself.

The findings of this study have implications for clinical practice. First, it questions the current conventional view that desire for therapy to change sexual orientation is always succumbing to societal pressure and irrational internalized homophobia. For some individuals, changing sexual orientation can be a rational, self-directed goal. Second, it suggests that the mental health professionals should stop moving in the direction of banning therapy that has as a goal a change in sexual orientation. Many patients, provided with informed consent about the possibility that they will be disappointed if the therapy does not succeed, can make a rational choice to work toward developing their heterosexual potential and minimizing their unwanted homosexual attractions. In fact, the ability to make such a choice should be considered fundamental to client autonomy and self-determination.

These findings of considerable benefits and no obvious harms in the study sample suggest that the current recommendation by the American Psychiatric Association (2000) that "ethical practitioners refrain from attempts to change individuals sexual orientation" is based on a double standard: It implies that it is unethical for a clinician to provide reparative therapy because there is inadequate scientific evidence of effectiveness, whereas it assumes that it is ethical to provide gay affirmative therapy for which there is also no rigorous scientific evidence of effectiveness and for which, like reparative therapy, there are reports and testimonials of harm (Gonsiorek, 1982; Throckmorton, 2002).

The author concurs with the American Psychiatric Association Position Statement on Therapies Focused on Attempts to Change Sexual Orientation (American Psychiatric Association, 2000) that "encourages and supports research by the National Institute of Mental Health and the academic research community to further determine 'reparative' therapy's risks versus its benefits." Clearly, it is only this kind of research that can provide the information that both clinicians and potential patients need to have to make informed decisions about reparative therapy. What is needed is a prospective outcome study of reparative therapy in which a consecutive series of volunteer individuals are evaluated before starting therapy and after several years. Such a study could provide data as to how often significant change in sexual orientation is reported. It could also examine how often individuals who are unsuccessful in the therapy are harmed in some way and the magnitude of the harm. Unfortunately, given the cost of conducting such a complex study, its necessarily long duration, and the current consensus of the mental health professions that reparative therapy is both ineffective and harmful, it is extremely unlikely that such a useful study will be conducted in the near future.

In this self-selected sample, almost all of the participants reported substantial changes in the core aspects sexual orientation, not merely overt behavior. Even individuals who made a less substantial change in sexual orientation reported that the therapy was extremely beneficial in a variety of ways. Change in sexual orientation should be seen as complex and on a continuum. Some people appear able to change only sexual orientation self-identity. Others appear also able to change overt sexual behavior. This study provides evidence that some gay men and lesbians are able to also change the core features of sexual orientation.

APPENDIX

Interview questions for the 10 change measures:

1. "We have a sexual attraction scale with 100 only to a man/woman [same sex] and 0 being only to a woman/man [opposite sex]. In the year (before you started therapy/last year), how would you rate yourself?"

     If a subject had difficulty answering the question an additional question was asked: "Suppose each time you saw someone that you were sexually attracted to, you noted whether they were a man or a woman. After you did this 100 times, how many times would it be a man and how many times a woman?"
2. "In the (year before you started therapy/last year) how often did you yearn for romantic emotional intimacy with a [same sex]?"
3. "In the (year before you started therapy/last year) how often did you look with lust at a [same sex] or daydream about having sex with a [same sex], which could include your partner?"
4. "In the (year before you started therapy/last year) on what percent of these occasions [masturbating] were you, without trying, fantasizing a sexual experience with a [opposite sex]?"
5. "In the (year before you started therapy/last year) on what percent of these occasions [masturbating] were you fantasizing a sexual experience with a [same sex]?"
6. "In the (year before you started therapy/last year) on what percent of the occasions, when you were having this sex with a [opposite sex], did you at some time think with lust of a [same sex]?"
7. "In the (year before you started therapy/last year), how often did you have homosexual sex?"
8. "The next scale also goes from 100 to 0 but is a global scale of homosexual-heterosexual that takes into account not only sexual attraction but also how you think about yourself—your identity. On this scale, in the (year before you started therapy/the last year), how would you rate yourself?"

9. "In the (year before you started therapy/last year) how much were you bothered by unwanted homosexual feelings?"

Interview questions about three marital variables:

1. "In the (year before you started therapy/last year) how often did you have sex with your (wife, husband)?"
2. "In the (year before you started therapy/last year) how emotionally satisfying was your relationship with your (wife, husband)?"
3. "In the (year before you started therapy/last year) how physically satisfying was sex with your wife?

NOTES

1. Data were missing for 15 participants who could not answer this question.
2. Data were missing for 4 subjects who could not answer this question.

REFERENCES

Adams, H.E. & Sturgis, E.T. (1977), Status of behavioral reorientation techniques in the modification of homosexuality: A review. *Psychological Bulletin,* 84: 1171-1188.

American Academy of Pediatrics (1983), Policy statement: Homosexuality and adolescence. *Pediatrics,* 92:631-634.

American Counseling Association (1998), Resolution adopted by the Governing Council of the American Counseling Association: On appropriate counseling responses to sexual orientation. Available upon request from the American Counseling Association.

American Psychiatric Association (1999), Position statement on psychiatric treatment and sexual orientation. *American J. Psychiatry,* 156:1131.

American Psychiatric Association (2000), Position statement on therapies focused on attempts to change sexual orientation (reparative or conversion therapies), *American J. Psychiatry,* 157:1719-1721.

American Psychological Association(1997), Resolution on appropriate therapeutic responses to sexual orientation. Retrieved January 23, 2003, from http://www.apa.org/pi/sexual.html.

Barlow, D.H. & Agras, W.S. (1973), Fading to increase heterosexual responsiveness in homosexuals. *J. Applied Behavior Analysis,* 6:355-366.

Baumeister, R.F. (2000), Gender differences in erotic plasticity: The female sex drive as socially flexible and responsive. *Psychological Bulletin,* 126:347-374.

Beckstead, A.L (2001), Cures versus choices: Agendas in sexual reorientation therapy. *J. Gay & Lesbian Psychotherapy,* 5:87-125. Reprinted in: *Sexual Conversion Therapy: Ethical, Clinical and Research Perspectives,* eds. A. Shidlo, M. Schroeder, & J. Drescher. Binghamton, NY: The Haworth Press, 2001, pp. 87-125.

Berger, J. (1994), The psychotherapeutic treatment of male homosexuality. *American J. Psychotherapy,* 48:251-261.

Bieber, I., Dain, H., Dince, P., Drellich, M., Grand, H., Gundlach, R., Kremer, M., Rifkin, A., Wilbur, C., & Bieber T. (1962), *Homosexuality: A Psychoanalytic Study.* New York: Basic Books.

Bieschke, K.J., McClanahan, M., Tozer, E., Grzegorek, J.L. & Park, J. (2000), Programmatic research on the treatment of lesbian, gay, and bisexual clients: The past, the present, and the course for the future. In: *Handbook of Counseling and Psychotherapy with Lesbian, Gay, and Bisexual Clients,* eds. R.M. Perez, K.A. DeBord, & K.J. Bieschke. Washington, DC: American Psychological Association, pp. 309-335.

Callahan, E. J. (1976), Covert sensitization for homosexuality. In: *Counseling Methods,* eds. J. Krumboltz & C.E. Thoresen. New York: Holt, Rinehart and Winston, pp. 234-245.

Diamond, L. (2003), Was it a phase? Young women's relinquishment of lesbian/bisexual identities over a 5-year period. *J. Personality & Social Psychology,* 84:352-364.

Drescher, J. (2001), Ethical concerns raised when patients seek to change same-sex attractions. *J. Gay & Lesbian Psychotherapy,* 5(3/4):181-210. Reprinted in: *Sexual Conversion Therapy: Ethical, Clinical and Research Perspectives,* eds. A. Shidlo, M. Schroeder, & J. Drescher. Binghamton, NY: The Haworth Press, 2001, pp. 181-210.

Ellis, A. (1959), A homosexual treated with rational psychotherapy. *J. Clinical Psychology,* 15:338-343.

Forstein, M. (2001), Overview of ethical and research issues in sexual orientation therapy. *J. Gay & Lesbian Psychotherapy,* 5(3/4):167-180. Reprinted in: *Sexual Conversion Therapy: Ethical, Clinical and Research Perspectives,* eds. A. Shidlo, M. Schroeder, & J. Drescher. Binghamton, NY: The Haworth Press, 2001, pp. 167-180.

Freeman, W. & Meyer R.G. (1975), A behavioral alteration of sexual preferences in the human male. *Behavior Therapy,* 6:206-212.

Friedman, R.C. & Downey, J.I. (2002), *Sexual Orientation and Psychoanalysis: Sexual Science and Clinical Practice.* New York: Columbia University Press.

Goetze, R. (2001), Homosexuality and the possibility of change: An ongoing research project. Retrieved October 16, 2002, from http://www.newdirection.ca/research/index.html.

Golwyn, D.H. & Sevlie, C.P. (1993), Adventitious change in homosexual behavior during treatment of social phobia with phenelzine. *J. Clinical Psychiatry,* 54:39-40.

Gonsiorek, J. (1982), The use of diagnostic concepts in working with gay and lesbian populations. *J. Homosexuality*, 7:9-20.

Hadden, S. B. (1966), Treatment of male homosexuals in groups. *International J. Group Psychotherapy*, 17:13-22.

Hadfield, J. A. (1958), The cure of homosexuality. *British Medical J.*, 58:1323-1326.

Haldeman, D.C. (2001), Therapeutic antidotes: Helping gay and bisexual men recover from conversion therapies. *J. Gay & Lesbian Psychotherapy*, 5(3/4):117-130. Reprinted in: *Sexual Conversion Therapy: Ethical, Clinical and Research Perspectives*, eds. A. Shidlo, M. Schroeder, & J. Drescher. Binghamton, NY: The Haworth Press, 2001, pp. 117-130.

Hatterer, L. (1970), *Changing Homosexuality in the Male*. New York: McGraw-Hill.

Isay, R.A. (1996), *Becoming Gay: The Journey to Self-Acceptance*. New York: Pantheon.

Kitzinger, C. & Wilkinson, S. (1995), Transitions from heterosexuality to lesbianism: The discursive production of lesbian identities. *Developmental Psychology*, 31:95-104.

Liss, J.L. & Welner, A. (1973), Change in homosexual orientation. *American J. Psychotherapy*, 27:102-104.

MacIntosh, H. (1994), Attitudes and experiences of psychoanalysts in analyzing homosexual patients. *J. American Psychoanalytic Association*, 42:1183-1207.

Mahoney, M.J. (1991), *Human Change Processes: The Scientific Foundation of Psychotherapy*. New York: Basic Books.

Masters, W.H. & Johnson, V.E. (1979), *Homosexuality in Perspective*. Boston: Little, Brown.

McCrady, R.E. (1973), A forward-fading technique for increasing heterosexual responsiveness in male homosexuals. *J. Behavior Therapy & Experimental Psychiatry*, 4:257-261.

Mintz, E.E. (1966), Overt male homosexuals in combined group and individual treatment. *J. Consulting Psychology*, 30:193-198.

Murphy, T.F. (1992), Redirecting sexual orientation: Techniques and justifications. *J. Sex Research*, 29:501-523.

National Association of Social Work (1997), *Social Work Speaks: National Association of Social Workers Policy Statements*, Fourth Edition. Washington, DC: NASW Press.

Pattison, E.M. & Pattison, M.L. (1980), "Ex-gays": Religiously mediated change in homosexuals. *American J. Psychiatry*, 137:1553-1562.

Poe, J.S. (1952), The successful treatment of a 40-year old passive homosexual based on an adaptational view of sexual behavior. *Psychoanalytic Review*, 39:23-33.

Shechter, R.A. (1992), Treatment parameters and structural change: Reflections on the psychotherapy of a male homosexual. *International Forum Psychoanalysis,* 1:197-201.

Shidlo, A. & Schroeder, M. (2002), Changing sexual orientation: A consumers' report. *Professional Psychology: Research & Practice,* 33(3):249-259.

Socarides, C.W. (1978), *Homosexuality.* New York: Jason Aronson.

Spanier G.B. (1976), Measuring dyadic adjustment: New scales for assessing the quality of marriage and similar dyads. *J. Marriage & the Family,* 38:15-28.

The Surgeon General's call to action to promote sexual health and responsible sexual behavior (2001), Retrieved October 16, 2002, from http://www.surgeongeneral. gov/library/sexualhealth/call.htm.

Throckmorton, W. (2002), Counseling practices as rated by clients seeking sexual reorientation counseling. Manuscript submitted for publication.

van den Aardweg, G.J.M. (1986), *On the Origins and Treatment of Homosexuality.* Westport, CT: Praeger.

Wolpe, J. (1969), *The Practice of Behavior Therapy.* New York: Pergamon Press.

Section III:
Commentaries on the Spitzer Study
and Dr. Spitzer's Response from
Archives of Sexual Behavior

5

Can Sexual Orientation Change?
A Long-Running Saga

John Bancroft

The issue of whether people can change their sexual orientation has been obscured by moral controversy ever since homosexual orientation was "constructed" in the late nineteenth century (Bancroft, 1989, 1994). On the one hand, any evidence that such change has occurred has been used by those who condemn homosexuality as evidence of its "acquired" nature which, they would argue, is consistent with it being sinful; on the other hand, those who defend the homosexual reject evidence of such change on the grounds that those changed cannot have been true homosexuals in the first place (e.g., Ellis, 1915). Rational debate about the extent to which people can change, and what characteristics might predict the potential for such change, therefore becomes rapidly buried.

I am more than familiar with this long-running controversy. In the 1960s, early in my career as a budding behaviorist, I carried out research to assess whether behavioral techniques, such as aversion therapy or systematic desensitization, could modify sexual preference in men (no women presented themselves for such treatment). My experiences fairly quickly led me to conclude that such interventions were ineffective, but in reporting my findings (Bancroft, 1974), I came under attack from members of the Gay Rights Movement for attempting to impose societal norms on those with a homosexual orientation, and in the process reinforcing the social stigma. Thus, some-

---

This chapter appeared originally under the same title in *Archives of Sexual Behavior* 32(5):419-421. Copyright 2003 Kluwer Academic/Plenum Publishers. Reprinted with permission.

doi:10.1300/5503_05

what unwittingly, I found myself in the midst of this moral controversy. This, needless to say, caused me to reflect (Bancroft, 1975). In
no way had I rejected homosexuality as a sexual lifestyle nor had I regarded it as pathological. In my innocence, I was responding to the requests of some homosexual men to help them to change and escape
from the social stigma their sexuality brought upon them. Also, as a
researcher, I wanted to know whether the claims of "reorientation"
that were being made by other behavior therapists, in particular Mac-
Culloch and Feldman (1967), could be substantiated. The use of such
interventions did not imply that homosexuality was a pathology, but
rather an aspect of behavioral responsiveness that might be modifi-
able with these new behavioral techniques that were based on so-
called "modern learning theory."

Times were different then. The Gay Rights Movement was early in
its development and it was much more likely than it is today that individuals would seek such change. But on reflection, I realized that,
whereas I was genuinely trying to help the individual, in the process I
was aligning myself with those who reinforced homophobic attitudes
and all the consequences of the stigma that ensued. It did not continue
to be a dilemma for me, as my own results gave me no reason to continue to use such simplistic interventions.

Then, in 1973, the American Psychiatric Association (APA) removed homosexuality from the DSM, in the process rejecting the notion that it was inherently pathological (Bayer, 1981). Although revealing considerable division of opinion within the psychiatric
profession on this issue, this step could be regarded as the official end
of the medicalization of homosexuality, which up to that time had
been pursued steadfastly by the medical profession. As if to reinforce
this "demedicalization," the APA has since periodically issued statements about the immutability of sexual orientation, and that it is unethical for clinicians to attempt to change it with therapy (American
Psychiatric Association, 2000). What has happened since 1973 is that
"the Church," in many of its manifestations, has stepped into the
breach, reviving religious opposition to homosexuality in terms of
immorality rather than pathology. Given that Spitzer played a key
role in the APA's demedicalization of homosexuality in the 1970s, it
is interesting that he has recently paused to reconsider, if not the
pathology of homosexuality, at least its immutability.

What can we learn from Spitzer's study? Its principal strength is the substantial size of his sample, much larger than most comparable studies. I also have no reason to doubt Spitzer's sincerity in carrying out this study. But there are some major limitations.

First and foremost, the sample consists of men and women who principally sought treatment because of their religious beliefs and who were presenting themselves as evidence that such change was both possible and desirable for others (for 93 percent, religion was extremely or very important, and 78 percent had spoken in public about their "conversion," in many cases in their churches). Assessment of change was entirely based on their recall of how things were before treatment. Given their powerful agenda of promoting such treatment, it would be surprising if they did not overestimate the amount of change. A similar problem exists with the evaluation of any treatment for which the patient has a vested interest in proving its worth. Spitzer addresses this issue by pointing out that simple bias of this kind would have produced a more clear-cut picture of reorientation and no gender difference. He is partially right, but he cannot justifiably conclude that because distortion was not maximum, that distortion did not occur.

Second, it is very difficult to discern from this study just what the "reparative therapy" had involved. At best, it had been a long process, with a substantial minority still continuing in ongoing therapy after many years. A few hints at specific interventions were given, mainly of the "self-control" variety (e.g., "thought stopping," "avoiding tempting situations"), and an intriguing passing reference, at least for homosexual men, to "the demystification of the male and maleness," resulting in a decrease of romanticization and eroticization of men, but for the most part, there seemed to be a more general process involving group pressure and therapist reinforcement of the determination to be different and, as a result, less immoral.

It was not clear how these subjects were recruited, although unquestionably they constitute a highly unrepresentative sample of those who had come under the influence of religion-driven "reparative therapy." I could also take issue with Spitzer's criteria of change, and his title, which states that 200 participants reported a change from homosexual to heterosexual orientation, when the article reports a less substantial change for many if not most of them.

So where does this leave us? Let me put aside, for one moment, the politics and ethics of "reparative therapy." There are good grounds, apart from this study, for concluding that sexual orientation is not always fixed early and immutable. Whereas the large majority of us identify as homosexual or heterosexual at a relatively early age, never change, and have no inclination to attempt to change, a minority of unknown size exists whose sexual behavior is less bound by an "orientation" or who are less certain about their sexual identity and who may go through processes of change without any involvement in "reparative therapy" or the like. It is noteworthy that Kinsey (Kinsey, Pomeroy, and Martin, 1948) proposed his scales to capture the variability of sexual preference, not only across individuals but also within the same individual over time. As the Gay Rights Movement gathered momentum, Kinsey's view was rejected in favor of a clear dichotomy of "straight or gay," with those who identified as bisexual regarded as deceiving themselves (e.g., Robinson, 1976). In the past 15 years, the flexibility of sexual identity has again been acknowledged. In the AIDS era, the concept of "men who have sex with men" is used as a more general descriptor than "homosexual."

Every now and then, I see someone in my clinic who presents himself (and, more occasionally, herself) as confused or conflicted about sexual identity. Sometimes these individuals are struggling with the idea of bisexuality. "Does bisexuality exist?" they might ask. In some cases, their sexuality is compartmentalized (e.g., "I find certain types of men very sexually arousing, but I can't imagine being in a loving sexual relationship with another man")—what might be described as a failure to incorporate one's sexuality into one's capacity for a close dyadic relationship, a problem by no means confined to those with homosexual orientation. How do I react to such patients after a career of reflection on this issue? I now have no doubts about how to respond and this involves some crucial sequential steps:

> *Step 1.* Make it absolutely clear that, whatever the patient's values or beliefs might be, I have no difficulty whatsoever in accepting and valuing either a homosexual or a heterosexual or a bisexual identity. The issue is which is right for that person. Insofar as I have personal values, they apply to issues of responsibility and the use of sex to foster intimacy in a close ongoing relationship. Neither is dependent on the gender of

those involved. It behooves the therapist to be explicit about her or his moral values as they impact on the treatment process so that the patient can choose whether to work with that therapist or not.

Step 2. Make it clear that in order to find out what type of sexual relationship works best, it may be necessary to experience more than one type of relationship, involving partners of either gender. Furthermore, during a lifetime, more than one successful relationship may occur, involving same-sex and opposite-sex partners at different times.

Step 3. Emphasize the need to take time to work out what is right. The therapist, who is better designated as a counselor in this context, facilitates this process of search and discovery as appropriate. This may involve helping the patient to identify the different "compartments" of his or her sexuality, and how to incorporate them into a sexually rewarding, intimate, and loving relationship. This is more education than therapy.

Some of the subjects in Spitzer's study may have gone through some comparable process, except that it is clear that at no time was the acceptability of a homosexual or bisexual solution ever on the agenda. Others sound as though they are still battling with the conflict between what feels sexually right for them and what is morally acceptable to them (and their therapist).

The concept of "reparative therapy," as described, raises some key ethical issues, the most fundamental being the distinction between medical treatment for a pathological condition and the imposition of moral values under the guise of medical treatment. If there were any grounds for regarding homosexual orientation as a pathology rather than a variant of human sexual expression, then treating the pathology might be justified. I would assert that no such grounds exist, and hence providing treatment on that basis is professionally unethical and, according to my value system, immoral. There is a long and disturbing history of medical practitioners imposing their moral values through their professional practice. The imposition of moral values, explicitly or implicitly, that is, urging someone to undergo change because his or her current sexual orientation is immoral, should not be regarded as "therapy," and in any case raises other ethical and moral issues. I would strongly advocate Surgeon General David Satcher's

The Surgeon General's Call to Action to Promote Sexual Health and Responsible Sexual Behavior (U.S. Department of Health and Human Services, 2001). This calls for responsibility in our sexual lives (responsibility toward ourselves and our sexual partners), coupled with a respect for diversity. Thus, someone who believes that homosexuality is wrong is entitled to that opinion, but is not entitled to impose it on others, particularly if those others exercise responsibility in their sexual lives. Thus, the principle of responsibility facilitates the acceptance of diversity.

Spitzer's findings are consistent with the idea that some people do change their sexual orientation in some respects during the course of their lives, but his findings do not justify the existence of "reparative therapy." As defined, this constitutes vigorous reinforcement of homophobia and the social stigma experienced by those with homosexual identities in our society. Together, this results in widespread suffering for homosexual minorities and, no doubt, for many who are pressured into attempting such change, considerable conflict and unhappiness.

REFERENCES

American Psychiatric Association (2000), Commission on Psychotherapy by Psychiatrists (COPP): Position statement on therapies focused on attempts to change sexual orientation (Reparative or conversion therapies). *American J. Psychiatry,* 157:1719-1721.

Bancroft, J. (1974), *Deviant Sexual Behavior: Modification and Assessment.* Oxford, England: Oxford University Press.

Bancroft, J. (1975), Homosexuality and the medical profession: A behaviorist's view. *J. Medical Ethics,* 1:176-180.

Bancroft, J. (1989), *Human Sexuality and Its Problems.* Edinburgh, Scotland: Churchill Livingstone.

Bancroft, J. (1994), Homosexual orientation: The search for a biological basis. *British J. Psychiatry,* 164:437-440.

Bayer, R. (1981), *Homosexuality and American Psychiatry: The Politics of Diagnosis.* New York: Basic Books.

Ellis, H. (1915), *Studies in the Psychology of Sex:* Volume 2. *Sexual Inversion.* Philadelphia: Davis.

Kinsey, A.C., Pomeroy, W.B., & Martin C.E. (1948), *Sexual Behavior in the Human Male.* Philadelphia: W.B. Saunders.

MacCulloch, M.J. & Feldman, M.P. (1967), Aversion therapy in the management of 43 homosexuals. *British Medical J.,* 2:594-597.

Robinson, P. (1976), *The Modernization of Sex*. New York: Harper & Row.

U.S. Department of Health and Human Services (2001), *The Surgeon General's Call to Action to Promote Sexual Health and Responsible Sexual Behavior*. Washington, DC: U.S. Government Printing Office.

6

Understanding the Self-Reports of Reparative Therapy "Successes"

A. Lee Beckstead

It should not be surprising that individuals who identify as "ex-gay" would report positive results when invited to participate in a study designed to support their position. It would be more informative, however, to understand how and why they came to those conclusions. My commentary on Spitzer's study will involve reinterpreting his data in light of my research regarding individuals who reported successful experiences and those who reported harms from sexual reorientation therapy. My commentary will also clarify several misunderstandings that Spitzer made regarding my research.

My article that Spitzer cited (Beckstead, 2001a) was not meant to be a comprehensive summary of my findings or methodology but was written to describe the variety of agendas involved in sexual reorientation therapy. The methods I used in my investigations have been detailed in Beckstead (1999, 2001b) and Beckstead and Morrow (2003). Briefly, the whole of my research in this area includes two qualitative investigations involving 45 men and 5 women who held a wide range of perspectives regarding sexual reorientation. Participants described their experiences at different points between 1997 and 2001 through interviews, prospective personal journals written during their therapy, four focus groups, and a multidimensional assessment (Coleman, 1987) of past, present, and intended future sexual orientations. Participants verified and also influenced my analysis of their experi-

This chapter appeared originally under the same title in *Archives of Sexual Behavior* 32(5):421-423. Copyright 2003 Kluwer Academic/Plenum Publishers. Reprinted with permission.

Published by The Haworth Press, Inc., 2006. All rights reserved.
doi:10.1300/5503_06

ences by reading preliminary results and correcting misinterpreta-
tions. Throughout these multiple interactions, participants described
when they first discovered their attractions, how they dealt with these
attractions while growing up, what motivated them to seek reorientation therapy, what their experiences were of such therapy, how therapy had affected them, how they currently managed their attractions,
and what changes had occurred since the beginning of the study. Unlike Spitzer's investigation, my studies also asked participants about
their reasons for being involved with this type of research. All participants were asked the same questions during the interviews but were
allowed to describe their experiences without any leading questions
or direction. Similar to a structured interview, this method allowed
for consistency and comparability among participants but also permitted exploration and the opportunity for participants to respond in
their own terms.

The primary difference between my studies and Spitzer's study is
that my research was designed to analyze the meanings of participants' experiences and understand the context of their struggles and
how they cognitively or behaviorally resolved their conflicts. Spitzer
used his participants' self-reports, however, to prove the efficacy of
reparative therapy. Because of my research focus and methodology, I
learned that a variety of alternate reasons exist, besides the efficacy of
reorientation treatments, as to why and how such participants claim
success. I learned foremost that participants could identify as heterosexual because they were provided in the course of therapy with
causal theories and interventions that helped them dissociate from a
gay or lesbian identity. Such techniques included teaching participants that they were heterosexuals who had sexualized their emotional needs to be close to the same sex. Participants could then
reframe their same-sex sexual fantasies as "admiration" rather than
eroticism and believe they were heterosexual by eliminating their
homosexual behaviors and maintaining their commitments to their
family and religion.

Participants described being successful in reducing homosexual
thoughts and behaviors; however, my results demonstrated ambiguity
and inconsistencies in participants' reports of their sexual orientation.
For example, some participants indicated they were "exclusively heterosexual" but specified experiencing limited heterosexual attractions. Some would describe themselves as "heterosexuals with a ho-

mosexual past," or as no longer having homosexual attractions, but only because they now avoided certain situations, such as "cruising" areas or being alone with same-sex individuals. These same inconsistencies may also be found in Spitzer's findings when some could not answer the question regarding labeling their sexual identity. Successful reports of reorientation in my studies were also in contrast to participants' journal entries, which monitored their attractions and motivations throughout their therapy experience. Several wrote about homosexual and heterosexual longings but later denied or disregarded them, which seemed to depend upon their current thinking process and circumstance. Because of these discrepancies in self-reports, it was difficult to say exactly how many participants experienced an increase in heterosexual attraction following therapy.

It became apparent during my analysis as well that participants' sexuality could not be measured on a unidimensional scale, as Spitzer used, because their homosexual attractions seemed mutually exclusive to their heterosexual attractions. That is, if a participant described himself or herself as "less homosexual," it would not necessarily mean she or he was "more heterosexual." Spitzer claimed that my definition was arbitrary of what constitutes a significant increase in heterosexual arousal. However, I conceptualized sexual orientation by using Freund's (1974) definition as "the erotic preference for the body of one sex over that of the other" (p. 26). Participants in my studies reported that, at the end of therapy, they could still be aroused erotically to the body shape of same-sex individuals and, indeed, that this arousal pattern exceeded that toward opposite-sex individuals *despite calling themselves heterosexuals.* Participants reported that therapy helped them change their thinking about and expression of homosexuality and sexuality but not their actual sexual orientation. As well, even those participants who reported having an increase in heterosexual attraction described those attractions as oriented only to their spouse and different from their homosexual arousal. This difference in attraction and intimacy was described by one "converted" participant in this way:

> I use the comparison of a campfire versus a forest fire. That maybe my emotional response to men would be like a forest fire and that it's very . . . it's been very intense and dangerous and out of control and perhaps damaging or hurtful. But my relationship with my wife is more like the campfire. It's warm and comfort-

able and happy and reassuring and protective and although it probably doesn't have the same emotional intensity that the physical relationship with a man might bring, you know, I think maybe it's good.

Some participants enjoyed sexual intercourse with the opposite sex; some stated that sexual intercourse with the opposite sex felt unnatural. In addition, participants reported that their same-sex attractions and conflicts became a non-issue because they became less focused on their sexuality and more focused on careers and relationships.

Several other reasons exist concerning why we should not accept these clients' self-reports uncritically. As Spitzer noted, self-reports are unreliable measures. Freund (1960, 1977) and Conrad and Wincze (1976), for example, found that clients' self-reports of favorable re-orientation outcomes tended to be imprecise, deny certain facts, and were not supported by objective data. Spitzer seemed to believe that he has assessed sexual attraction; yet, he has only measured participants' subjective experiences of their attractions. Phallometry would be a more reliable and valid measurement of sexual orientation because it distinguishes erotic arousal patterns in men. In addition, men can suppress responses in such assessments but not produce false ones (Kuban, Barbaree, and Blanchard, 1999; see also Chivers, 2000). A man who is primarily attracted to children and who wants to avoid punishment would more than likely tell others that he has changed, but measuring the degree of his arousal may indicate otherwise.

Demand characteristics and social and cognitive dissonance theories suggest that participants in my research and in Spitzer's would also need to tell themselves and others that they were not failures. Given the extreme internal and external motivations and the amount of time and energy they have invested, participants would want to feel successful.

To illustrate this, I talked with an individual, "Steven" (personal communication, January 26, 2003), who participated in a study conducted by Shidlo and Schroeder (2002), which was similar to mine and to Spitzer's. Steven stated that he was asked by his therapist to participate in this study and "give a good report." Steven stated that he felt confident at the time of his interview that he was doing the right thing and was making progress. Therefore, he told the interviewer that he had made significant improvements in his pre and post ratings.

Steven also stated, however, that, in retrospect, his report was "inflated" and based on his need for approval and validation:

> I wanted to be NARTH's poster child. I wanted to fit in and there was so much at stake. I wanted to boost my morale and tell others that I was doing well . . . I downplayed my sexuality. I lied enough so it would be believable to myself and the researcher. I also believed I could become [heterosexual], and I saw a glimmer that it was true. I convinced myself because I sometimes felt it, and there was enough hope that it was or could be true.

Steven stated that because he was behaving heterosexually, could be aroused with stimulation, was delaying the times between ejaculations, and loved his wife, he felt heterosexual. He also described sex with his wife as satisfying because it kept his family together, met religious and societal standards, and was preferable to the extreme guilt associated with the brief sexual encounters he had with men. He also stated that he struggled with labels: "I've slept with 1 woman 100 times and 100 men 1 time. Am I bisexual?" Steven stated that although he stopped sexualizing his thoughts about men, his dreams manifested erotic preferences for them. Furthermore, Steven stated that his self-report was political: "Gay-affirmative research was taking away our right to our beliefs. I needed to defeat these people and stand up for our beliefs and for the crusade." Steven's experiences are similar to those described by my participants and suggest that Spitzer's data collection may be invalid, ignoring important contextual factors and the shifts these individuals may make in perspectives and individual development.

An additional limitation of Spitzer's study is his selective reporting of clients' experiences. His research fails to describe the experiences of those individuals for whom reparative therapy does not work. By contrast, my research included the significant harms that occurred when hopes and assurances of a lasting cure turned false and the person continued to be "plagued" by same-sex attractions after sincere efforts to change had failed. These failures were internalized and reported to increase self-hatred, hopelessness, and fear, even leading some participants to attempt suicide. In addition, reparative therapy tended to reinforce extreme, negative stereotypes of the lives of lesbian, bisexual, and gay individuals, which seemed to cause still more self-hatred, discrimination, and difficulties in intimacy. Spouses and families also blamed themselves or the client for not changing enough and further pain, separation, and depression followed. These harms are not superficial ones. They require clarification and accuracy in portraying how the underpinnings and current practice of such therapy have the potential for serious negative consequences. Spitzer espouses reparative therapy, but missed the larger picture because he limited his focus on a highly self-selected, nonrepresentative portion of the population who may seek out such treatments.

Spitzer's data are important, however, in that they demonstrate that a subset of same-sex attracted individuals can adapt successfully to live in a heterosexual relationship. Spitzer is inaccurate when he wrote that I would consider these individuals as therapy failures. In fact, I have advocated and developed a broader-based treatment plan in which such clients can explore a wide range of options and develop individualized solutions to integrate their sexual and social selves in a healthy manner. My biggest concern is that Spitzer's description of his data is misleading. Policymakers, religious leaders, families, and individuals in conflict may believe that all homosexual or bisexual individuals could (and therefore should) be heterosexual if they just tried hard enough. In fact, Spitzer's study has been widely cited as proof that gay men and lesbians can change their sexual orientation. A more accurate interpretation of his results would suggest, however, that only a rare proportion of same-sex attracted individuals can find ways to live satisfactorily in a heterosexual relationship.

REFERENCES

Beckstead, A.L. (1999), "Gay is Not Me": Seeking Congruence Through Sexual Reorientation Therapy. Unpublished master's thesis, University of Utah, Salt Lake City, UT.

Beckstead, A.L. (2001a), Cures versus choices: Agendas in sexual reorientation therapy. *J. Gay & Lesbian Psychotherapy,* 5(3/4), 87–115. Reprinted in: *Sexual Conversion Therapy: Ethical, Clinical and Research Perspectives,* eds. A. Shidlo, M. Schroeder, & J. Drescher. New York: The Haworth Press, 2001, pp. 87-115.

Beckstead, A.L. (2001b), The Process toward Self-acceptance and Self-identity of Individuals who Underwent Sexual Reorientation Therapy. Unpublished doctoral dissertation, University of Utah, Salt Lake City, UT.

Beckstead, A.L. & Morrow, S.L. (2003), Clients' Experiences of Conversion Therapy: The Need for a New Treatment Model. Manuscript submitted for publication.

Chivers, M.L. (2000), Genital and Subjective Sexual arousal in Heterosexual, Bisexual, and Lesbian Women. Unpublished master's thesis, Northwestern University, Evanston, IL.

Coleman, E. (1982), Developmental stages of the coming-out process. *J. Homosexuality,* 7(3):41-43.

Coleman, E. (1987), The assessment of sexual orientation. *J. Homosexuality,* 14(1):9-24.

Conrad, S.R. & Wincze, J.P. (1976), Orgasmic reconditioning: A controlled study of its effects upon the sexual arousal and behavior of adult male homosexuals. *Behavior Therapy,* 7:155-166.

Freund, K. (1960), Some problems in the treatment of homosexuality. In: *Behavior Therapy and the Neuroses,* ed. H.J. Eysenck. Oxford: Pergamon Press, pp. 312-326.

Freund, K. (1974), Male homosexuality: An analysis of the pattern. In: *Understanding Homosexuality: Its Biological and Psychological Bases,* ed. J.A. Loraine. Lancaster, England: Medical and Technical Publishing, pp. 26-81.

Freund, K. (1977), Psychophysiological assessment of change in erotic preferences. *Behaviour Research & Therapy,* 15:297-301.

Kuban, M., Barbaree, H.E., & Blanchard, R. (1999), A comparison of volume and circumference phallometry: Response magnitude and method agreement. *Archives Sexual Behavior,* 28:345-359.

Shidlo, A. & Schroeder, M. (2002), Changing sexual orientation: A consumers' report. *Professional Psychology: Research & Practice,* 33:249-259.

7

The Malleability of Homosexuality: A Debate Long Overdue

A. Dean Byrd

Is homosexuality innate and immutable? Or can a person with a homosexual sexual orientation make significant changes in the direction of becoming heterosexual? Are the official statements issued by the major national mental health associations—which declare that no published evidence exists demonstrating that homosexuals can significantly alter their sexual attractions—in fact, accurate? Such questions take center stage in any discussion of sexual orientation and change.

Studies published in some peer-reviewed journals have attempted to demonstrate that homosexuality is so strongly compelled by biological factors that it must be indelibly ingrained in a person's core identity. Therefore, such studies imply that sexual orientation is not amenable to change; however, critical reviews of those studies and subsequent acknowledgments by the researchers themselves yield only one conclusion: that biology alone is not sufficient to explain the development of homosexuality (Byne and Parsons, 1993; Friedman and Downey, 1993; Hamer and Copeland, 1994; LeVay, 1996). Rather, homosexuality—as with most other complex attractions and behaviors—is almost certainly polygenic and multifactorial in origin. Given this likely genesis of homosexuality, what potential is there for change for those individuals who are motivated to seek such change?

Sexual plasticity in homosexual men is not a new or novel idea. More than 30 years ago, Freund (1963, 1971), using penile plethysmog-

This chapter appeared originally under the same title in *Archives of Sexual Behavior* 32(5):423-425. Copyright 2003 Kluwer Academic/Plenum Publishers. Reprinted with permission.

doi:10.1300/5503_07

raphy, found that some homosexual men could voluntarily alter their penile responses to respond to heterosexual stimuli without ever receiving reorientation therapy. Although it would be erroneous to generalize from such a clinical sample to suggest that homosexual orientation is malleable in all people, still, historical and current research would suggest that it is equally erroneous to conclude that change in sexual orientation is not possible for *some* men.

In addition, the recent research by Diamond (2000) on lesbians has demonstrated that sexual orientation in females is far from fixed in those women who are not exclusively heterosexual. My own research and clinical experience for more than 30 years suggests that some homosexual men are able to make and sustain significant changes in core aspects of their homosexual orientation, including fantasy and sexual arousal—not just behavior. Such individuals are able to develop and then maintain heterosexual attractions (Byrd and Nicolosi, 2002; Nicolosi, Byrd, and Potts, 2000). Sexual plasticity in homosexual men and women has not received adequate attention within our profession. Indeed, a number of writers have decried the political activism that silences opposing viewpoints within the mental health arenas (Halpern, Gilbert, and Coren, 1996; Sarason, 1986). In a recent lead article in the *American Psychologist,* Redding (2001) made a strong case for the lack of sociopolitical diversity in psychology, the bias that results in research and publications, and the de facto discrimination that disfavors clinicians who hold unpopular views (such as the belief that clients who seek sexual reorientation should be supported).

This confounding of politics, psychology, and therapeutics has occurred, I believe, because of antihomosexual bias in some cases and gay activism in others. In both instances, there has been a confusing co-mingling of facts and theories by anti- or prohomosexual political groups—both of which claim to have science on their side—and the ideas expressed do not appear to be representative of beliefs held by most therapists.

Frustrated with such activism, a former president of the American Psychological Association (APA), Robert Perloff, exclaimed " . . . listen to the client . . ." (Murray, 2001). Indeed, patient self-determination is the cornerstone of the mental health professions, and it must take priority over political activism. In fact, in a rare public expression of anger and frustration at the American Psychological Association meeting in 2001, Perloff condemned the APA's narrow politicization. Of reorientation therapy with homosexuals, he said: "It is considered unethical. . . . *That's all wrong.* First, the data are not fully in yet. Second, if the client wants a change, listen to the client. Third, you're barring research" (Murray, 2001, p. 20).

Listening to the client and respecting his or her choices are essential to the mental health professions, and Spitzer has concluded that some individuals who seek to diminish their homosexual attractions are motivated by a rational, self-directed goal. They are not simply seeking change to conform to external pressures or because of internalized homophobia.

The Spitzer study essentially reopens the debate over whether homosexuality is mutable. His research has ignited a heated discussion about the possibility of diminishing a homosexual orientation and developing heterosexual attractions. Indeed, Spitzer provides evidence that some gay men and lesbians are not only able to change self-identity, but are able to modify core features of sexual orientation, including fantasies. Thus, his research makes an important contribution to a plethora of other studies and case reports on change (Throckmorton, 2002).

Spitzer's sample size was larger than those of most in prior studies. He carefully considered the affective components of the homosexual experience and was considerably more detailed in his assessment than were other studies. His use of a structured interview demonstrates clearly how the subjects were evaluated. He limited his pool of participants to those who reported at least 5 years of sustained change from a homosexual to a heterosexual orientation. Virtually any bias in the interview coding was eliminated by the near perfect interrater scores. A unique feature of his research is that the entire set of data is available to other researchers. And, finally, Spitzer has been and continues to be supportive of gay affirmative therapy and gay rights.

Much of the criticism of Spitzer's study is likely to focus on sample bias because many of his subjects were referred by religiously conservative organizations that promote the possibility of change; however, as astutely noted by Rosik (2003), this may actually be a strength of the research given that the clear majority of the studies on homosexuality and change used convenience samples solicited through gay-affirming organizations and media. Rosik (2003) further notes that "this suggests a skew in the existing literature as a whole, the degree of which can only be determined through a closer examination of individuals such as those in Spitzer's study" (p. 18).

A substantial majority of the participants in the Spitzer study valued and agreed with their traditional religious faiths, which view homosexual relationships as non-life-giving and outside of the will of God. Such value systems should not be dismissed, judged by the therapist to be improper, or overridden through therapeutic manipulation. Haldeman (2000) offers an interesting perspective in this regard:

> A corollary issue for many [clients] is a sense of religious or spiritual identity that is sometimes as deeply felt as is sexual orientation. For some it is easier, and less emotionally disruptive, to contemplate changing sexual orientation, than to disengage from a religious way of life that is seen as completely central to the individual's sense of self and purpose. However we may view this choice or the psychological underpinnings thereof, do we have the right to deny such an individual treatment that may help him to adapt in the way he has decided is right for him? I would say that we do not. (p. 3)

As LeVay (2000) explains it:

> First, science itself cannot render judgments about human worth or about what constitutes normality or disease. These are value judgments that individuals must make for themselves, while possibly taking scientific findings into account. Second, I believe that we should as far as possible, respect people's personal autonomy, even if that includes what I would call misguided desires such as the desire to change one's sexual orientation. (p. 12)

Spitzer's research has demonstrated that, contrary to the prevailing climate, the data on homosexuality are far from complete. Ethicality would suggest that the suppression of data and discouragement of further scientific research should not be tolerated. With appropriate guidelines in place (institutional review boards), it is not only ethical but well within the purview of science to encourage the study of issues such as change from homosexuality. The well-intentioned caretakers of our national organizations slide down a slippery slope when advocating what amounts to a virtual censorship of scientific investigation of politically unpopular views. It is ironic that Spitzer—the original architect of the 1973 decision to remove homosexuality from the DSM—is once again, going against the prevailing winds of his time and advocating the avoidance of that slippery slope.

REFERENCES

Byne, W. & Parsons, B. (1993), Human sexual orientation: The biologic theories reappraised. *Archives General Psychiatry,* 50:228-239.

Byrd, A.D. & Nicolosi, J. (2002), A meta-analytic review of treatment of homosexuality. *Psychological Reports,* 90;1139-1152.

Diamond, L.M. (2000), Sexual identity, attractions, and behavior among young sexual-minority women over a 2-year period. *Developmental Psychology,* 36:241-250.

Freund, K. (1963), A laboratory method of diagnosing predominance of homo- or hetero-erotic interest in the male. *Behaviour Research & Therapy,* 17:451-457.

Freund, K. (1971), A note on the use of the phallometric method of measuring mild sexual arousal in the male. *Behavioral Therapy,* 2:223-228.

Friedman, R.C. & Downey, J.I. (1993), Neurobiology and sexual orientation: Current relationships. *J. Neuropsychiatry,* 5:131-153.

Haldeman, D.C. (2000, August), *Gay Rights, Patients Rights: The Implementations of Sexual Orientation Conversion Therapy.* Paper presented at the meeting of the American Psychological Association, Washington, DC.

Halpern, D.F., Gilbert, R., & Coren, S. (1996), PC or not PC? Contemporary challenges to unpopular research findings. *J. Social Distress & the Homeless,* 5:251-271.

Hamer, D. & Copeland, P. (1994), *The Science of Desire: The Search for the Gay Gene and the Biology of Behavior.* New York: Simon and Schuster.

LeVay, S. (1996), *Queer Science: The Use and Abuse of Research into Homosexuality.* Cambridge, MA: MIT Press.

LeVay, S. (2000), *Sexual Orientation: The Science and Its Social Impact.* Retrieved April 3, 2001, from http:members.aol.com/hta/slevay/page12.htm.

Murray, B. (2001), Same office, different aspirations. *Monitor on Psychology,* 32(11):20.

Nicolosi, J. & Byrd, A.D. (2000), Beliefs and practices of therapists who practice sexual reorientation psychotherapy. *Psychological Reports,* 86:689-702.

Nicolosi, J., Byrd, A.D., & Potts, R.W. (2000), Retrospective self-reports of changes in homosexual orientation: A consumer survey of conversion therapy clients. *Psychological Reports,* 86:1071-1088.

Redding, R.E. (2001), Sociopolitical diversity in psychology. *American Psychologist,* 56:205-215.

Rosik, C. H. (2003), Motivational, ethical, and epistemological foundations in the clinical treatment of unwanted homoerotic attraction. *J. Marital & Family Therapy,* 29:13-28.

Sarason, S.B. (1986), And what is the public interest? *American Psychologist,* 41: 899-905.

Throckmorton, W. (2002), Initial empirical and clinical findings concerning the change process for ex-gays. *Professional Psychology: Research & Practice,* 33:242-248.

8

A Methodological Critique of Spitzer's Research on Reparative Therapy

Helena M. Carlson

In Spitzer's study of the effectiveness of reparative therapy in changing sexual orientation, he reports that gay men and lesbians indicate that they have made major changes in their sexual orientation from homosexual to heterosexual. He also notes that even those who made only limited change in sexual orientation still found the therapy beneficial.

The criteria for acceptance into the study required subjects to have had a predominantly homosexual orientation before entering reparative therapy. They should be able to report that after reparative therapy they have sustained for at least 5 years some change toward a heterosexual orientation. The acceptance criteria also required participants to report in a telephone interview on their sexual behavior for the year before they entered reparative therapy and then also report on their behavior in the year before the current research interview. Spitzer reports that there was, on average, an interval of 12 years between the time of entry into reparative therapy and the telephone interview. This places a heavy burden on memory and Spitzer acknowledges that greater fallibility exists in such long-range memory.

Participants in the study come from a very narrow stratification of the population: 97 percent were Christian, 95 percent were Caucasian, the mean age for males was 42 years, the mean age for females was 44 years, 76 percent of the males were married, and 47 percent of

This chapter appeared originally under the same title in *Archives of Sexual Behavior* 32(5):425-427. Copyright 2003 Kluwer Academic/Plenum Publishers. Reprinted with permission.

Published by The Haworth Press, Inc., 2006. All rights reserved.
doi:10.1300/5503_08

the women were married. Some participants were directors of ex-gay ministries and some had publicly spoken favorably of efforts to change sexual orientation, often at their church. Thus, this is a population of highly religious, white, protestant, middle aged, and middle class men and women. There is little evidence that they are representative of a diverse gay community.

Participants in this study were asked in a telephone interview to report on their sexual fantasies, masturbation fantasies, lustful looks, use of gay pornography, homosexual thoughts, and overt sexual behavior. A key question is the credibility of the participants' self-report. It should be recognized that 93 percent of participants reported that religion was extremely or very important to them.

No consent form was administered and participants' identity was known to the interviewer. Ethical guidelines for informed consent for research issued by the American Psychological Association (2002) require not only protection of confidentiality for participants but that a consent form should clearly state that participants may withdraw from research at any time. Without a consent form, it is possible that participants were wary that their confidentiality would not be protected. The total reliance on self-report in this study can be disturbing when one considers that fundamentalist religious beliefs tend to be strongly opposed toward any acceptance of homosexuality.

Martin (2000) has pointed out that when the research topic is an emotion-laden issue, then individuals might not wish their true feelings to be known, particularly when these feelings differ from socially accepted practices in their community. It seems that this highly religious Christian sample would be particularly vulnerable to feelings of shame and embarrassment if they had to report that they had engaged in condemned behavior. A significant risk exists for self-deception and even lying in highly religious participants when responding to questions about sexual behavior that is strongly condemned by their religion. These participants would also be highly motivated to providing supportive data for the possibility of change of sexual orientation.

Another methodological concern is that all the telephone interviews were done by the investigator alone. This raises the methodological issue of interviewer bias. An interviewer can subtly influence respondent's answers by inadvertently indicating approval or disapproval (Cozby, 2001). Interviewers may also bring their own expectations to their interviews and that can bias their interpretation of responses. Although no research method is absolutely free of bias, the interview is more open to bias than most other research methods (Sommer and Sommer, 2002). It would have been better to have trained and used other interviewers, preferably those blind to the hypothesis of the study. A research assistant did independently rate audio recordings of 43 of the 200 interviews and Spitzer reports they achieved .98 interrater reliability based on this sampling. It would be helpful if one had some details on the background of the research assistant in order to evaluate more fully the interrater reliability.

Another issue of concern was the diversity and background of the therapies or counseling offered. Although all were described as reparative or conversion, with the goal to change sexual orientation from homosexual to heterosexual, the therapists came from different educational and training backgrounds. The majority (43 percent) were from ex-gay religious ministries, primarily protestant, who focused on conversion to heterosexuality; 23 percent came from a group of primarily psychoanalytic mental health professionals and lay people with the same focus; 9 percent were recruited as participants by their former therapists; and 25 percent were a variety of sexual reorientation counselors, including social workers, ministers, and lay people.

Despite the diverse educational and training background, Spitzer lumps all types of counseling together as reparative therapy. Since religious approaches may well be in the form of prayer, it is difficult to see how this form of counseling can be combined in data from the treatments used by trained psychoanalysts. This presents confusion since it is unclear to which particular type of therapy any reported changes can be attributed.

Spitzer used a numerical scale of sexual attraction to determine whether participants had a predominantly homosexual or heterosexual orientation before entering therapy and to assess any changes in sexual orientation by comparing scores on this measure after they had received reparative therapy. He defined participants in the study as predominantly homosexual if they scored at least 60 on the scale of sexual attraction before seeking therapy. He also required before acceptance in the study that participants report a change of at least 10 points, lasting at least 5 years, toward the heterosexual end of the scale.

It is difficult to assess data from this Sexual Attraction Scale, which appears to have been designed for this study. This is a 100 point scale (where 0 = *exclusively heterosexual* and 100 = *exclusively homosexual*). Spitzer defined a score ≥ 20 as homosexual (see Table 4.1) and used the same score on the Sexual Orientation Self-Identity Scale. It appears that, for example, participants who scored 25 on this scale will be recognized as homosexual and similar to participants who scored 100 on this scale.

Spitzer reported that married couples were mailed copies of the Dyadic Adjustment Scale (Spanier, 1976). They were asked to complete this questionnaire independently of their partner and to mail it in. Spitzer reported a 72 percent response rate from married participants and that, on average, subjects reported the same degree of marital adjustment as the instrument's normative reference group. It is difficult to assess data from this measure because no description was given of it, no complete reference for it was given, and no validity cited. There was also no control over when and how the respondents actually completed the measure.

No control group was included in this research, although admittedly that would be hard to obtain. This means that causality cannot be demonstrated. Spitzer acknowledged the fundamental methodological problems with the research but also claimed that it provides support for the possibility of reparative therapy to change sexual orientation from homosexual to heterosexual. Spitzer cited some nonsexual benefits from this therapy. He noted that participants reported that after therapy they had a greater sense of masculinity in males and femininity in females. This needs more clarification in light of the many studies of the complexities of gender roles (Crawford and Unger, 2000; Kilmartin, 2000).

In conclusion, even the limited hypothesis that some individuals whose orientation is predominantly homosexual can become predominantly heterosexual following reparative therapy is not supported by this study. It may be possible that some of the research participants might have a more fluid sexual orientation, such as bisexuality (Bohan, 1996).

REFERENCES

American Psychological Association (2002), Ethical principles of psychologists and code of conduct. *American Psychologist,* 57:1060-1073.

Bohan, J.S. (1996), *Psychology and Sexual Orientation: Coming to Terms.* New York: Routledge.

Cozby, P.C. (2001), *Methods in Behavioral Research,* Seventh edition. Mountain View, CA: Mayfield Publishing.

Crawford, M. & Unger, R.K. (2000), *Women and Gender: A Feminist Psychology,* Third edition. San Francisco, CA: McGraw-Hill.

Kilmartin, C.T. (2000), *The Masculine Self,* Second edition. San Francisco, CA: McGraw-Hill.

Martin, D.W. (2000), *Doing Psychology Experiments,* Fifth edition. Belmont, CA: Wadsworth.

Sommer, R. & Sommer, B. (2002), *A Practical Guide to Behavioral Research: Tools and Techniques,* Fifth edition. New York: Oxford University Press.

Spanier, G.B. (1976), Measuring dyadic adjustment: New scales for assessing the quality of marriage and similar dyads. *J. Marriage & the Family,* 38:15-28.

9

Are Converts to Be Believed?
Assessing Sexual Orientation "Conversions"

Kenneth M. Cohen
Ritch C. Savin-Williams

The realization that subject selection criteria significantly influence results when investigating socially stigmatized populations is one of the earliest and most frequently documented lessons learned by sexologists. Examples of the biasing influence of subject selection are legendary, including the early discovery that recruitment venue could determine outcomes, such as age of coming out, number of gay friends, and self-esteem level (Harry, 1986), and, more recently, that selecting gay youth from support groups (Savin-Williams and Ream, 2003) or with sex-atypical behavior (McDaniel, Purcell, and D'Augelli, 2001) escalates levels of reported suicidality. Reviewing problems inherent in sampling "homosexuality," Sandfort (1997) argued that "findings in a specific study depend heavily on the definition and operationalization of homosexuality adopted, and on the way the sample has been put together" (p. 261). Yet, sample selection remains one of the "unresolved issues in scientific sexology" reviewed by McConaghy (1999) several years ago in this Journal.

Nowhere is this issue more pertinent than in assessing the highly volatile issue of sexual orientation change following reparative therapy. As Spitzer noted in his literature review, the question of the ef-

This chapter appeared originally under the same title in *Archives of Sexual Behavior* 32(5):427-449. Copyright 2003 Kluwer Academic/Plenum Publishers. Reprinted with permission.

doi:10.1300/5503_09

fectiveness and consequences of "reorientation" therapy has been a source of vitriolic controversy. Because of this current debate, we believe that sexologists must be extra vigilant to conduct the most methodologically sophisticated, conservative investigations possible, which implies being particularly attentive to subject selection. We do not believe that it is justifiable for contemporary research scholars to presume their conclusions by selection criteria: Including subjects most likely to agree with the author's hypothesis while excluding those most likely to give disconfirming results. To permit conclusions about causality, which Spitzer denies making but nevertheless embraces ("change in sexual orientation following some kind of therapy does occur in some gay men and lesbians"), the scientific method must be fully embraced, for only then will it be possible to determine whether events (sexual orientation change) are the consequence of chance, untested variables, or the study's independent variable (reparative therapy). Scientific research also depends on the willingness of the researcher to question the truthfulness of subject claims. Given the failure of previous scientific attempts to demonstrate change in sexual orientation (versus sexual identity or behavior), the findings by Spitzer deserve close methodological scrutiny.

In this commentary, we ignore Spitzer's apparent conceptual misunderstanding about the purpose of his study (a title and literature review that promises a study about changes in sexual orientation from homosexual to heterosexual, but a proposed hypothesis that merely suggests shifts in sexual attractions, an event not uncommon among many sexual-minority individuals—see Diamond, 2003a). We also ignore several methodological procedures that create doubt about whether Spitzer used proper scientific methods to ensure the validity of his data, including his definition of sexual orientation, the lack of reliability and validity data on instruments, and the failure to behaviorally anchor response items. Instead, our focus is on subject selection biases that raise serious questions about the veracity of subject claims of reorientation. It is our contention that Spitzer selected a unique group of subjects who were decidedly invested in demonstrating the possibility and benefits of reparative therapy. This one fatal flaw seriously diminishes the internal and external validity of his study and necessarily precludes the very conclusions Spitzer offered: "The mental health professions should stop moving in the direction of banning sexual reorientation therapy" and that "many patients . . .

can make a rational choice to work toward developing their heterosexual potential and minimizing their unwanted homosexual attractions."

Who were Spitzer's subjects and how could this collective affect the internal and external validity of his findings? In terms of venue, volunteers were recruited through "repeated" notices to ex-gay religious ministries, therapies, and political organizations that promote biasing conditions. Subjects were clearly not blind to the study's hypothesis or purpose and most, if not all, had compelling motivations to provide data that would prove the hypothesis correct. Indeed, subjects *could not* participate in the study unless their perceived experience supported the study's hypothesis. Thus, subjects had a strong desire to change (including 19 percent who were directors of ex-gay ministries or mental health professionals), strong desire to witness to others (e.g., 78 percent publicly spoke in favor of efforts to change homosexual orientation, often at church functions), strong desire to affirm their religiosity (93 percent reported that religion was "very" or "extremely" important to them), and strong desire to believe that their own conversion was successful. These biasing conditions are not conducive or even normative to scientific investigations. The intent to eliminate or at least reduce social desirability as a potentially damaging influence on the veracity of results is standard fare for scientific research and yet it appears that Spitzer did everything within his power to *promote* if not *ensure* his intended responses. Thus, it is exceedingly difficult to take at face value the independence of the study's data.

Spitzer himself recognized this point by acknowledging that "subjects' and their spouses' high motivation to provide data supporting the value of efforts to change sexual orientation" was present, but he concluded that it was unlikely that their reports were "biased due to self-deception, exaggeration, or even lying." If subjects were biased, according to Spitzer, they would have reported a "rapid onset of change," a "complete or near complete change in all sexual orientation measures," marital adjustment scores "higher than that of the normative reference group," and no gender differences. Although the study's findings were sufficient "at least to the author" to rule out systematic bias, Spitzer provided no empirical or theoretical support for the reasoning underlying these assumptions. Furthermore, his reasoning is not self-evident. For example, when lie/faking scales are integrated into questionnaires (e.g., the MMPI-2), degree of deception falls along a continuum and only rarely are subjects distributed at either pole. Spitzer assumed that bias must be conscious, intentional, and deceitful, but we know of no evidence supporting this perspective which, naively, discredits the psychological sophistication of his subjects and ignores the possibility that unconscious defense mechanisms (e.g., repression, suppression, denial) are operative. Indeed, given the nature of the subject pool, it would be surprising if subjects did *not* engage in data manipulation.

This subject selection bias might also have contributed to a memory bias that could have further generated inflated reports of change. To the extent that PRE-therapy (average was 12 years before the interview) homoerotic feelings were emotionally disturbing, on recollection years later they would likely be remembered as greater or more omnipresent than they were at the time. When combined with a desire to minimize current homoerotic feelings, inflated PRE–POST differences might well be expected that would erroneously suggest greater reorientation change than that actually achieved. Also contributing to this expected inflation was Spitzer's reliance not on physiological measures of sexual orientation, which he recognized are rare in social science research, but on reports of behaviors and cognitions that are mostly under conscious control. Yet, comparing sexual behavior, attractions, masturbatory fantasies, and masturbatory orgasm fantasies, Cohen (1999) found that as same-sex attracted males progressed toward orgasm, and thus were less able to control fantasy content, greater quantity of homoerotic thoughts surfaced. This distinction becomes imperative when assessing subjects who find their homoeroticism exceedingly unacceptable and voluntarily attempt conversion by means such as intentional suppression. Thus, it is not surprising that Spitzer found the greatest change in those aspects of same-sex sexuality most under conscious control (behavior and identity), some change in sexuality under some control (attractions), and the least change in aspects least under conscious control (homoerotic content during masturbatory fantasies). Yet, even masturbation fantasy content must be carefully assessed. Spitzer accepted at face value claims of reduced homoeroticism and increased heteroeroticism during fantasies. Without probing, however, it is nearly impossible to verify the veracity of these claims because homoerotic content is easily obscured by heteroerotic images.

Finally, on another methodological note, it is curious that despite the reorientation power Spitzer ascribed to reparative therapy, he provided no credible evidence that therapy was actually the mechanism of reported changes. Although we contend that the study's design invalidates the data collected, if one were to believe the subjects' reports of changes in their sexuality, it would be just as valid (and perhaps more parsimonious, given prior research) to assert that numerous other uncontrolled, extraneous factors (e.g., time, history, maturation) significantly contributed to the "successful reorientation" changes during the *many* years subjects were in treatment. Given the myriad confounding variables that may have contributed to apparent therapy effects, including degree of homoeroticism, marital status, previous dissatisfaction with same-sex attractions, psychological vulnerability of subjects (depressed, suicidal, unhappily married, distressed by their sexuality, living a religious lie), church/therapy/support group involvement, length of therapy, need to proselytize, it is regrettable that Spitzer did not consider these possible contributors to reorientation. They might have explained more variance than the therapy itself.

In conclusion, a most basic and frequently documented lesson learned by sexologists investigating socially stigmatized populations cannot be overstated: Subject selection impacts research findings. As scientists we must disbelieve Spitzer's data because they are so compromised by subject selection bias as to raise serious objections to any claims Spitzer might make about their meaning and generalizability. Research that cannot be applied to nonstudy participants is of limited utility in the social and behavioral sciences.

REFERENCES

Cohen, K.M. (1999), The Biology of Male Sexual Orientation: Relationship Among Homoeroticism, Childhood Sex-Atypical Behavior, Spatial Ability, Handedness, and Pubertal Timing. Unpublished doctoral dissertation, University of Detroit Mercy, Detroit, MI.

Diamond, L.M. (2003a), Was it a phase? Young women's relinquishment of lesbian/bisexual identities over a 5-year period. *J. Personality & Social Psychology,* 84:352-364.

Harry, J. (1986), Sampling gay men. *J. Sex Research,* 22:21-34.

McConaghy, N. (1999), Unresolved issues in scientific sexology. *Archives Sexual Behavior,* 28:285-318.

McDaniel, J.S., Purcell, D., & D'Augelli, A.R. (2001), The relationship between sexual orientation and risk for suicide: Research findings and future directions for research and prevention. *Suicide & Life-Threatening Behavior,* 31(Suppl.): 84-105.

Sandfort, T.G.M. (1997), Sampling male homosexuality. In: *Researching Sexual Behavior: Methodological Issues,* ed. J. Bancroft. Bloomington, IN: Indiana University Press, pp. 261-275.

Savin-Williams, R.C. & Ream, G.L. (2003), Suicide attempts among sexual-minority male youth. *J. Clinical Child & Adolescent Psychology,* 32(4):509-522.

10

Reconsidering "Sexual Desire" in the Context of Reparative Therapy

Lisa M. Diamond

CLARIFYING THE QUESTION

First things first: Is Spitzer's study really "about" changing sexual orientation? In order to answer this question, we need to agree on a definition of sexual orientation and its defining criteria. But, of course, these issues have long been topics of heated debate (e.g., Bailey, 1995; Bem, 1996; Ellis, 1996; Golden, 1987; Rust, 1992; Veniegas and Conley, 2000). Is sexual orientation an innate sexual predisposition or a learned behavioral pattern? Does it primarily influence sexual desire or does it also shape affiliative preferences, affectional feelings, and gender-typed behavior? Such debates might seem shopworn at this point, but they are neither resolved nor irrelevant. To the contrary, the more we learn about the diversity of same-sex sexuality across different populations and contexts, the more we must regularly reevaluate our implicit and explicit models of this phenomenon and the hypotheses they prompt us to test.

Spitzer's central question—whether homosexuals can change into heterosexuals—presumes a fairly reductionistic sexual taxonomy that has garnered increasing scientific skepticism over the years. Kinsey et al. (1948) were perhaps the first and most famous to caution that "The world is not to be divided into sheep and goats" (p. 639) and empirical data increasingly buttress this perspective (Blackwood,

This chapter appeared originally under the same title in *Archives of Sexual Behavior* 32(5):429-431. Copyright 2003 Kluwer Academic/Plenum Publishers. Reprinted with permission.

2000; Murray, 2000). For example, representative studies of American adolescents (French et al., 1996; Garofalo et al., 1999) and adults (Laumann et al., 1994) have found that most individuals with same-sex attractions *also* report experiencing other-sex attractions, and both changes in, and disjunctures among, sexual behaviors, attractions, and identity are widespread (Baumeister, 2000; Diamond, 2000, 2003b; Golden, 1987; Pattatucci and Hamer, 1995; Rust, 1992; Stokes, Damon, and McKirnan, 1997; Weinberg, Williams, and Pryor, 1994).

Spitzer's research question and methodology do not acknowledge these complexities. Rather, he uncritically treats sexual attractions, fantasies, and emotional longings as coordinated indices of one's underlying "sheep" or "goat" status, despite the fact that (1) it is increasingly unclear whether these discrete types even *exist* as natural categories and (2) it is similarly unclear whether "sheepness" or "goatness" could ever be reliably diagnosed by coordinated and stable patterns of fantasy, desire, and affection. Given these problems, some researchers have argued that "it makes more sense to ask about specific aspects of same-gender behavior, practice, and feelings during specific periods of an individual's life rather than a single yes-or-no question about whether a person is homosexual" (Laumann et al., 1994, pp. 285-286). What, then, might we learn from Spitzer's study if we jettison extrapolations to "sexual orientation" and focus instead on domain-specific changes?

INTERPRETING THE FINDINGS: THE MEANING AND EXPERIENCE OF DESIRE

Unfortunately, a number of factors hamper interpretation of Spitzer's data, such as the significant and obvious problems of self-selection and self-report biases. Yet, I will leave aside these concerns, trusting that other commentators will address them in depth. Granting for the sake of argument that some of Spitzer's participants did, in fact, experience declines in their self-reported same-sex desires, how should we interpret such changes?

First of all, as previously noted, the phenomenon of plasticity in sexual desire over time has already been documented in several prospective studies, and is not newsworthy in and of itself (Diamond, 2000, 2003; Pattatucci and Hamer, 1995; Stokes et al., 1997; Weinberg et al., 1994). Spitzer, however, is more concerned with *effortful* changes effected through cognitive-behavioral strategies, such as "thought stopping," avoidance of situations that trigger same-sex attractions, and social support mobilization. Can these techniques actually alter one's subjective desires? Of course they can—just as attending Weight Watchers meetings and keeping "forbidden" foods out of the house can attenuate a dieter's natural, evolved cravings for salty, fatty, calorie-dense foods. Furthermore, any reader of Shakespeare or Jane Austen will recognize that these cognitive and behavioral techniques have been used for hundreds of years by individuals who had the misfortune of becoming attracted to partners of the right sex, but the wrong family, wrong social class, wrong nation, etc.

Yet, we are already ahead of ourselves—this entire discussion skirts a far more important but unanswered question lying just beneath the surface of this and other studies of sexual orientation: *Just what do we mean by "desire?"* Given that sexual desire is generally considered the primary indicator of one's sexual orientation (Marmor, 1980), one might expect that researchers would have spent considerable time validating and cross-checking our conceptualizations and measures of its phenomenology, but this has not been the case. Instead, we typically ask respondents to estimate their balance of same-sex and other-sex desires without clarifying what types of experiences "count" as desire, naively assuming that (1) these experiences are fairly uniform from person to person and (2) we all "know them when we feel them."

Yet, qualitative research increasingly demonstrates that individuals have strikingly different personal definitions and experiences of "desire" and "attraction" (Diamond and Savin-Williams, 2000; Tolman, 2002), including, for example, "liking to look at a woman's face or body," "the urge to have sex," "a fluttery feeling in my belly," "wanting to be physically near someone," "not needing to care about her personality," "feeling really really happy around someone," "electric energy," or "wanting to talk all night long." Such ambiguity makes it impossible to reliably interpret self-report data on everything from "age of first attractions" to "ratio of same-sex to other-sex attractions" to—most notably—"stability of attractions."

Which types of feelings might Spitzer's respondents have been talking about? How might it influence our interpretation of his findings if, for example, an individual's "fluttery belly feelings" exhibited little change, but "liking to look at face/body" changed markedly? How exactly do these phenomena relate to the specific frequency with which one's sexual fantasies are populated with same-sex versus other-sex individuals? We currently have no empirical or theoretical basis on which to interpret such phenomenological nuances and their relevance for models of sexual orientation, just as we have long lacked clear-cut conceptualizations of the specific relevance of love and affection for such models (Diamond, 2003b). Without greater empirical and theoretical rigor, we will remain hamstrung in our attempts to interpret the causes and implications of *any* self-reported changes in same-sex sexuality.

FINAL EVALUATIONS: WHAT GETS REPAIRED?

Where does this leave us? Does reparative therapy work? What does it work *on?* On this point, it bears noting that perhaps the most salient and striking changes recollected by Spitzer's research participants concerned their overall happiness and self-concept. Prior to the therapy, they were bothered by their same-sex feelings, they were at odds with their own personal or religious beliefs, many were unhappily unmarried, and one third were suicidal. After the therapy, over 75 percent of the men and over 50 percent of women were married, less than 10 percent reported that they were still bothered by their same-sex attractions, and measures of "heterosexual functioning" (participation in a "loving" heterosexual relationship, regular and satisfying sex with partner, etc.) had apparently improved markedly.

Are these successful outcomes? For individuals embedded in social-relational contexts that fundamentally forbid same-sex sexuality and prioritize traditional marriage, how can they not be? Of course, such outcomes could have been achieved through therapeutic interventions *other* than effortful control, redirection, and reconditioning of sexual and affectional feelings; at the very least, these individuals might have attempted to change—or escape—their stigmatizing and restrictive social contexts instead of their sexuality.

But for some this is not an option. Living in Salt Lake City (the worldwide headquarters of the Church of Latter Day Saints), I have come to know numerous men and women who have struggled with the gulf between their same-sex sexuality and their passionate devotion to the Mormon faith, *both* of which may be experienced as inextricably woven into one's deepest sense of self. As long as some individuals' chosen communities (whether based on faith, ethnicity, geography, etc.) invalidate the possibility of living openly with same-sex desires, clinicians must develop, analyze, test, and validate different approaches for helping members of those communities to make peace with, and decisions about, their irreconcilably conflicting life choices and chances.

At the very least, our evaluations of "reparative" interventions must be scrupulously attentive to clients' motives and the unique nature of their experiences in order to guard against inappropriate generalizations about "sexual orientation." Studies such as Spitzer's provide valuable information about how individuals with stigmatized experiences actively manage those experiences, in concert with their own narratives of adjustment, coping, and personal growth. In the final analysis, however, such studies have little to tell us about "change in sexual orientation" or even "change in sexual desire." If anything, Spitzer's findings should prompt sex researchers to revisit our own assumptions about the phenomenology and ontology of same-sex and other-sex desires, fantasies, and attractions in order to improve the validity and interpretability of future research on these phenomena over the life course.

REFERENCES

Bailey, J.M. (1995), Biological perspectives on sexual orientation. In: *Lesbian, Gay, and Bisexual Identities over the Life Span*, eds. A.R. D'Augelli & C.J. Patterson. New York: Oxford University Press, pp. 102-135.

Baumeister, R.F. (2000), Gender differences in erotic plasticity: The female sex drive as socially flexible and responsive. *Psychological Bulletin*, 126:347-374.

Bem, D.J. (1996), Exotic becomes erotic: A developmental theory of sexual orientation. *Psychological Review*, 103(2):320-335.

Blackwood, E. (2000), Culture and women's sexualities. *J. Social Issues*, 56:223-238.

Diamond, L.M. (2000), Sexual identity, attractions, and behavior among young sexual-minority women over a 2-year period. *Developmental Psychology*, 36:241-250.

Diamond, L.M. (2003), What does sexual orientation orient? A biobehavioral model distinguishing romantic love and sexual desire. *Psychological Review*, 110:173-192.

Diamond, L.M. & Savin-Williams, R.C. (2000), Explaining diversity in the development of same-sex sexuality among young women. *J. Social Issues,* 56:297-313.

Ellis, L. (1996), The role of perinatal factors in determining sexual orientation. In: *The Lives of Lesbians, Gays, and Bisexuals: Children to Adults,* eds. R.C. Savin-Williams & K.M. Cohen. Fort Worth, TX: Harcourt Brace, pp. 35-70.

French, S.A., Story, M., Remafedi, G., Resnick, M.D., & Blum, R.W. (1996), Sexual orientation and prevalence of body dissatisfaction and eating disordered behaviors: A population-based study of adolescents. *International J. Eating Disorders,* 19:119-126.

Garofalo, R., Wolf, R.C., Wissow, L.S., Woods, E.R., & Goodman, E. (1999), Sexual orientation and risk of suicide attempts among a representative sample of youth. *Archives Pediatrics & Adolescent Medicine,* 153:487-493.

Golden, C. (1987), Diversity and variability in women's sexual identities. In: *Lesbian Psychologies: Explorations and Challenges,* ed. Boston Lesbian Psychologies Collective. Urbana, IL: University of Illinois Press, pp. 19-34.

Kinsey, A.C., Pomeroy, W.B., & Martin C.E. (1948), *Sexual Behavior in the Human Male.* Philadelphia: W.B. Saunders.

Laumann, E.O., Gagnon, J.H., Michael, R.T., & Michaels, S. (1994), *The Social Organization of Sexuality: Sexual Practices in the United States.* Chicago: University of Chicago Press.

Marmor, J., ed. (1980), *Homosexual Behavior: A Modern Reappraisal.* New York: Basic Books.

Murray, S.O. (2000), *Homosexualities.* Chicago: University of Chicago Press.

Pattatucci, A.M.L. & Hamer, D.H. (1995), Development and familiality of sexual orientation in females. *Behavior Genetics,* 25:407-420.

Rust, P.C. (1992), The politics of sexual identity: Sexual attraction and behavior among lesbian and bisexual women. *Social Problems,* 39:366-386.

Stokes, J.P., Damon, W., & McKirnan, D.J. (1997), Predictors of movement toward homosexuality: A longitudinal study of bisexual men. *J. Sex Research,* 34:304-312.

Tolman, D.L. (2002), *Dilemmas of Desire: Teenage Girls Talk about Sexuality.* Cambridge, MA: Harvard University Press.

Veniegas, R.C. & Conley, T.D. (2000), Biological research on women's sexual orientations: Evaluating the scientific evidence. *J. Social Issues,* 56:267-282.

Weinberg, M.S., Williams, C.J., & Pryor, D.W. (1994), *Dual Attraction: Understanding Bisexuality.* New York: Oxford University Press.

11

The Spitzer Study
and the Culture Wars

Jack Drescher

On May 9, 2001, Spitzer presented the [study that is being discussed in this book], in oral form, at the annual meeting of the American Psychiatric Association (APA) in New Orleans and created an international media sensation (Lund and Renna, 2003). With the study's publication, history may repeat itself. Given the manner in which subjects were recruited, much of this study's social impact hinges on whether or not one believes their accounts. Spitzer not only believes his subjects, he offers his own belief as "evidence" that some people can change a homosexual orientation.

Although he is not a sex researcher, the media is interested in Spitzer's beliefs because of what he symbolizes. In the 1970s, he served on the APA's Task Force on Nomenclature and Statistics, which recommended to the Board of Trustees that they remove homosexuality from the DSM. When the Board did so, dissenting psychiatrists, mostly psychoanalysts, petitioned the APA to hold a membership referendum on the matter. The APA membership voted to support the Board (Bayer, 1981). Although many psychiatrists were involved in that process over several years (Robert Campbell, Lawrence Hartmann, Judd Marmor, Richard Pillard, and John Spiegel, to name a few), Spitzer was singled out as a favored bête noire of the dissenters (Socarides, 1995).

This chapter appeared originally under the same title in *Archives of Sexual Behavior* 32(5):431-431. Copyright 2003 Kluwer Academic/Plenum Publishers. Reprinted with permission.

doi:10.1300/5503_11

In the following decades, these dissenters were gradually marginalized from the mental health mainstream. In the early 1990s, however, some began to speak publicly—both to and as representatives of—segments of society that regard homosexuality as an unacceptable form of social expression. In the contemporary debate known as the "culture wars" (Drescher, 2002a, 2002b; Dreyfuss, 1999; Shidlo, Schroeder, and Drescher, 2001), the clinical argument that homosexuality is an illness meshed seamlessly with a social-conservative, political message: Heterosexuality is the only normal expression of human sexuality and accepting homosexuality is harmful to society (Socarides, 1994).

These clinicians' antihomosexual arguments, however, are not directed toward a mental health mainstream that vigorously supports gay and lesbian civil rights, but toward lay audiences and policymakers (Lund and Renna, 2003). They are intended to counter growing public and political acceptance of homosexuality by challenging the popular belief that homosexuality is "biological" and "immutable." The recitation that one is not "born gay" because some people can change sexual orientation has become a mantra of those opposed to civil rights protections for gay men and women. Despite its religious roots, however, this movement does not use religion alone to deliver its antihomosexual message. Using the model of creation scientists (Tiffen, 1994), groups such as the National Association for Research and Therapy of Homosexuality (NARTH) cite scientific data selectively to support their theories regarding the causes and treatments of homosexuality.

NARTH members have argued on the op-ed page of *The Wall Street Journal* that individuals unhappy about their homosexual feelings should have the right to seek treatment for change (Socarides, et al., 1997). Their claims of supporting homosexual civil rights notwithstanding, sexual conversion therapists filed affidavits in support of Colorado's antigay Amendment Two (Socarides, 1993). They also supported unsuccessful defenses of sodomy laws in Tennessee in 1995 and Louisiana in 1998 (Cohen, 1998a, 1998b). Why do these therapists want to criminalize homosexuality, even though they believe it to be an illness? NARTH's current President says, "We believe harm would be done if our laws were to affirm homosexuality as indistinguishable from heterosexuality" (Nicolosi, 2000).

So what does this have to do with Spitzer's study? Spitzer's revamping of the American psychiatric diagnostic system in the DSM-III (American Psychiatric Association, 1980) gave him a standing among the international scientific community that no sexual conversion therapist has ever achieved. And, although once reviled by reparative therapists as "someone who crosses far over the line, from science to open advocacy of a political position" (Socarides, 1995, p. 166), antihomosexual social forces now seek to harness Spitzer's reputation—and the media attention he attracts—to legitimize their own.

Why so much media attention to this study? At the 2001 meeting of the APA, before Spitzer even presented his preliminary findings, conservative political groups used the event to put out the message to the press that the man who had removed homosexuality from the DSM had changed his mind. However, the media message was ambiguous—perhaps deliberately so—and it was not entirely clear what Spitzer had changed his mind about! It was the public relations machine's implicit message—that Spitzer had changed his mind about homosexuality not being an illness—which drove the media frenzy around his study and left scores of mental health professionals scrambling to respond to misleading headlines. Buried in the small print, however, was Spitzer's now-official change of view: "Like most psychiatrists," says Dr. Spitzer, "I thought that homosexual behavior could be resisted—but that no one could really change their sexual orientation. I now believe that's untrue—some people can and do change" (Nicolosi, 2001). The story here is obviously Spitzer's change of heart. But did he actually change his mind?

It seems unlikely since, in 1973, it was Spitzer's suggestion that the DSM-II (American Psychiatric Association, 1968) replace homosexuality with a new diagnosis, sexual orientation disturbance (SOD). According to SOD criteria, only those "bothered by," "in conflict with," or who "wished to change" their homosexuality had a mental disorder. SOD, however, had two conceptual problems. First, the diagnosis could apply to heterosexuals, although no cases of unhappy heterosexuals seeking psychiatric treatment to become gay were reported. In 1980, with Spitzer chairing the Task Force on Nomenclature and Statistics, SOD was modified in the DSM-III and replaced by ego-dystonic homosexuality (EDH). This new diagnosis, however, did not resolve the second, thornier issue of making patients' subjective distress about homosexuality the determining factor in making a diagnosis. Although SOD and EDH were a compromise in the 1973 debate, they were incongruous with an evidence-based approach to psychiatric diagnosis. In 1987, with Spitzer's reluctant approval, EDH was removed from the DSM-III-R (American Psychiatric Association, 1987; Krajeski, 1996; Spitzer, personal communication, January 23, 2003).

If Spitzer did not previously believe in the possibility of changing homosexuality, why did he invent the DSM disorders of SOD and EDH? In 1984, I heard Spitzer speak at a New York conference on homosexuality at which he defended the still-extant EDH diagnosis, saying "If a guy comes to me and says he wants to change his homosexuality, I believe he should have the right to try and change." Thus, despite what the conversion therapy publicists would have the media and the public believe, it seems unlikely that Spitzer himself has undergone the conversion he now claims. Clearly, he has always supported trying to change same-sex attractions.

In 1965, songwriter Tom Lehrer wrote, "Once, the rockets are up who cares where they come down / that's not my department / says Wernher von Braun." Anecdotal reports of harm done to patients is the reason the American Psychiatric Association (2000) deemed conversion therapies unethical. However, Spitzer dismissed this issue, stating he did not interview anyone who was harmed (cf. Shidlo and Schroeder, 2002). However, the question has been raised whether researchers should consider any potential social harm that might arise from their scientific research (Byne et al., 2002). To his credit, Spitzer has been willing to speak out against political misuse of his study. In September 2001, the Finnish Parliament debated a bill intended to grant same-sex couples the right to civil unions. With opponents of the bill citing Spitzer's study as "proof " that homosexuality could be changed, Spitzer's letter to the Finnish parliament was published in a major Finnish newspaper. Spitzer explained that while his report was "based on a very unique sample," such results "are probably quite rare, even for highly motivated homosexuals" (Hausman, 2001). He added in his letter to the parliament member that "it would be a serious mistake to conclude" from his research that homosexuality is a "choice." He emphasized that he is concerned with "scientific issues" related to sexual orientation, and that he "personally favor[s] anti-discrimination laws and civil unions for homosexuals" (Hausman, 2001).

After Spitzer's intervention, the Finnish civil unions bill passed (Stålström and Nissinen, 2003). With the publication of his study, one can only hope that when Spitzer's "rockets" land elsewhere he will find ample time and opportunity to respond to those situations as well.

REFERENCES

American Psychiatric Association (1968), *Diagnostic and Statistical Manual of Mental Disorders,* Second edition. Washington, DC: American Psychiatric Press.

American Psychiatric Association (1980), *Diagnostic and Statistical Manual of Mental Disorders,* Third edition. Washington, DC: American Psychiatric Press.

American Psychiatric Association (1987), *Diagnostic and Statistical Manual of Mental Disorders,* Third edition—Revised. Washington, DC: American Psychiatric Press.

American Psychiatric Association (2000), Commission on Psychotherapy by Psychiatrists (COPP): Position statement on therapies focused on attempts to change sexual orientation (Reparative or conversion therapies). *American J. Psychiatry,* 157:1719-1721.

Bayer, R. (1981), *Homosexuality and American Psychiatry: The Politics of Diagnosis.* New York: Basic Books.

Byne, W., Schuklenk, U., Lasco, M., & Drescher, J. (2002), The origins of sexual orientation: No genetic link to social change. In: *The Double-Edged Helix: Social Implications of Genetics in a Diverse Society,* eds. J.S. Alper, C. Ard, A. Asch, J. Beckwith, P. Conrad, & L.N. Geller. Baltimore: Johns Hopkins University Press, pp. 197-214.

Cohen, R. (1998a), Voir dire testimony taken before the Honorable Carolyn Jefferson, Judge, State of Louisiana, Civil District Court for the Parish of Orleans, CDC No. 94-9260, Section 5, Division A, Friday, October 30.

Cohen, R. (1998b), Testimony taken before the Honorable Carolyn Jefferson, Judge, State of Louisiana, Civil District Court for the Parish of Orleans, CDC No. 94-9260, Section 5, Division A, Friday, October 30.

Drescher, J. (2002a), Sexual conversion ("reparative") therapies: A history and update. In: *Mental Health Issues in Lesbian, Gay, Bisexual, and Transgender Communities (Review of Psychiatry,* 21:4), eds. B.E. Jones & M.J. Hill. Washington, DC: American Psychiatric Press, pp. 71-91.

Drescher, J. (2002b), Ethical issues in treating gay and lesbian patients. *Psychiatric Clinics of North America,* 25(3):605-621.

Dreyfuss, R. (1999) The holy war on gays. *Rolling Stone,* March 18, pp. 38-41.

Hausman, K. (2001, December 21), Finland's Parliament assesses U.S. reparative-therapy study. *Psychiatric News,* 36(24):11.

Krajeski, J. (1996), Homosexuality and the Mental Health Professions. In: *Textbook of Homosexuality and Mental Health,* eds. R.P. Cabaj & T.S. Stein. Washington, DC: American Psychiatric Press, pp. 17-31.

Lund, S. & Renna, C. (2003), An analysis of the media response to the Spitzer study. *J. Gay & Lesbian Psychotherapy,* 7(3):55-67.

Nicolosi, J. (2000, February 4), [Letter to the editor]. *Psychiatric News,* 35(3):13, 25.

Nicolosi, L.A. (2001), *Historic Gay Advocate Now Believes Change is Possible.* Retrieved March 13, 2003, from National Association for Research and Treatment of Homosexuality, http://www.narth.com/docs/spitzer3.html.

Shidlo, A. & Schroeder, M. (2002), Changing sexual orientation: A consumers' report. *Professional Psychology: Research & Practice,* 33:249-259.

Shidlo, A., Schroeder, M. & Drescher, J., eds. (2001), *Sexual Conversion Therapy: Ethical, Clinical and Research Perspectives.* New York: The Haworth Press, Inc.

Socarides, C.W. (1993), District Court, City and County of Denver, Colorado. Case No. 92 CV 7223. Affidavit of Charles W. Socarides, M.D., *Evans. v. Romer.*

Socarides, C.W. (1995), *Homosexuality: A Freedom Too Far.* Phoenix, AZ: Adam Margrave Books.

Socarides, C.W., Kaufman, B., Nicolosi, J., Satinover, J. & Fitzgibbons, R. (1997, January 9), Don't forsake homosexuals who want help. *The Wall Street Journal.*

Stålström, O. & Nissinen, J. (2003), The Spitzer study and the Finnish parliament. *J. Gay & Lesbian Psychotherapy,* 7(3): 83-95.

Tiffen, L. (1994), *Creationism's Upside-Down Pyramid: How Science Refutes Fundamentalism.* Amherst, NY: Prometheus Books.

– 12 –

Sexual Orientation Change:
A Study of Atypical Cases

Richard C. Friedman

This study must be understood in historical and sociocultural context.

ANTIHOMOSEXUAL BIAS

Although antihomosexual bias has recently diminished, much work remains to be done in order to eliminate it entirely. The mental health professions have been helpful in combating discrimination. However, for many years they were unfortunately responsible for adding fuel to the prejudicial fires. In the first edition of the *Diagnostic and Statistical Manual of Mental Disorders* (DSM) (American Psychiatric Association, 1952), homosexuality was included in the category of Sociopathic Personality Disorders. At that time, the view of the psychiatric establishment was that a person who was homosexual inevitably had a defective conscience. The second edition of the DSM (American Psychiatric Association, 1968) included it with the sexual perversions, such as pedophilia, sexual sadism, and fetishism. Public policy decisions were made on the basis of these clinical judgments. These decisions adversely influenced the lives of gay/lesbian people and contributed to negative stereotypes depicted in the media (Gonsiorek and Weinrich, 1991).

This chapter appeared originally under the same title in *Archives of Sexual Behavior* 32(5):432-434. Copyright 2003 Kluwer Academic/Plenum Publishers. Reprinted with permission.

During the decades following World War II, homosexual desires were believed to be symptoms motivated by unconscious irrational anxiety about heterosexuality. It was thought that psychotherapy would cause these fantasies to melt away and the patient would become heterosexual. Universal heterosexuality was seen as biologically based and normative (Bieber et al., 1962; Socarides, 1978). This model rested on a scant data base, but was accepted not only by most psychoanalysts, but by most psychiatrists, psychologists, and other mental health professionals. Hooker's (1957) well-known study of socially well-adjusted homosexual men demonstrated that unconscious conflicts attributed by most psychotherapists to homosexuality per se were, in fact, not demonstrable among *nonpathological* homosexual men. This research dramatized the necessity to distinguish between clinical and nonclinical samples in conceptualizing sexual orientation.

Perhaps more to the point of the Spitzer study, data about the frequency of change of sexual orientation as a result of psychotherapy were also lacking. In his article, Spitzer cites Bieber et al.'s (1962) outcome data. Two aspects of the study by Bieber et al. warrant commentary. The first is that the investigators studied overt sexual behavior and not fantasy; hence, the outcome data refer to heterosexual competency but not heterosexual/homosexual desire. Second, the majority of patients in the Bieber et al. study who were predominantly or exclusively homosexual did not, in fact, become predominantly or exclusively heterosexual. Interestingly, Freund (1963, 1971) also observed that in a laboratory setting some homosexual men could voluntarily alter penile responses to respond to heterosexual stimuli. Both Bieber et al.'s and Freund's data suggested that a minority of men may have some degree of plasticity of response to an erotic stimulus. Although the entire body of literature prior to the Spitzer study has many defects, it suggests that for *most* men, homosexual orientation is more or less fixed, but that for some—almost certainly a small minority—it seems more plastic. More women appear to be plastic with respect to erotic stimuli than men (Baumeister, 2000). Hence, more women than men would be likely to have the capacity to alter sexual orientation in response to some type of intervention.

REPARATIVE THERAPY

Nicolosi (1991) hypothesized that homosexuality was a reaction to a defect in the masculine self. Nicolosi's clinical experience was based on patients who were frequently devout Christians and who sought to change their sexual orientation either for religious reasons or because they disapproved of a "gay" lifestyle. Similar to the orthodox psychoanalysts of the 1950s and 1960s, Nicolosi used clinical samples to make generalizations about all homosexual people. By the 1990s, however, ideas about homosexuality generally accepted by mainstream mental health professionals, including psychoanalysts, had changed (Friedman, 1988; Isay, 1989; Marmor, 1980). The pathological model of homosexual orientation had been or was soon about to be repudiated by the vast majority of psychotherapists. Moreover, it had become apparent that many patients had suffered harm because of misguided efforts to alter their fixed sexual orientations (Duberman, 1991). I have seen many such patients in consultation over the years. The idea that homosexuality generally is a product of a masculine self-defect was abhorrent to many and reparative therapy was strongly criticized by mental health professionals (American Psychiatric Association, 2000). A belief became increasingly popular among therapists that a homosexual orientation should always be considered normal and that attempts to change it ill-considered and even unethical.

HOMOPHOBIA AND INTERNALIZED HOMOPHOBIA

Patients who seek reparative therapy have a conflict between their erotic desires and conscience/value systems. In order to understand this group from a clinical perspective, it is necessary to have a sociocultural and historical grasp of homophobia, and a psychodynamically informed understanding of "internalized homophobia." The latter term refers to negative internalizations about being homosexual that become part of the self concept during development as a consequence of interactions with homophobic/heterosexist others (Malyon, 1982). Limitations of space interdict extensive discussion of these topics here, and we refer interested readers to Friedman and Downey (2002) and Herek (1996). Suffice it to say that for many nonheterosexual people, the primary psychopathological problem is not with their sexual orientations, but rather with rigid, irrationally punitive superegos formed during childhood which undermine the well-being of the older person. Most such people can be helped by gay affirmative psychotherapy and some by more exploratory dynamic psychotherapy. During therapy, sexual orientation does not change, but the person's pathological conscience structure is modified to be compatible with his or her present life philosophy. A different clinical subgroup, however, consists of people—often religious fundamentalists—whose value systems are not compatible with a homosexual orientation. These people reject the suggestion that their values should be modified, and insist on their right to personal/religious values that are not gay affirmative—or are even antigay affirmative. It is primarily from a *subgroup* (e.g., positive responders) of these individuals that Spitzer found volunteers for his investigation.

THE SPITZER STUDY

In order to appreciate the contribution of this investigation, it is necessary to have a clear idea of its limitations. The study did not assess the techniques of reparative therapy itself. The particular sample reported on was not representative of those who seek such interventions. The research was not designed to ascertain the effectiveness of reparative therapy nor did it assess complications resulting from such intervention. It is possible, for example, that most people who requested the intervention were either not helped by it or actually harmed in some fashion. The design of the study was such that these issues were intentionally not addressed. As a single point study of people selected to have benefited from the treatment, the sample was obviously highly biased. The data base reported on in the study therefore does not support any generalizations about reparative therapy per se. Spitzer cites estimates of success in sexual orientation change by Socarides and Nicolosi, but their global impressions do not meet scientific standards for acceptable data.

THE USEFULNESS OF THE STUDY

This is an investigation of sexual histories taken in a detailed and systematic manner of an unusual sample. It has three major strengths. First, the structured interview used is comprehensive and carefully constructed. Second, the data are available and open to inspection by others. This type of transparency and sharing of information is a welcome advance, supporting scholarly values at a time when political correctness often dominates academic discourse. Finally, the data support inferences already available to therapists and scientists but obscured by controversy. Some degree of plasticity with respect to the object of sexual desire appears possible for some people. This was already known by the scientists and clinicians, but because the possibilities for abuse of the majority through misguided application of "reparative" principles has been so great, this point has recently been obscured. Scientific and clinical judgment suggest that even among a delimited universe of highly religious men, meaningful change is probably impossible for most. The small minority for whom such change is possible, however, have rights and the subgroup of that minority who have psychiatric disabilities also have clinical needs that must be appropriately responded to by therapists. The needs and attributes of this minority, however, must not be taken as applicable to those of most gay/lesbian people.

CONCLUSION

Systematic investigation of unusual cases has always been an integral part of academic-clinical work. The findings of the Spitzer study are part of this tradition. The fact that this research was carried out is even more important than its findings. It is necessary for reasoned inquiry to proceed during periods of social unrest when pressures toward censorship are particularly great.

REFERENCES

American Psychiatric Association (1952), *Diagnostic and Statistical Manual of Mental Disorders*. Washington, DC: American Psychiatric Association.

American Psychiatric Association (1968), *Diagnostic and Statistical Manual of Mental Disorders,* Second edition. Washington, DC: American Psychiatric Press.

American Psychiatric Association (2000), Commission on Psychotherapy by Psychiatrists (COPP): Position statement on therapies focused on attempts to change sexual orientation (Reparative or conversion therapies). *American J. Psychiatry,* 157:1719-1721.

Baumeister, R.F. (2000), Gender differences in erotic plasticity: The female sex drive as socially flexible and responsive. *Psychological Bulletin,* 126:347-374.

Bieber, I., Dain, H., Dince, P., Drellich, M., Grand, H., Gundlach, R., Kremer, M., Rifkin, A., Wilbur, C., & Bieber T. (1962), *Homosexuality: A Psychoanalytic Study.* New York: Basic Books.

Duberman, M. (1991), *Cures: A Gay Man's Odyssey.* New York: Dutton.

Freund, K. (1963), A laboratory method of diagnosing predominance of homo- or hetero-erotic interest in the male. *Behaviour Research & Therapy,* 17:451-457.

Freund, K. (1971), A note on the use of the phallometric method of measuring mild sexual arousal in the male. *Behavioral Therapy,* 2:223-228.

Friedman, R.C. (1988), *Male Homosexuality: A Contemporary Psychoanalytic Perspective.* New Haven, CT: Yale University Press.

Friedman, R.C. & Downey, J.I. (2002), *Sexual Orientation and Psychoanalysis: Sexual Science and Clinical Practice.* New York: Columbia University Press.

Gonsiorek, J.C. & Weinrich, J.D., eds. (1991), *Homosexuality: Research Implications for Public Policy.* Newbury Park, CA: Sage.

Herek, G. (1996), Heterosexism and homophobia. In: *Textbook of Homosexuality and Mental Health,* eds. R.P. Cabaj & T.S. Stein. Washington, DC: American Psychiatric Press, pp. 101-115. Washington, DC: American Psychiatric Press.

Hooker, E. (1957), The adjustment of the male overt homosexual. *J. Projective Techniques,* 21:18-31.

Isay, R.A. (1996), *Becoming Gay: The Journey to Self-Acceptance.* New York: Pantheon.

Malyon, A.K. (1982), Psychotherapeutic implications of internalized homophobia in gay men. *J. Homosexuality,* 7:59-69.

Marmor, J., ed. (1980), *Homosexual Behavior: A Modern Reappraisal.* New York: Basic Books.

Nicolosi, J. (1991), *Reparative Therapy of Male Homosexuality: A New Clinical Approach.* Northvale, NJ: Jason Aronson.

Socarides, C.W. (1978), *Homosexuality.* New York: Jason Aronson.

13

The Politics of Sexual Choices

John H. Gagnon

The decision, recorded in the article by Spitzer, for people who
have a well established history of sex with persons of the same gender
to seek professional help and religious encouragement to start a life
of having sex with persons of the other gender, becomes remarkable
only in particular political and scientific circumstances. I will not discuss the methodology or substance of the article in any detail. This
will undoubtedly be the topic of a number of other commentaries. My
concern is how the political and scientific contexts shape the way in
which individual changes in gender preference in erotic relationships
are understood. Only two comments about the changers—the folks
who made the change seem to have done so for reasons that have to do
with becoming more conventional in their social performances rather
than for a more satisfying "sexual," in the narrow sense, life. And it
may well be that the amount of "sturm and drang" involved is a function of the moral condition (which is a consequence of its political
status) of their prior sexual lives—sinners always proclaim the difficulty of giving up their sins as they return to the moral community, in
this case the moral community of straightness.

Let me first address the problem of politics. There are those who
believe that it is possible to study "homosexuality" without addressing the political context of their research, but I am not one of them.
Although survey evidence shows that antigay prejudice is less than it
once was, there still remains a substantial number of persons who are
actively antigay and a still larger number whose latent antigay senti-

This chapter appeared originally under the same title in *Archives of Sexual Behavior*
32(5):434-436. Copyright 2003 Kluwer Academic/Plenum Publishers. Reprinted with
permission.

doi:10.1300/5503_13

ments can be mobilized by provocative political campaigns. At the present time, important positions in the U.S. federal government are occupied by persons of these antigay persuasions.

Many gay men and lesbian women feel threatened by these circumstances. These fears are not fanciful. Thus, the availability of programs to "help" persons who are unhappy with the fact that they are having sex with persons of the same gender can reasonably be construed as the beginning of the proverbial "slippery slope." A slippery slope that may lead to the prescription of behavior change programs for all persons who continue to maintain a sexual life with partners of the same gender. This appears to be the most benevolent option.

This is the political context. A number of antigay folks feel that having same-gender partners is both sinful and psychologically pathological and they are actively seeking to make folks who have same-gender partners sufficiently unhappy that they will try to change the gender of their preferred sexual partner.

Let me use an analogy. Consider being Jewish. As with a preference for a same-gender sexual partner, being Jewish is for the child who grows up in a Jewish family "unchosen." Even when surrounded by Christians (or Muslims or atheists), being Jewish, for the growing child, is part of the natural order of things. At some point, the young person realizes that there is a political context around being a Jew, that there is a cost to this "unchosen" preference. In less politically fraught circumstances, this may only result in housing or work discrimination, but as the level of fraughtness increases it may result in forced conversion to the majority religion (or even "voluntary" conversions—see the composer Arnold Schoenberg or the philosopher Karl Popper—or simply name changing to avoid identification by hostile others) or in most terrifying circumstances, being exterminated in camps constructed for the purpose.

So Jews are anxious about the survival of their practices (and, in certain circumstances, their very selves). They worry about "Jews for Jesus," they are concerned about political attacks on the State of Israel, and they discuss rates of marital exogamy as threats to the existence of Judaism. One may differ about the level of danger, but one cannot quarrel with the notion that this small minority that has been victim of systematic and murderous persecution has the right to feel nervous about the intentions of the majority.

Men who have had sex with persons of the same gender have had similar experiences with these practices (from discrimination to mass murder in Germany, but with discrimination to imprisonment and state encouraged violence in other countries). Prejudice against lesbian women has not been as intense, but antilesbian practices have been both common and in many cases violent.

So that is, in brief, the political context.

And now for the issue of rates of change between one significant social practice to another. A change that occurs within the political context has to be understood within that context.

Human beings change their membership groups at very high rates and often do so with great success (and such changes usually occur in coercive political and economic circumstances). Thus, vast numbers of persons from very different "native" cultures have crossed national borders and have become, for the most part, satisfactory members of the new cultures to which they have moved. In the nineteenth century, millions of rural, non–English-speaking peoples, who often lived in societies with quite different political, economic, religious, reproductive, and sexual regimes moved to the United States and learned to live in urban settings, operate in a market economy, work in factories, tolerate other religions, reduce their family size, change their sexual lives, and give up one language and learn another. For some, it took three generations to become "Americans"; some never succeeded and fell afoul of the prisons and the mental hospitals, others went home (in the millions), but most became "Americans" (indeed some so quickly succeeded that positive programs of discrimination in elite universities had to be created to prevent them from succeeding). All found themselves both objects of oppression and discrimination as well as enlightened attempts to "Americanize" them, both of which shaped their individual and collective adaptations.

Becoming an American was not an easy task and many worried about the abandonment of old ways. The compound names for most American ethnic groups (Irish-Americans, German-Americans, Japanese-Americans, and the like) reflect both collective and individual ambivalence about becoming American. Marrying out of the group was one of the great markers of the betrayal of the old and the triumph of the new. Marriage across ethnic, religious, skin color, and class lines were the central dramas of the American cinema of the 1930s. The lament of mothers and fathers as they watched their children rise in the world and abandon them, their religion, and their views of family life is a chronic dirge in the American story. Even in the present day, the notion of "giving back to the community," which is ritual expectation of members of minority groups who are becoming Americans, is a measure of the attempts of an older, usually oppressed social world, to hold on to their members.

But what does this example of culture change have to do with sex, particularly that aspect of sex that has to do the gender of the partner one prefers (aka homosexuality and heterosexuality)? If one believes that sexual partner preferences are fundamentally different than all other preferences, a position marked the choice of the phrase "sexual orientation" or the belief that there is direct pathway from a gene (or complex of genes or mixture of chemicals) and the like to desiring to have sex with someone who has similar genitals, the answer is nothing. But, if you believe, as I do, that the complex of sex practices is learned in a particular historical and cultural situation, then the idea of comparing sexual practices with other social practices is not very mysterious.

It is clear from the Spitzer study that some persons who have long (and perhaps exclusive) histories of sex with same-gender partners move, often with religious and other "therapeutic" supports, to lives in which they have sex with persons of the other gender. From prior studies, we know that substantial numbers of persons who have had long (and perhaps exclusive) lives with partners of the other gender have voluntarily (sometimes describing the experience as finding their true selves) and sometimes with therapeutic support moved on to lives in which they have sex exclusively or nearly exclusively with persons of the same gender. This movement back and forth in partner preferences is not unexpected given the general movement of humans from one to another deeply seated and "unchosen" life way or practice.

Most of our early life is "unchosen." We learn whatever is expected of us, sometimes well, sometimes poorly, sometimes we learn what adults want of us, sometimes we learn the opposite. Religious parents raise atheists as well as believers, parents raise children who speak English, who then learn French and emigrate, working-class parents raise children who go to Harvard and learn to exploit the working class, rich parents raise children who become communists. These are all minority outcomes, but they happen. If you believe, as I do, that language, religion, and gender learning are as deeply embedded in a person (as un-chosen, if you will) as the specific sexual preference of the gender of the sexual partner, then in adulthood when some ways of life seem uncomfortable and choices are apparent (sometimes hard choices), it is not surprising that changes take place.

It is the politics of the change that shape most of the debate. The actual process is quite understandable and expectable. Whether such change should happen, what direction it should take, whether it should be encouraged, and who should decide whether it is a good or bad thing for either individuals or communities is the political question.

14

Too Flawed: Don't Publish

Lawrence Hartmann

I think Spitzer's paper is too flawed to publish, and is likely to do harm. Yet, here it is, being published.

The area of change in sexual orientation is an interesting one, worth study, and one in which little is known but in which many think they know, and in which many have passionate commitments to what they think they know. The area is embedded in so much context, history, bias, passion, self-delusion, and even lying that it deserves a higher level than Spitzer provides of careful and detailed openness, skepticism, and multiple levels of scrutiny.

Too many problems, major and minor, exist in the article to discuss in reasonable detail in a brief commentary. I will touch on only a few. Some of the problems are technical; others are of emphasis or skepticism, of definitions, of numbers, and of ethics. Some of these problems were pointed out to Spitzer by many very critical peers when he presented the paper at a May 2001 panel at the meeting of the American Psychiatric Association. He has not fixed them. The article remains a failure at establishing what it says it establishes: that some gay people can be changed to straight.

One might, from this article (from some of its interesting and energetic outreach attempts, data, careful-looking psychiatric research apparatus, and discussion of possible problems), and from my following numerical calculations, legitimately conclude that a *minute* number of gay people *may* be able to change their sexual orientation somewhat in some way, *perhaps related to* interventions designed to

---

This chapter appeared originally under the same title in *Archives of Sexual Behavior* 32(5):436-438. Copyright 2003 Kluwer Academic/Plenum Publishers. Reprinted with permission.

doi:10.1300/5503_14

help them change. Modesty and accuracy demand "may," not "can," and "perhaps related to," not "caused by." And a *minute* number is a key element in this potential legitimate conclusion—and that is very different from the loose common word "some." (That the vast majority of gay people probably cannot change orientation is essentially left out of this study.)

Spitzer rightly recognizes that credibility of his subjects is a basic and significant potential problem, but I think his statements are rather naive and underconcerned about it. Also, the selection of subjects is worth far more scrutiny than it gets. A study designed around the question "Can I find any people who say 'x' about themselves?," especially in an area people feel strongly about and have fought about, is particularly vulnerable to (and pretty much invites) pressure, distortion, bias, self-delusion, and lying. Spitzer does not protect adequately against this, as even he seems to know.

Selection/inclusion criteria and procedures are not made clear enough. No prospective study was done. No controls. No independent observations or measurements at all: physiological, psychological, social. Spitzer relies wholly on self-reporting and on one 45-minute telephone interview, which is understandably convenient and cheap, but allows rather easy evasion, distortion, and lies.

In addition, and a differently cogent matter, Spitzer nearly never puts "reparative therapy" in proper distancing quotation marks. That is, he repeatedly takes a strong side on the central question he is ostensibly studying. (To many colleagues, "reparative therapy" is neither reparative nor therapy; it is, rather, destructive pseudotherapy. Relatively neutral words could have been used, such as "intervention aimed at changing sexual orientation," or, simply, "reparative therapy" in quotes.) Spitzer also seems implicitly to accept, uncritically, the high percentages of cure or change (which are widely considered unreliable, probably wishful at best, and much exaggerated) estimated by the rather notorious Bergler, Socarides, and Nicolosi.

Another matter, and one of several ethical issues, is Spitzer's statement that he found no evidence of harm of "reparative therapy" in these 200 people. This is misleading and breathtaking in its blinkered view and its omission of the relevant groups: (1) the many more (10 times as many? 100 times? Far more?) who have had some form of "reparative therapy" and who do not think it helped them. In addition to recent less-than-pleased-or-changed ex-patients of "reparative therapists," excluded by Spitzer, how many gay or bisexual people were in analysis or dynamic psychotherapy heavy with "reparative" elements from, say, 1930 to 1980 or 1990? These should be looked at carefully for harm. I know many, and I have treated several. And (2) the wider population at large, straight and gay. Most mental health professionals I know consider that the semisanctioned existence of "reparative therapy" probably harms millions of nontreated gay people.

There is inevitably continual spillover from "reparative therapy's" narrowly defined into (1) many psychotherapies (much psychoanalysis and dynamic psychotherapy of the twentieth century contained significant doses of such spillover and "therapeutic" first cousins) and (2) public policy, law, values, definitions of illness, etc. Even if "reparative therapy" helps a few people in some ways, as I think it may, it nearly certainly harms a far larger number of people, and that is a major ethical issue relevant to Spitzer's study but apparently not seriously considered by him.

Then numbers: One large aspect of the study pretty well *proves* just about *the opposite* of what it says it shows. Spitzer scoured the United States for several years ("actively for 2 or 3 years," he told me in 2001). He is an experienced social-psychiatric researcher attached to a major university, and he went energetically and repeatedly to all the antigay groups he could find: to the National Association for Research and Therapy of Homosexuality (NARTH), to all the religious change-gay-to-straight programs he could find, all the "reparative therapists" he could find, in all the United States, to find all the gay-to-straight ex-patients he could find. That yielded about 200 people he felt could be used for his study. 200. Let us leave aside for the moment that, in my fairly educated view, I suspect that of the 200 many were heavily biased and were probably distorting and/or lying since there was clearly pressure on many to do so, and nearly certainly many had some coaching as to how to do so. Spitzer's idea that it was probably proof of reliability that many said they had only partly changed seems to me wishful and naive. But even if I am very dubious about many of them, 200 is the number Spitzer offers.

Numbers matter. Two hundred out of how many? Taking the United States population over the age of 18 at about 210 million, and taking the gay population (never precisely definable but still estimatable) as about 3 to 10 percent, that gives us a figure of about 6 to

21 million gay people in the United States. Spitzer, after two or three years of energetic research seeking, found 200 possible sex-orientation-changed people out of 6 to 21 million gay people. That means we are talking about possible changes in not 1 percent, not one-tenth of a percent, not one-hundredth of 1 percent, but about one one-thousandth of 1 percent (.000009 to .00003) of the adult gay population. If any form of cancer had a cure rate of one in 100,000, it would not be called evidence that that cancer is curable; rather, to call it curable on that basis would be considered a cruel delusion and false promise.

As a further relevant issue of numbers, consider bisexuals. There are probably millions of Americans who are, by generally acceptable if imprecise criteria (e.g., postpubertal behavior, feelings, fantasies), bisexual. For reasons little understood, a great many of them vary in their sexual behavior styles and/or enthusiasms from one point in their lives to another. Certainly many thousands or hundreds of thousands are more heterosexual now than they were a few years ago, and certainly many thousands or hundreds of thousands are more homosexual than they were a few years ago. Nearly certainly, many thousands of such people are in some form of psychotherapy, and of those, some probably attribute various changes in themselves to the therapy. That little understood area alone would be expected to produce far larger numbers of what may look like changes in sexual orientation than did Spitzer's 200, and Spitzer does nearly nothing to acknowledge or help understand this area or to note that it vastly overshadows his 200.

The context of possible changes of sexual orientation is heavy with the history of demonizing, criminalizing, pathologizing, scapegoating, guilt-inducing—and otherwise socially, economically, physically, and emotionally harming—not hundreds of people but millions. Much of it, even if more subtly than in some past times and places, still goes on now in much of the world, and in much of the United States. This matters, and Spitzer largely ignores it.

Spitzer's article implies, without solid scientific support, something that has great and perhaps all-but-irresistible appeal to the popular press, to many politicians, and to many members of the public: that therapy can change gayness to straightness. Spitzer alerted the popular press before presenting part of this paper at the meeting of the American Psychiatric Association in 2001 and the popular press did some harm then. It is very likely to do more harm now, with the study's publication.

Spitzer's article, for all its dignified-looking data, scientific journal format, and partial disclaimers, is in essence irresponsible and unscientific. It does not constitute scientific evidence that gayness can be changed.

15

Evaluating Interventions to Alter Sexual Orientation: Methodological and Ethical Considerations

Gregory M. Herek

Consider this scenario:

A pharmaceutical company claims its new dietary supplement can change left-handed people to right-handers. Medical associations oppose the supplement on the grounds that it harms many people who use it. Noting that there is no reason for left-handed people to try to change, they urge their members not to recommend or administer the product to their patients. To test the drug company's claim, a researcher conducts brief telephone interviews with self-proclaimed "ex-lefties." He recruits respondents mainly through the drug company, which promotes his study to individuals who have given public testimonials about the product's effectiveness. They say they tried the supplement because they felt miserable as left-handers in a right-handed world. Most claim they now function as right-handers, although many report occasional thoughts about using their left hand and some occasionally lapse into left-handedness. The researcher's findings are based entirely on the one-time interviews in which he asked the ex-lefties to rate their handedness prior to taking the supplement (12 years earlier, on average) and during the previous year. Respondents' ratings of their past and current handedness are

This chapter appeared originally under the same title in *Archives of Sexual Behavior* 32(5):438-439. Copyright 2003 Kluwer Academic/Plenum Publishers. Reprinted with permission.

significantly different. The researcher concludes that the supplement does indeed change left-handers to right-handers in some cases. Meanwhile, other researchers and clinicians report anecdotally that the food supplement does not change most left-handers to right-handers, but many who tried the supplement report serious negative side effects.

The main questions raised by this hypothetical story concern whether the researcher's data are valid, whether the product's harmful effects would justify its use even if it is sometimes effective, and why left-handers should be encouraged to change in the first place. Similar questions arise from Spitzer's study of self-reported change from homosexuality to heterosexuality following participation in an intervention. Because of space limitations, this comment discusses only four of the many criticisms that can be made of Spitzer's article.

RELIANCE ON SELF-REPORT

Spitzer's data are ultimately the testimonials of a highly select sample of activists from groups whose raison d'etre is to promote efforts to change homosexuals into heterosexuals. It is difficult to imagine how his recruitment strategy would have yielded anything other than reports of substantial shifts to a heterosexual orientation. Despite his acknowledgment of its serious methodological inadequacies, Spitzer asks readers to take it on faith that his respondents were both willing and able to report accurately on their past and current thoughts, feelings, and behaviors.

This represents a curious abdication of the scientist's obligation to design a study in a way to avoid known sources of bias. Recognizing that even subtle and unintentional biases can affect the data, researchers routinely adopt elaborate safeguards to prevent their own expectations and those of their research subjects from affecting a study's outcomes. Spitzer's study lacked such safeguards, despite the obvious threats to validity inherent in his sampling procedures.

Even if Spitzer's respondents sincerely tried to give true accounts of their feelings and daily behaviors from (on average) 12 years prior to the interview, their reports cannot be assumed to be reliable. People often are inaccurate when recalling earlier mental states, especially when their emotions, goals, or beliefs have changed in the interim

(Levine and Safer, 2002). Memories of past beliefs, attitudes, and behaviors are affected by many factors, including personal theories about one's own behavior change over time (e.g., Ross, 1989). For this reason, asking research participants to recall their preintervention thoughts and feelings is always problematic, even when they are unaware of the study's purpose and have no ideological stake in its outcome. Given the inherently biased nature of Spitzer's sample, his failure to make even minimal attempts to assess the data's reliability (e.g., by assessing internal consistency within interviews and through follow-up interviews) and validity (e.g., through third party ratings or independent personal interviews with the respondent's spouse) seriously compromises the study.

CONCLUSIONS ABOUT CAUSATION

The title of Spitzer's paper is somewhat misleading. Few would dispute that some people's sexual orientation changes during their lifetime. Indeed, many lesbians and gay men report living as a heterosexual before recognizing or developing their homosexual orientation. The question at issue is not whether sexual orientation can change but whether interventions can be designed to bring about such change.

Spitzer's methodology is incapable of answering this question. Even if we were to accept the respondents' self reports as valid, simply asking people why they changed their behavior cannot establish what caused that change. Personal testimonials for the benefits of useless treatments abound. Some people genuinely believe that crystals healed them, laetrile cured their cancer, a psychic foretold their future, or a fad diet reduced their weight. Scientists, however, recognize that testimonials do not prove that an intervention works. People who undergo an intervention are often highly motivated to attest to its effectiveness. Their willingness to overstate (or actually lie about) its benefits is greater still when they have a financial or ideological stake in the intervention's success. Even when respondents sincerely attempt to be accurate, they (like all of us) remain unaware of many of their mental processes and, consequently, their accounts of the causes of their behaviors are not always reliable (e.g., Jacoby, Lindsay, & Toth, 1992; Nisbett & Wilson, 1977). This is why we use experimental designs to determine causation.

At most, Spitzer's data could demonstrate a correlation between reporting change and undergoing an intervention. Spitzer argues that a rigorous experimental study would be expensive and would take a long time to complete. These inconveniences, however, do not justify his ignoring the fact that a correlation does not establish a causal relationship.

RISK AND HARM

The hypothetical dietary supplement posed substantial risks to users. So do interventions to change homosexual orientation. As he acknowledges, Spitzer's selection criteria excluded those who had tried to change their sexual orientation without success. He dismisses those "failures" as outside the purview of his study, since his intention was to document that interventions change some homosexuals into heterosexuals, but just as with the hypothetical dietary supplement, the question of harm is important. To be sure, the risks associated with interventions to change homosexual orientation have not been experimentally demonstrated either. Concerns about such risks are based on anecdotal accounts from clinicians and self-reports by individuals who were subjected to the interventions (e.g., Haldeman, 2001; Shidlo & Schroeder, 2002).

Nonetheless, the standards for demonstrating harm are different from those for demonstrating efficacy. If harm seems to be at all likely, we have an ethical obligation to investigate the actual risk to patients before offering them an intervention. Indeed, clinical trials are structured to establish a treatment's safety before testing its efficacy. And if risks of harm exist, we must consider whether they are offset by the intervention's potential benefits. These considerations are reflected in the resolutions concerning sexual orientation change interventions passed by both the American Psychological Association and the American Psychiatric Association. Although Spitzer's article refers to those resolutions, he ignores the issue of harm except to note that (not surprisingly) his subjects did not report having experienced it.

HOMOSEXUALITY IS NOT AN ILLNESS

We recognize today that trying to change left-handers into right-handers is misguided. Left-handedness is not an illness. Neither is homosexuality. Yet, antigay activists promote a belief in homosexual-to-heterosexual "conversions" with missionary zeal. Why? A key reason is that an unpopular status or condition is more readily stigmatized to the extent that it is perceived as freely chosen. Recent religious campaigns selling so-called reparative therapy perpetuate the myths that homosexuality is a sickness and that gay people can (and should) become heterosexual. They are mainly about reinforcing the stigma experienced by gay men and lesbians, and blocking attempts to secure legal protections from discrimination on the basis of sexual orientation.

This is not to argue that Spitzer conducted his study to foster antigay stigma. But his article is oddly insensitive to this issue. Although he notes in passing that sexual orientation change "may be a rare or uncommon outcome of reparative therapy," it seems inevitable that activists from NARTH, Exodus, Focus on the Family, and similar groups will attempt to use the study to support their political agenda.

CONCLUSION

Spitzer's study is methodologically flawed and disturbingly silent about ethical concerns. It is disappointing that the *Archives* elected to publish it.

REFERENCES

Haldeman, D.C. (2001), Therapeutic antidotes: Helping gay and bisexual men recover from conversion therapies. *J. Gay & Lesbian Psychotherapy,* 5(3/4):117-130. Reprinted in: *Sexual Conversion Therapy: Ethical, Clinical and Research Perspectives,* eds. A. Shidlo, M. Schroeder & J. Drescher. Binghamton, NY: The Haworth Press, 2001, pp. 117-130.

Jacoby, L.L., Lindsay, D.S. & Toth, J.P. (1992), Unconscious influences revealed: Attention, awareness, and control. *American Psychologist,* 47:802-809.

Levine, L.J. & Safer, M.A. (2002), Sources of bias in memory for emotions. *Current Directions in Psychological Science,* 11:169-173.

Nisbett, R.E. & Wilson, T.D. (1977), Telling more than we can know: Verbal reports on mental processes. *Psychological Review,* 84:231-259.

Ross, M. (1989), Relation of implicit theories to the construction of personal histories. *Psychological Review,* 96:341-357.

Shidlo, A. & Schroeder, M. (2002), Changing sexual orientation: A consumers' report. *Professional Psychology: Research & Practice,* 33:249-259.

16

Guttman Scalability Confirms the Effectiveness of Reparative Therapy

Scott L. Hershberger

Spitzer presents compelling evidence that a homosexual orientation can be changed to a heterosexual orientation by reparative therapy. The best of evidence is found in changes following reparative therapy in (a) homosexual sex, (b) homosexual self-identification, and (c) homosexual attractions and fantasies. In this commentary, I will focus on the more dramatic results for men, although the results for women also support the effectiveness of reparative therapy.

Most therapists would agree that it is easiest to lower or eradicate participation in homosexual sex, somewhat harder to change self-identification from homosexual to heterosexual, and hardest of all to lower or eradicate homosexual attractions and fantasies. In Spitzer's study, changes in sexual behavior, self-identification, and attractions and fantasies toward a predominately heterosexual orientation confirm this expected order. After reparative therapy, homosexual sex was lowered for 98 percent of those who had previously engaged in homosexual sex, heterosexual identity was affirmed by 78 percent more individuals, and homosexual attractions or fantasies were experienced by 47 percent fewer individuals. Spitzer also categorized individuals as having changed or not changed by dichotomizing each of the three measures "at a point that the author regarded as indicating more than a slight level of homosexuality" (p. 408).

This chapter appeared originally under the same title in *Archives of Sexual Behavior* 32(5):440. Copyright 2003 Kluwer Academic/Plenum Publishers. Reprinted with permission.

doi:10.1300/5503_16

We can quantify the close match between the expected pattern of change with the observed pattern of change by thinking of sex, self-identification, and attraction and fantasies as three items whose order conforms to that of a Guttman scale. For the items to form a Guttman scale, everyone who has significantly fewer homosexual attractions and fantasies should also be more likely to self-identify as a heterosexual, and all those who now self-identify as a heterosexual should be more likely to have reduced the number of their homosexual sex experiences. The coefficient of reproducibility *(CR)* can serve as a measure of goodness of fit between the observed and predicted change patterns. The *CR* is defined as

$$CR = 1 — \Sigma \, e/N \, k$$

where *e* is the number of individuals whose item order does not conform to that of a Guttman scale, *N* is the sample size, and *k* is the number of items (Dunn-Rankin, 1983). The *CR* ranges from 0 to 1, with 1 denoting perfect conformity to a Guttman scale.

In order to compute the *CR*, data at the individual level are required. Spitzer clearly states in his article that his raw data are available to others, but the data were not available at the time this commentary was written. Thus, the following procedure was used to obtain an estimate of the *CR* for these data. Data were first created for 133 individuals by requiring that, for each item, the simulated data have some proportion of individuals who changed as in the observed data. For example, 47 percent of the individuals in the observed data reduced their homosexual fantasies; therefore, the simulated data for this item was also defined to have 47 percent of the sample change. Although the simulated data can reflect the correct proportions of change for the items, it is impossible to specify for any one person the specific pattern of change. To overcome this difficulty, 1,000 bootstrap samples of 133 individuals each were created to provide an estimate of the true *CR*. From the 1,000 samples, the *CR* ranged from 0.83 to 0.95, with a mean of 0.92 and a *SD* of 0.03.

Does a mean *CR* of 0.92 indicate a good fit? No value of *CR* has been defined that is universally accepted as a dividing line between acceptable and unacceptable goodness of fit, although Guttman (1947) originally defined a value of 0.85 as the dividing line. Other authors (e.g., Torgerson, 1958) suggested that a *CR* above 0.90 is a better standard. Therefore, the mean *CR* of 0.92 indicates that the pattern of change among the measures does fit a Guttman scale well. The goodness of fit of the Guttman scale to the three items is even more impressive when one considers that the mean CR of 0.92 is certainly an underestimate of its true value in the real data: the data set from which each of the bootstrap samples was drawn was created by randomly specifying whether an individual changed or not on *each item separately*. Therefore, each individual's entire item pattern was random.

The orderly, lawlike pattern of changes in homosexual sexual behavior, homosexual self-identification, and homosexual attraction and fantasy observed in Spitzer's study is strong evidence that reparative theory can assist individuals in changing their homosexual orientation to a heterosexual orientation. Now it is up to those skeptical of reparative therapy to provide comparably strong evidence to support their position. In my opinion, they have yet to do so.

REFERENCES

Dunn-Rankin, P. (1983), *Scaling Methods.* Hillsdale, NJ: Erlbaum.

Guttman, L. (1947), The Cornell technique for scale and intensity analysis. *Educational & Psychological Measurement,* 7:247-280.

Torgerson, W.S. (1958), *Theory and Methods of Scaling.* New York: Wiley.

17

Methodological Limitations Do Not Justify the Claim That Same-Sex Attraction Changed Through "Reparative Therapy"

Craig A. Hill
Jeannie D. DiClementi

The study by Spitzer suffers from substantial limitations that render his conclusions virtually meaningless. The main problems are methodological and relate to demand characteristics, sampling, lack of control, and validity of measurement.

The problem of demand that pervades the study is a fundamentally confounding factor. The sample most likely consisted of individuals who have experienced intense anxiety and guilt to the extent that this sets them apart from a majority of other lesbians and gay men who are dealing with identity issues. Consequently, the reports of change provided by these participants may originate from a combination of erotophobia (negative emotional reactions to sexual issues) and remorse over perceived violations of religious doctrine or culturally and family-based values, rather than representing a self-enhancing change in erotic and romantic nature.

Individuals who are unhappy with their attraction to the same sex and who have gone to great lengths to change will be motivated for their attitudes to become consistent with their public behavior, in line with cognitive dissonance theory. Reports of attitude change may not

This chapter appeared originally under the same title in *Archives of Sexual Behavior* 32(5):440-442. Copyright 2003 Kluwer Academic/Plenum Publishers. Reprinted with permission.

doi:10.1300/5503_17

be enduring over the long haul when they are related to such compelling issues as attraction and sexual desire.

The desire to change one's lesbian or gay sexual orientation is typically based on deeply entrenched negative attitudes about one's same-sex feelings, frequently called *internalized homophobia,* "the most insidious of the minority stress processes, . . . leading to a devaluation of the self and resultant internal conflicts and poor self-regard" (Meyer and Dean, 1998, p. 161). Meyer and Dean note that "men in the early stages of coming out and men who have sex with men but have not accepted their homosexuality are likely to have higher levels of internalized homophobia than their counterparts" (p. 179). The important role of traditional mainstream religions in promoting the internalization of homophobia is demonstrated in Meyer and Dean's study of 912 gay men. The men who were religious, but who were not associated with gay churches or synagogues, experienced higher levels of internalized homophobia than men who were religious, but who were associated with gay religious organizations; in fact, these latter men were equivalent in homophobia to nonreligious men, suggesting a beneficial influence of gay-affirming beliefs.

The effect of such conflict and anguish very likely distorts assessments made by individuals who have gone to great lengths to seek help. In response to antigay attacks, individuals with high levels of internalized homophobia likely experience their orientation as a source of pain, rather than as a source of pleasure, love, and intimacy. Antigay attacks are therefore often interpreted as justified punishment for being lesbian or gay and this may contribute to the process of wanting to change their sexual orientation (Garnets, Herek, and Levy, 1990).

Contrary to claims made by Spitzer, bias could account for a substantial portion of the changes reported by his respondents. Sexuality researchers have been concerned for some time about the potential for biases that diminish the accuracy of information, both in self-report methods (Meston, et al., 1998) and in interviews (Catania, 1999). Such biases are likely due to nonconscious self-enhancing or social desirability processes (Brown and Sinclair, 1999). Such distortion never occurs in a form in which all individuals skew their reports perfectly in line with the desirable standard, an argument Spitzer employed to dismiss the probability that bias affected the results of his study. Rather, bias is identified by differences in group averages. The variability within groups is never close to zero, with all members of a group falling extremely close to one end of the dimension. This is true even in validity research in which participants are requested to distort their responses by the researcher (Holden and Jackson, 1981). Therefore, substantial distortion could have occurred in self-reports of respondents in the Spitzer study which would not be evidenced by all respondents rating themselves at the "perfect" (i.e., heterosexual) end of the scales.

In contrast to the argument advanced by Spitzer, which was also intended to discount the possibility of bias, gender differences can be found in distortion, *especially* with respect to sexuality. One example of this is that men report greater numbers of sexual partners than do women of the same age, which cannot be entirely or even substantially attributed to larger numbers of men having sex with a small number of women (Brown and Sinclair, 1999). Furthermore, according to the availability heuristic (Kahneman and Tversky, 1973), the salience of an event biases judgment about the frequency of the event. For example, adolescent same-sex experimentation is quite common, but for the individual who is horrified at the thought that she or he may be gay, one or two such contacts could easily be perceived as excessive, and consequently the perception, and subsequent reports, of homosexual activity are gross overestimates. Such a possibility suggests that the participants in the Spitzer study may not actually be gay to begin with, or they are bisexual; in either case, their reports of change therefore would not really reflect a change of sexual orientation among lesbians and gay men. The most plausible explanation is that a nonconscious cognitive distortion affects judgments about sexual experiences for both sexes (Brown and Sinclair, 1999; Meston et al., 1998).

Given the possibility of distortion and the demand for attitude-behavior consistency, issues related to sampling and control should be elevated to the highest level. Simply locating people who claim to have changed does not provide convincing data. It would be possible to locate people who claim and sincerely believe any number of phenomena that are not easily verifiable empirically and about which many professionals are skeptical. All participants were obtained from organizations or therapists who are extremely committed to the efficacy of reparative therapy and only people who contacted the researcher were included in the study. These people are by definition those who believe in the effectiveness of the reparative techniques and earnestly need the technique to be effective both from a spiritual and an emotional perspective. Moreover, basic to any behavior change research is the inclusion of persons who attempted behavior change and failed.

Effort to employ the highest degree of control is incumbent upon researchers of such sensitive topics. Assignment of participants to experimental conditions is not the only means of enhancing control. Because of the problems with a hypothesis-biased population, it is critical to establish the nature of the sample obtained in terms of theoretically relevant characteristics; it is important as well to compare these individuals to other samples of lesbians and gay men to determine exactly the ways in which they are similar or different. Such critical characteristics should include homophobia, erotophobia, sex guilt, emotional stability, psychological disorders, self-esteem, social functioning, and religious guilt, to name but a few.

A comparison could involve matching therapy participants with nontherapy participants to determine the extent to which nontherapy participants had attempted sexual orientation changes in the past. With only one group purporting to experience change and with no comparison group, little confidence can be placed in claims that change occurred specifically due to therapeutic intervention and not due to some other factor. Moreover, change based on retrospective reports related to therapeutic progress are highly suspect in terms of validity, again especially given the incredible demand for change inherent in the life situation of these respondents, and given the fact that the pretherapy period was on average 12 years prior to the data-collection period.

In addition to emotionally based cognitive distortions, the issue of bias in assessment of current heterosexual relationships must be considered. When an individual who desperately wants to be heterosexual is finally involved in a heterosexual relationship and is asked, "Are you emotionally satisfied with your relationship?" what the researcher may actually be measuring is relief at achieving this greatly desired goal and not necessarily what most individuals mean by satisfaction with a relationship. The same can be said for the question about physical satisfaction. What is not investigated is the effort that goes into becoming physically aroused, because anecdotal reports suggest that "ex-lesbians" or "ex-gays" often must spend a great deal of effort achieving levels of arousal sufficient to engage in heterosexual sexual behavior.

The only conclusion that is indisputable in Spitzer's study is that he has identified a subset of lesbians and gay men (who in fact may actually be more appropriately considered bisexual) who claim to have changed their overt sexual behavior; the nature of the change, and the process through which it occurred, has not been convincingly established. Given the importance of this issue for individuals struggling with their sexual orientation, to claim otherwise is misleading and dangerous.

REFERENCES

Brown, N.R. & Sinclair, R.C. (1999), Estimating number of lifetime sexual partners: Men and women do it differently. *J. Sex Research,* 36:292-297.

Catania, J.A. (1999), A framework for conceptualizing reporting bias and its antecedents in interviews assessing human sexuality. *J. Sex Research,* 36:25-38.

Garnets, L.D., Herek, G.M. & Levy, B. (1990), Violence and victimization of lesbians and gay men: Mental health consequences. *J. Interpersonal Violence,* 5:366-383.

Holden, R.R. & Jackson, D.N. (1981), Subtlety, information, and faking effects in personality assessment. *J. Clinical Psychology,* 37:379-386.

Kahneman, D. & Tversky, A. (1973), On the psychology of prediction. *Psychological Review,* 80:237-251.

Meston, C.M., Heiman, J.R., Trapnell, P.D. & Paulhus, D.L. (1998), Socially desirable responding and sexuality self-reports. *J. Sex Research,* 35:148-157.

Meyer, I.H. & Dean, L. (1998), Internalized homophobia, intimacy, and sexual behavior among gay and bisexual men. In: *Stigma and Sexual Orientation: Understanding Prejudice Against Lesbians, Gay Men, and Bisexuals,* ed. G.M. Herek. Thousand Oaks, CA: Sage, pp. 160-186.

18

Initiating Treatment Evaluations

Donald F. Klein

Spitzer presents face valid evidence that changes in homosexual behavior and feelings of desire and satisfaction can be achieved by some, to varying degrees, via "reparative therapy."

These reports, which Spitzer quite logically argues are convincing, are necessary preliminaries to an open trial, which enrolls a series of appropriate subjects, treats them all, and records the results. This allows an estimate of the proportion of good outcomes, although it does not establish that the therapy caused the benefit since patients may improve in spite of their treatment. Volunteers who claim successful outcomes do not yield an estimate of the proportion benefited. Also, just how common such reported successes are remains obscure.

Spitzer calls for a consecutive series who perceive homosexuality as a problem of theirs they wish fixed, who have been evaluated before and after treatment. I agree this is the correct next step. Apparently, Nicolosi and Byrd claim to have such data. If this is more than therapist self-serving, they have an obligation to present their data or to stop making such important claims. Such strictures also apply to the range of official groups that assert the uselessness and damaging effects of "reparative therapy" for homosexuality. Where are their data? If it is nothing but anecdotes and presumptions, how can they claim they are being professionally responsible? Relevant observations are needed to raise hopes that a treatment is worth evaluating. Spitzer provides the level of evidence appropriate to the initial stages

This chapter appeared originally under the same title in *Archives of Sexual Behavior* 32(5):442-443. Copyright 2003 Kluwer Academic/Plenum Publishers. Reprinted with permission.

doi:10.1300/5503_18

of therapeutic evaluation with regard to a heuristically important issue.

Spitzer, pessimistically, but perhaps accurately, states that this methodologically correct next step, the evaluation of the treatment of a well-defined consecutive series of homosexual patients, is unlikely to occur. However, cost and duration are really not to the point, considering other trials that have received NIMH funding. Concerns about patient safety may be more to the point but apparently these concerns are more theory driven than data substantiated. A data safety monitoring board would provide an adequate safeguard.

The trepidation in this area may arise from concern about the "re-pathologization" of homosexuality. This is fostered by the term "reparative therapy," which is both vague and presumptuous. However, if it was renamed, say, "role modification," would that help? Effective change techniques do not necessarily imply illness (e.g., cosmetic surgery).

The American Psychiatric Association (APA) states that it supports such research, but ethical practitioners should refrain from attempts to change individual's sexual orientation until the research findings are at hand. Such a data-based orientation with regard to psychotherapeutic efforts can only be welcomed. Of course, if this criterion was consistently applied, the APA would have to be substantially more critical about other more favored psychotherapies.

Treatment evaluation aspires to demonstrate specific benefits through determinate causes. Spitzer suggests that the causal efficacy of reparative therapy may never be shown because it is extremely unlikely that patients would enter a long placebo-controlled trial. However, the point of a placebo controlled trial is to address the null hypothesis that the entire effect of the treatment is due to the nonspecific combined effects of being in treatment, having one's hopeful expectations raised in a congenial environment, and the natural history of the condition.

However, controlled dismantling comparisons allow causal inferences. Behavioral activation, which may account for the benefits of cognitive behavior therapy, is a reasonable comparison. Reparative therapy might be compared to its components, such as incremental heterosexual pleasures, avoidance of exposure to homosexual pleasures, or any other credible component of the currently ill-defined reparative therapies. If it turns out that complex reparative therapy was more effective than its credible components, and if it were unlikely that the components were toxic, this suggests causal efficacy for reparative therapy, even though specific causal agents remain obscure.

To engage in such meticulous research would require a very convincing body of data from the simpler longitudinal, complete, series of treated and evaluated subjects. Those who claim therapeutic success have the responsibility for providing the supportive data. Spitzer's study provides the necessary minimum for future studies to be considered feasible and perhaps fruitful.

Some claim that they know that the mere publication of this report will cause grievous social, political, and personal harms. This amounts to a call for censorship rather than meeting the issues on factual and logical grounds. History is replete with often successful attempts to quash questions about the conventional wisdom. This accounts for their infrequency. Initiating questions, in the framework of fostering objective studies, rather than asserting prior knowledge of the truth, has an honored place in science.

19

A Positive View of Spitzer's Research and an Argument for Further Research

Richard B. Krueger

Spitzer demonstrates that some individuals who have undergone "reparative" therapy report that they have changed their sexual orientation from homosexual to heterosexual for at least a 5-year period. His study obviously has many limitations, being retrospective, relying on telephone interviewing, and without any objective measurements of sexual arousal, such as penile plethysmography or vaginal photoplethysmography, which he fully discusses.

Arguably, one's fantasies, including masturbatory fantasies, are the best reflection of one's sexual arousal pattern compared with questions involving one's history of sexual interest or behavior. It is notable that in this study, among those who masturbate post-therapy, 68 percent of males and 41 percent of females still report same-sex fantasies on 20 percent or more of masturbatory occasions and only 31 percent of males and 72 percent of females report opposite-sex fantasies on 20 percent or more of masturbatory occasions. This masturbatory data suggest that change in one's sexual arousal pattern is difficult.

Spitzer, as well as the various national organizations cited in his article, suggests that more research could be done to further determine "reparative" therapy's risks versus its benefits. However, he then says that, realistically, it is unlikely, given the costs of such a study, that such research will be conducted in the future. Although "reparative"

This chapter appeared originally under the same title in *Archives of Sexual Behavior* 32(5):443-444. Copyright 2003 Kluwer Academic/Plenum Publishers. Reprinted with permission.

therapy concerns itself with change in sexual orientation, other therapies, such as cognitive behavioral therapy, concern themselves with the control or elimination of unwanted sexual behaviors and arousal, such as those present in the paraphilias or in individuals who are sexually compulsive (Abel et al., 1992; Benotsch, Kalichman, and Kelly, 1999; Kalichman, Greenberg and Abel, 1997). Further study of behavioral and/or pharmacological therapy to help such individuals seems indicated and appropriate. I think that Spitzer has made a substantial contribution, given limited resources, and would hope that more funding for the study of therapies involving not only the change and control of unwanted sexual behavior, but its origins and development, will become available.

REFERENCES

Abel, G.G., Osborn, C., Anthony, D., & Gardos, P. (1992), Current treatment of paraphiliacs. *Annual Review Sex Research,* 3:255-290.

Benotsch, E.G., Kalichman, S.C., & Kelly, J.A. (1999), Sexual compulsivity and substance use in HIV-seropositive men who have sex with men: Prevalence and predictors of high-risk behaviors. *Addictive Behaviors,* 24:857-868.

Kalichman, S.C., Greenberg, J., & Abel, G.G. (1997), HIV-seropositive men who engage in high-risk sexual behavior: Psychological characteristics and implications for prevention. *AIDS Care,* 9:441-450.

20

Penile Plethysomography
and Change in Sexual Orientation

Nathaniel McConaghy

In his article, Spitzer pointed out that reported change in sexual orientation in men and women following therapy would have benefited from use of penile or vaginal plethysmography. Outcome changes in men's penile volume responses to films of nude men and women were reported in a series of studies evaluating aversive therapies aimed at changing sexual orientation, administered over one week. The men were investigated prior to as well as at follow-up, at six months to three years. Their self-reports showed changes following treatment similar to, though less strong than, those reported by Spitzer. Of 40 men consecutively treated in the first study (McConaghy, 1970), at follow-up of one to three years, 15 percent reported an increase and 30 percent a possible increase in heterosexual desire. Thirty-two percent reported a reduction, and 15 percent a possible reduction in homosexual desire. Prior to treatment, 38 had homosexual relations with a number of partners, with 18 having been arrested for homosexual behavior on one or more occasions. Following treatment, 27 percent had no homosexual relations, and 32 percent reduced their frequency; 7 percent continued heterosexual relations at the same frequency, and 27 percent initiated them or continued them at an increased frequency. They showed significantly reduced mean penile volume responses to men; however, although they showed significant mean increase in penile responses to the films of women, this

This chapter appeared originally under the same title in *Archives of Sexual Behavior* 32(5):444-445. Copyright 2003 Kluwer Academic/Plenum Publishers. Reprinted with permission.

doi:10.1300/5503_20

change was only present in men who prior to treatment had shown negative responses to those films, not in the men who prior to treatment had shown positive responses to them.

Some men who remained exclusively homosexual following treatment reported they were no longer continuously preoccupied with homosexual thoughts and felt more emotionally stable and able to live and work more effectively. Others were able to control compulsions to make homosexual contacts in public lavatories, which had previously led to their being arrested. Of nine married men, six stated their marital sexual relationship had markedly improved. They included two of three who had ceased having intercourse with their wives some years before treatment. Related studies were carried out on a further 40 men (McConaghy, Proctor, and Barr, 1972) and 46 men (McConaghy and Barr, 1973). The changes in self-report and penile volume responses of the men following treatment were comparable with those found in the first study. Again, the increase in penile volume of the treated men to pictures of women was due to reduction of negative penile responses rather than an increase in positive penile responses. It was considered that the aversive procedures produced reduction in homosexual feelings, but no actual increase in heterosexual feelings. The increase in heterosexual feelings and behaviors reported by treated patients was attributed to their increased awareness of previously existing heterosexual feelings when their homosexual feelings were reduced.

It was attempted to increase the heterosexual feelings of homosexual men by showing them slides of nude women in temporal association with slides of nude men to which they were sexually aroused. It was expected this would lead by conditioning to the pictures of women becoming sexually arousing. The men seeking sexual reorientation were randomly allocated, 15 to receive the conditioning procedure and 16 to receive aversive therapy (McConaghy, 1975). The men's penile volume responses throughout treatment were monitored. No increase in the men's penile volume responses to the pictures of women were produced by the conditioning procedure and it was concluded it was therapeutically ineffective. At one-year follow-up, slightly more men reported increase in heterosexual feelings and markedly more men reported reduction in homosexual feelings and reduction or cessation of homosexual behavior following the aversive rather than the conditioning procedure, the difference with behavior being statistically significant. Since the conditioning procedure was ineffective, it was concluded that it acted as a placebo therapy and the significant reduction in men's homosexual behavior following aversive therapy was a specific effect.

As in previous studies, the men's mean penile volume responses were significantly greater to the moving films of women and less to those of men at the year follow-up compared to their responses prior to treatment, with the changes being equivalent following the aversive and the conditioning procedure. As the conditioning procedure appeared to have no therapeutic effect, the changes in penile volume responses following it could not be an effect of therapy and were considered due to the men consciously or unconsciously modifying their penile volume responses to conform with their wishes to be more heterosexual. As the changes in the men's penile volume responses following the aversive therapy were no greater than those following the conditioning procedure, it was concluded they also were not specific effects of the treatment, but due to similar attempts by the men to modify their responses.

Freund (1971) found that 20 percent of homosexual men when requested could produce penile volume responses that indicated they were predominantly heterosexual. In the four studies reported previously, of the men assessed prior to treatment, 117 showed penile volume responses indicating predominantly homosexual and 33 predominantly heterosexual orientation. Following treatment, 53 showed predominantly heterosexual orientation. Hence, 17 percent of men showed the change to predominant heterosexuality, less than the 20 percent of homosexual men Freund showed could produce this change voluntarily. It was concluded that aversive therapy produced a reduction in men's homosexual feelings and behaviors without altering their physiologically assessed sexual arousal to women as compared to men. An alternative theory was advanced that aversive therapies acted not by modifying physiological sexual arousal, but by reducing compulsive homosexual urges and behaviors. These changes were experienced as reduction in homosexual feelings, allowing some subjects to be more aware of and express their heterosexual feelings.

It is possible that the subjects investigated by Spitzer experienced similar changes without change in the core item of physiological sexual arousal to men as compared to women. Though he found much stronger changes than those in the men in the four studies reported, it is possible that men and women with strong changes were more likely to have volunteered for Spitzer's study. A number of men and women, presumably at times without treatment, can change what Spitzer termed core features of sexual orientation. The representative sample of the United States population investigated by Laumann et al. (1994) showed a steady reduction in homosexual behavior with age. It was reported respectively by 6.4 percent of men and 3.5 percent of women in their adolescence, 4.1 percent of men and 2.2 percent of women in the past five years, and 2.7 percent of men and 1.3 percent of women in the previous year. About 1 percent of men and 0.3 percent of women were aware of equal bisexual or predominant homosexual feelings but identified as heterosexual, as did 16 percent of the 2.4 percent of men who were exclusively attracted to the same sex. Exclusive homosexual activity was rare, reported by only 0.2 percent of women and 0.6 percent of men since puberty. Hence, less than a quarter of the 1.4 percent of women and 2.7 percent of men who identified as homosexual or bisexual had never had sexual activity with members of the opposite sex. Dunne et al. (2000) found that 20 percent of male and female twins reported homosexual behavior or awareness of some homosexual feelings; 97 percent of all the men and 96 percent of all the women had been sexually attracted to someone of the opposite sex at some time in their life. Hence, an ability to identify as heterosexual, to experience heterosexual attraction, and to have heterosexual activity is present in a significant percentage of men and women with homosexual feelings or behaviors.

On the basis of the theory that aversive therapies acted to reduce compulsions, an alternative nonaversive therapy, imaginal desensitization, was developed and shown in a randomized control trial to reduce men's compulsive sexual feelings and activity to a greater extent than an aversive procedure (McConaghy, Armstrong, and Blaszczynski, 1985). Imaginal desensitization was recommended to reduce preoccupations with homosexual fantasies and compulsive homosexual behaviors, in men and women unable to accept a homosexual adjustment (McConaghy, 1993). Behavioral therapy for anxiety concerning homosexual activity, and where appropriate, referral to a trained opposite-sex surrogate therapist, were recommended to increase heterosexual interest and activity. The book containing these recommendations was reviewed in a number of psychiatry and sexuality journals. No reviewers objected to the recommendations. It is possible that the majority of psychiatrists are not opposed to the use of therapies aimed at changing what Spitzer termed core features of sexual orientation of men and women who cannot accept a homosexual lifestyle. It could be argued that physiological arousal to members of one's own sex versus the opposite sex is the core feature of sexual orientation, particularly when the evidence presently available indicates that such arousal cannot be modified with therapy. However, this would seem a semantic issue, irrelevant to whether or not therapies aimed at modifying homosexual feelings and behaviors produce changes experienced positively by the men and women treated. The evidence from studies carried out over the past 40 years indicates that they do. Spitzer's concurrence with the recommendation to evaluate the risks versus the benefits of such therapies may be shared by many colleagues.

REFERENCES

Dunne, M.P., Bailey, J.M., Kirk, K.M., & Martin, N.G. (2000), The subtlety of sex-atypicality. *Archives Sexual Behavior,* 29:549-565.

Freund, K. (1960), Some problems in the treatment of homosexuality. In: *Behavior Therapy and the Neuroses,* ed. H.J. Eysenck. Oxford: Pergamon Press, pp. 312-326.

Laumann, E.O., Gagnon, J.H., Michael, R.T., & Michaels, S. (1994), *The Social Organization of Sexuality: Sexual Practices in the United States.* Chicago: University of Chicago Press.

McConaghy, N. (1970), Subjective and penile plethysmograph responses to aversion therapy for homosexuality: A follow-up study. *British J. Psychiatry,* 117: 555-560.

McConaghy, N. (1975), Aversive and positive conditioning treatments of homosexuality. *Behaviour Research & Therapy,* 13:309-319.

McConaghy, N. (1993), *Sexual Behavior: Problems and Management.* New York: Plenum.

McConaghy, N., Armstrong, M.S., & Blaszczynski, A. (1985), Expectancy, covert sensitization and imaginal desensitization in compulsive sexuality. *Acta Psychiatrica Scandinavica,* 72:176-187.

McConaghy, N. & Barr, R.F. (1973), Classical, avoidance and backward conditioning treatments of homosexuality. *British J. Psychiatry,* 122:151-162.

McConaghy, N., Proctor, D., & Barr, R.F. (1972), Subjective and penile plethysmography responses to aversion therapy for homosexuality: A partial replication. *Archives Sexual Behavior,* 2:65-78.

21

Finally, Recognition
of a Long-Neglected Population

Joseph Nicolosi

As a clinical psychologist who has worked almost exclusively with homosexual men for over 15 years, and as the originator of the term "reparative therapy," I am very grateful to Spitzer for giving a voice to ex-gays. Although this client population remains little recognized, there are hundreds of ex-gay men and women whose quiet and heroic struggles have been assisted by the clinicians associated with the National Association of Research and Therapy of Homosexuality (NARTH). Some NARTH clinicians see same-sex attraction as a developmental disorder; others do not. But whether or not they hold to the "disorder" theory, all of these clinicians have agreed to support clients who choose to diminish their unwanted homosexuality and develop their heterosexual potential.

Who, then, is this client that seeks out "reparative" or "reorientation" therapy? Is he or she a self-hating person whose problem is rooted in internalized homophobia? It is essential to understand that there are radically different understandings of the term "homophobia." Some see it as self-hatred and rejection of one's core identity whereas others define it as the recognition that something is disordered about one's sense of self and way of relating to others with respect to gender.

Recently, Rosik (2003) noted that usually a difference in beliefs exists about the source of moral value that separates clients who seek

---

This chapter appeared originally under the same title in *Archives of Sexual Behavior* 32(5):445-447. Copyright 2003 Kluwer Academic/Plenum Publishers. Reprinted with permission.

doi:10.1300/5503_21

sexual reorientation from those who seek gay-affirming therapy. Clients who seek gay-affirming therapy tend to emphasize a sexual morality that sees the individual as his own autonomous source of moral truth. This is the "ethic of autonomy," which envisions sex as being moral as long as it is consensual. By contrast, argues Rosik, those who seek reorientation therapy tend to approach the subject more from a moral domain emphasizing the "ethic of divinity" and/or "ethic of community," both of which assume a universal moral order grounded in religious values given by God or community. The act of giving one's consent, for those who hold to this ethic, does not make a sexual act moral. Some expressions of sexuality, according to this view, convey an intrinsic harm to personhood—whether or not this harm is measurable by psychology or actually perceived by the person.

A considerable body of psychodynamic theory—supported by empirical evidence—is available to buttress reparative-drive theory and reparative therapy. Reparative theory views homosexual attractions as generated by unmet same-sex attachment needs (Moberly, 1983; Nicolosi, 1991, 1993). In fact, in the 30 years since the removal of homosexuality from the DSM, any alternative, credible, non-traumatic model of development that results in homosexuality has yet to emerge. The only serious attempt to formulate a developmental model is the model offered by Bem (1996), and I elsewhere have listed my objections to Bem's "Exotic Becomes Erotic" model (Nicolosi and Byrd, 2002).

Are there other, purely practical reasons for leaving a gay lifestyle? Male eroticism—which is by its very nature promiscuous—seems to pose an inevitable problem of infidelity. McWhirter and Mattison (1984) conducted an in-depth study of the quality and stability of 156 long-term homosexual couplings that had lasted from one to 37 years. Two-thirds of the respondents had entered the relationship with the expectation of faithfulness, but not one of those couples was able to maintain sexual fidelity for more than five years. For this and other reasons, it is not so surprising that many of Spitzer's subjects reported a deep dissatisfaction with gay life. I believe that the deficit-driven nature of homosexual attraction limits two men to constant cycles of intense infatuation that never have the chance to ripen beyond good friendship into mature, sexually faithful love.

One of my clients who has had over 2,000 anonymous contacts admits gay sex is "incredibly intense—no doubt the most pleasurable thing in my life." Yet, this man confesses that afterward he is "wiped out, depressed, sad, and discouraged." Another former client (who married and now has grown children) explains why he left a gay lifestyle:

> The sexual experience with a man is like taking an opium drug. It's soothing, it's anesthetizing, and it's a "quick fix." This can make it very difficult to leave homosexuality. When we have sexualized those emotional needs—when we have already learned to get those needs temporarily met in a sexual way—we've taken a normal, legitimate, God-given need [same-sex bonding and affection] and met it with a "drug." That's one of the things that I've had to recognize and admit to myself: a same-sex relationship wasn't meant to have that kind of zing. The "zing" is artificial, but it is very compelling—and it is what keeps a lot of men in the gay life.

So, if it is true that for many people, gay relationships simply don't "work," then the next question must be: Is change possible? As Spitzer astutely notes, change should be viewed not in terms of erasing all unwanted desires but as a matter of diminishing homosexual attractions and increasing heterosexual responsiveness.

Spitzer is not the only recent researcher who has observed the potential fluidity of sexuality. Diamond (2000) found that "for sexual-minority women, nonexclusivity in attraction is the norm, rather than the exception" (p. 247). Half of the lesbian, bisexual, and "unlabeled" women in her study reported at two-year follow-up that they had changed sexual identities more than once. Haldeman (2000), who has been critical of reorientation therapy because he sees homosexuality as part of a person's core nature, has stated that "the categories of homosexual, heterosexual, and bisexual, considered by many researchers as fixed are in reality very fluid for many."

Typically, with men who have left a gay lifestyle and developed heterosexual attractions, we almost always see that these newly developing attractions are of lesser intensity than their former homosexual feelings. For many years I was unable to understand why, nor did I know why ex-gay men typically say they are sexually attracted to their wives, but much less so to other women (good news, of course, for the wives). I came to realize that this was not so much a problem of arousal as of trust. Male homosexuality is often associated with the boy's narcissistic emotional enmeshment with the mother in which the son feels responsible for the mother's feelings (Socarides, 2002). The resulting fear and anger is projected onto all women, whom he expects will be manipulative and engulfing and will take away his masculine power. The challenge for the ex-gay man is to enter into a relationship with a woman while maintaining a sense of self-possession. As he gets closer to a woman, this anxiety manifests itself as a fear of sexual performance. Therefore, almost without exception, the ex-gay man cannot develop a sexual relationship with a woman unless he first develops a friendship. Only when he knows he can trust the woman with his vulnerability will his latent heterosexual feelings become manifest.

Almost all the clients I have known who transition away from homosexuality describe a more subtle heterosexual response, one which has, as my former client says, less "zing." But even though they are of less intensity, these experiences are richer, fuller, and more emotionally satisfying. These men describe a feeling of "rightness" and a natural compatibility. As one ex-gay and now-married client said, "When I compare my intimate experiences with my wife to my homosexual experiences, it seems like we were little boys playing in the sandbox." Rather than feeling depleted, he is renewed, feels good about himself, and experiences himself as an integral part of the heterosexual world.

Wyler (2002) captures an experience of sexual reorientation similar to many of the individuals interviewed in Spitzer's study:

> Where once we felt sexual lust [for other men], today we feel brotherly love. Where once we felt fear of heterosexual men and estrangement from them, today we feel trust and authentic connection. Where once we felt self-hate and a feeling of never being "man enough," today we feel self acceptance and a strong and confident masculine identity. We experienced this profound change by uncovering and healing the underlying pain and alienation from men, masculinity and God that, we found, had caused so much of our homosexual symptoms. . . .

We can only speak for ourselves—about our own experience, about what was right for us, about what brought about change in our lives . . . and what brought us joy.

There is no doubt that reorientation therapy is not for everybody. Many clients choose to live out their same-sex attractions—and respect for client diversity and autonomy require that gay-affirming therapy be available. But reorientation therapy must be offered for those who do believe that gay is not who they really are. This group—the population Spitzer studied—are the men and women who seek to live out a different understanding of the meaning of gender and wholeness.

REFERENCES

Bem, D.J. (1996), Exotic becomes erotic: A developmental theory of sexual orientation. *Psychological Review,* 103(2):320-335.

Diamond, L.M. (2000), Sexual identity, attractions, and behavior among young sexual-minority women over a 2-year period. *Developmental Psychology,* 36:241-250.

Haldeman, D.C. (2000, August), *Gay Rights, Patients Rights: The Implementations of Sexual Orientation Conversion Therapy.* Paper presented at the meeting of the American Psychological Association, Washington, DC.

McWhirter, D. & Mattison, A. (1984), *The Male Couple: How Relationships Develop.* Englewood Cliffs, NJ: Prentice Hall.

Moberly, E. (1983), *Homosexuality: A New Christian Ethic.* Greenwood, SC: Attic Press.

Nicolosi, J. (1991), *Reparative Therapy of Male Homosexuality: A New Clinical Approach.* Northvale, NJ: Jason Aronson.

Nicolosi, J. (1993), *Case Stories of Reparative Therapy.* Northvale, NJ: Jason Aronson.

Nicolosi, J. & Byrd, A.D. (2002), A critique of Bem's "exotic becomes erotic" theory of sexual orientation development. *Psychological Reports,* 90:931-946.

Rosik, C. H. (2003), Motivational, ethical, and epistemological foundations in the clinical treatment of unwanted homoerotic attraction. *J. Marital & Family Therapy,* 29:13-28.

Socarides, C.W. (2002), Advances in the psychoanalytic theory and therapy of homosexuality. In: *Objects of Desire: The Sexual Deviations,* eds. C.W. Socarides & A. Freedman. Westport, CT: International Universities Press, pp. 3-40.

Wyler, R. (2002), www.peoplecanchange.com.

22

Sexual Orientation Change and Informed Consent in Reparative Therapy

Bruce Rind

Spitzer concluded that reparative therapy can sometimes change homosexuals to heterosexuals and, therefore, the movement toward banning this type of therapy is wrong-headed. He argued that using this therapy should be the patient's choice. Such choice, when based on informed consent, should be seen as fundamental to client self-determination. In this commentary, I examine the validity of his claim for *actual* change in sexual orientation and then evaluate his arguments concerning informed consent.

Spitzer's assertion that his study is a significant improvement over previous research in this area is correct. His measures of sexual orientation were more diverse, including not just surface aspects (e.g., overt behavior, self-labeling), but features that appear to get to the core (e.g., feelings, yearnings, fantasies). His sample size was impressive, his interview schedule was well designed, and his offer to share all his data, including audio recordings, with the research community was very much in the scientific spirit. His results are clear in indicating that his subjects did change in important ways. For instance, extending his report to an effect size analysis, change in self-reported sexual attraction from before to after therapy was 3.40 *SDs* for men and 4.04 for women, values that are enormous compared to average psychotherapy effects, which Smith and Glass (1977) estimated to be 0.68 *SDs* in their seminal meta-analysis. Effect sizes

---

This chapter appeared originally under the same title in *Archives of Sexual Behavior* 32(5):447-449. Copyright 2003 Kluwer Academic/Plenum Publishers. Reprinted with permission.

doi:10.1300/5503_22

were similarly huge for other measures in Spitzer's study. Thus, on its surface, the study appears to show dramatic effects of therapy in changing sexual orientation. The key issue, as Spitzer himself noted, is the credibility of the self-reports.

Spitzer stated that he believed his subjects' self-reports, claiming these did not appear to be lies or self-deceptions. Most likely the subjects did believe what they reported (so they were not lying), but what about self-deception? Spitzer argued that if self-deception obtained, then one would have expected findings such as reports of complete or near complete change, rapid change, and similar change in men and women. Since these did not hold, he rejected self-deception. These arguments are unconvincing. Why must self-deception produce the perception of only complete and rapid change rather than partial and gradual change? Cannot men and women self-deceive differently to reach different perceptions of change, given that they are known to think differently about many sexual and nonsexual issues? More important, what about social psychological research on cognitive dissonance and social cognition (Festinger, 1957; Myers, 2000), which shows that self-deception frequently occurs in situations of conflict? Festinger (1957) described cognitive dissonance as a state of negative arousal resulting from conflict between important beliefs, which motivates attempts at dissonance reduction through means such as altering and even distorting the conflicting beliefs to make them consonant. Much experimental research has supported his theory. Social cognition research similarly has demonstrated multifarious routes to self-deception as a means of adapting to current needs and pressures (Myers, 2000).

Patients in Spitzer's study fit classically into the cognitive dissonance dilemma. On the one hand, their sexual attractions were homosexual. On the other, their religious beliefs were antihomosexual. Religion was core to their identities (93 percent said religion was very or extremely important in their lives) and its tenets caused serious conflicts with their sexual orientation (79 percent said that this conflict was a major motivation for wanting to change their sexual orientation). Resolving conflicts between such powerful forces is difficult, but subjugating homosexual expression to religion in some cases should not be seen as surprising. Volumes could be written on the power of religion to overcome one's basic nature. Suffice it to say that because of religious beliefs, men have frequently overcome survival instincts (e.g., Muslim suicide hijackings and bombings). In sexuality, men have frequently yielded to anti-body, antisex religious philosophies (e.g., Christian priests and monks, including the three most conspicuous early theorists: Origen, who cut off his testicles with a rock to destroy his sexual urge; Augustine, who abandoned sexual pleasure completely despite having enjoyed it so much previously; and Chrysostom, who lived as an ascetic hermit in the desert to avoid all temptation). In short, beliefs about the value of one's life and one's sexuality can readily become subservient to strong religious beliefs. Such yielding, however, does not alter one's biological nature; it just suppresses it. In this sense, strongly religious patients who accept their religion's antihomosexual view and then under therapy change their attractions and fantasies may be merely suppressing their true nature rather than altering it.

The alternative explanation then is that Spitzer's subjects, clearly in conflict, resolved their cognitive dissonance (and thus felt happier after the therapy) by rejecting homosexual feelings, thoughts, and behavior while embracing heterosexual ones. But this rejection represented an effortful suppression rather than an alteration of their basic core nature. Let us examine the therapy itself and some of Spitzer's measures in this regard. We are told that three of the most important elements of the therapy that helped produce change were linking childhood experiences to later sexual feelings, thought stopping, and avoiding tempting situations. The first of these likely reinforced the religious motive to change and added credibility to the therapy, teaching patients that their true nature is heterosexual just as their religions have insisted, that their diversion to homosexual "pathology" is attributable to their having been "victims" of abuse or neglect, and that now they can finally be "healed." The second and third provided the cognitive and behavioral controls to suppress homosexual yearnings and avoid them. Maintaining these controls and behaving heterosexually were then fueled by the relief provided by ending the decades-long cognitive dissonance.

A gay man sees another male who previously would have excited him; he rejects feeling aroused and acknowledging that the male is sexually attractive. He thinks about the other male when alone; he stops this thinking before it becomes a fantasy. He is alone and begins to yearn for homosexual sex, but stops himself, feeling resolutely now that this is intolerable. He sees a woman and tells himself she is attractive, and feels a rush of self-esteem for living up to Christian virtue. The problem is that these apparently involuntary reactions are actually under conscious, cognitive control. The man is playing out a role rather than expressing his true nature, which is suppressed (cf. Goffman, 1959). In short, these measures, it seems, assess surface rather than core change. The man's beliefs are tied to the surface, to the role he feels compelled to play, and to the extent that the core differs, his self-reports are self-deception. What are needed are measures of involuntary response to various actual stimuli, rather than just self-reports that reflect essentially volitional behavior. Put the man back into tempting situations of the kind that formerly aroused him or expose him to gay pornography of the type that used to excite him. Measure his arousal with plethysmography. Expose him to heterosexual situations that he claims attract him or expose him to heterosexual pornography and then measure the arousal in the same way. Have him self-report reactions to a researcher not in the reparative therapy camp. If he responds more as a homosexual, then his therapeutically induced beliefs are not genuine. If he responds more as a heterosexual, then reparative therapy may be seen as perhaps working.

Spitzer called for professionals to steer away from banning reparative therapy. The inconclusiveness of his measures, which could be reflecting self-deception, weakens this call. This aside, another problem with his recommendation concerns whether patients truly are giving informed consent, as they should be according to Spitzer. Informed consent requires knowing the odds of success, a result not derivable from Spitzer's data. More important, psychotherapy patients generally put trust in their therapists as medical patients do in their doctors—they assume the treatment is scientifically valid. Reparative therapists teach their patients that homosexual orientation is the product of childhood seduction or negative family events. Such teaching is *not* based on scientific research but stems from theory (usually psychoanalytic) combined with unsystematic observation that dubiously claims to be scientific. But empirical research, as opposed to clinical anecdotes, does *not* support seduction or any family environment variables as causative (e.g., Bell, Weinberg, and Hammersmith, 1981). Patients provided with myth presented as scientific fact are not giving true informed consent.

Finally, important reasons exist to urge caution in mental health treatment of "deviant" sexuality, given the field's history of medicalizing sex based on morality rather than approaching it scientifically (Kinsey, Pomeroy, and Martin, 1948; Szasz, 1990). If it is important for homosexual patients to give true informed consent, then therapy from psychologists and psychiatrists should be informed by the full range of knowledge we have about homosexuality, which extends far beyond the clinic or pulpit. Historical, cross-cultural, and cross-species perspectives are essential. The first shows clearly that the Judeo-Christian condemnation of homosexuality is socially constructed rather than divinely inspired, based on cultural and political events combined with idiosyncratic philosophy (Johansson, 1990). The first two perspectives show that homosexuality in certain forms has been accepted as normal and even functional rather than condemned as sinful and sick in a majority of human societies across time and place (Ford and Beach, 1951; Greenberg, 1988). The third perspective suggests that it has a natural if not genetic basis, as its expression increases systematically in the primate order as one moves from prosimians to New World monkeys to Old World monkeys to apes and finally to humans (Vasey, 1995). In the conflict between the Judeo-Christian attitude and homosexuality, it appears, scientifically speaking, that it is the former, not the latter, that is out of sink with nature. Therapy should be informed by these perspectives so that patients can give true informed consent.

REFERENCES

Bell, A.P., Weinberg, M.S., & Hammersmith S.K. (1981), *Sexual Preference: Its Development in Men and Women.* Bloomington, IN: Indiana University Press.

Festinger, L. (1957), *A Theory of Cognitive Dissonance.* Stanford, CA: Stanford University Press.

Ford, C.S. & Beach, F.A. (1951), *Patterns of Sexual Behavior.* New York: Harper & Row.

Goffman, E. (1959), *The Presentation of Self in Everyday Life.* Garden City, NY: Doubleday.

Greenberg, D. (1988), *The Construction of Homosexuality.* Chicago, IL: The University of Chicago Press.

Johansson, W. (1990), Kadesh. In: *The Encyclopedia of Homosexuality,* Volume 1, eds. W. Dynes, W. Johansson, & W. Percy. New York: Garland Publishers, pp. 653-656.

Kinsey, A.C., Pomeroy, W.B., & Martin C.E. (1948), *Sexual Behavior in the Human Male*. Philadelphia: W.B. Saunders.

Myers, D.G. (2000), *Exploring Social Psychology*, Second edition. Boston: McGraw-Hill.

Smith, M.L. & Glass, G.V. (1977), Meta-analysis of psychotherapy outcome studies. *American Psychologist*, 32:752-760.

Szasz, T.S. (1990), *Sex by Prescription: The Startling Truth About Today's Sex Therapy*. Syracuse, NY: Syracuse University Press.

Vasey, P.L. (1995), Homosexual behavior in primates: A review of evidence and theory. *International J. Primatology*, 16:173-203.

23

Reparative Science and Social Responsibility: The Concept of a Malleable Core As Theoretical Challenge and Psychological Comfort

Paula C. Rodríguez Rust

Spitzer's article is reminiscent of constructions of homosexuality as an illness, heterosexuality as normal and healthy, and "reparative therapy" as a treatment. Spitzer presents evidence that individuals' sexual attractions and sexual self identities, as well as sexual behaviors, can change over time, and he interprets this as a change in core sexual orientation resulting from reparative therapy. In the current theoretical climate, it would be easy for critics to reject the findings on methodological grounds, to disagree with the conclusion that core sexual orientation changes occurred, or to dismiss Spitzer's argument for its complicity with outdated views of homosexuality. It is important, however, to distinguish methodological criticisms from criticism of Spitzer's underlying moral perspective, and to refrain from using the former to undercut the latter.

Although there are sources of bias in Spitzer's methods, the findings that individuals' sexual attractions, responses, self identities, and behaviors can change are consistent with findings of other contemporary researchers. Comparable research has been conducted under different theoretical guises, including research on coming out, "situational homosexuality," and the multidimensionality of sexuality. Research

This chapter appeared originally under the same title in *Archives of Sexual Behavior* 32(5):449-451. Copyright 2003 Kluwer Academic/Plenum Publishers. Reprinted with permission.

on coming out documents shifts over the life course from heterosexual to lesbian, gay, or bisexual (LGB) self identities, feelings, and behaviors (e.g., Coleman, 1982; Rosario et al., 1996; Rust, 1993; Savin-Williams, 1995). Research on situational homosexuality explains same-sex activity among individuals otherwise cast as heterosexual, such as prison inmates (e.g., Giallombardo, 1966; Ward and Kassebaum, 1965; Wooden and Parker, 1982) and women in the sex trade (e.g., McCaghy and Skipper, 1969; see Rust, 2000a). Research on sexual multidimensionality documents imperfect and shifting correlations among sexual attraction, response, behavior, and identity (e.g., Blumstein and Schwartz, 1976a, 1976b, 1977; Diamond, 2000; Ekstrand et al., 1994; Rust, 1996a; Weinberg, Williams, and Pryor, 1994, 2001). Most research on coming out, situational homosexuality, and sexual multidimensionality involves the same methodological weaknesses as Spitzer's research, including reliance on retrospective self-reports (cf. Diamond, 2000; Weinberg et al., 1994, 2001). With one exception that I will discuss, I find Spitzer's acknowledgment of, and efforts to minimize, methodological bias thorough and fair. These biases must be considered, but they do not uniquely discredit Spitzer's findings.

Spitzer found greater changes among women than men. Numerous researchers have found greater variability in sexual feelings, identities, and behaviors over the life course among women than among men (e.g., Laumann et al., 1994; Weinberg et al., 1994) and less consistency among the dimensions of sexuality among women, particularly a tendency for women to identify themselves in ways inconsistent with their sexual attractions and behaviors (e.g., Diamond, 2000; Rust, 1992). It has been suggested that the greater variability and inconsistency in women's sexualities reflect greater social restrictions placed on their sexual behavior, greater dependence of sexual feelings on situational factors, and the importance of social relationships in defining women's identities (e.g., Pillard, 1990; Rust, 2000b; Schwartz and Blumstein, 1998). Whereas men might base their sexual identities primarily on their sexual feelings and experiences, women are socialized to subject their attractions to social considerations and to define themselves in terms of their relationships to others, resulting in greater socially induced changes in women's experiences of their sexualities and more frequent changes in their self identities.

Although social influences might be stronger for women, I (Rust, 1996b) have argued that both men and women develop situationally dependent attractions to others, derive identity from their social circumstances, and change their identities as social circumstances change (Rust, 2001). Cass (1996) argued that sociocultural settings have "indigenous psychologies" such that "psychological functioning and human behavior is specific to the sociocultural environment in which people live" (p. 229). Spitzer's findings that both men and women, but particularly women, experience changes in their sexual feelings, behaviors, and identities during reparative therapy is entirely consistent with these social constructive arguments. Religious teachings, social support from ex-gay organizations and other-sex spouses, and cultural encouragement of heterosexual relationships are circumstances that might influence individuals' sexualities.

Some of Spitzer's own findings appear to undermine his conclusions. For example, Spitzer reported that 85 percent of male and 70 percent of female respondents "did not find life as a gay man or lesbian emotionally satisfying." Although this could be interpreted as evidence that these individuals' pretherapy core sexual orientations were not homosexual, and that the shift toward heterosexual functioning is not, therefore, a shift in core orientation, I believe this would be a misinterpretation. The finding is not a lack of emotional satisfaction with a same-sex partner but with life as a gay man or lesbian. I see this as evidence of the social malleability of sexual feelings; life as a gay man or lesbian might be unsatisfying for Spitzer's respondents because same-sex relationships lack social recognition and do not fit the family image they covet. The lack of emotional satisfaction is social in origin, but leads to a perception of one's same-sex attractions as ego-dystonic, which motivates a reconstruction of the self as heterosexual. One might be attracted to one's own sex, but also to a heterosexual lifestyle, and one might generalize one's attraction to a heterosexual lifestyle into an attraction to an other-sex person.

The distinguishing feature of Spitzer's research is not the finding that changes occur, but the argument that they reflect changes in core sexual orientation. Researchers who document changes in sexuality generally do not infer changes in core sexual orientation. For example, coming out is usually described as a rejection of a false heterosexual identity in favor of a LGB identity that reflects one's true sexual orientation, rather than a change in core sexual orientation (cf. Dixon, 1984). The term "situational homosexuality" was developed to protect the notion of an immutable core sexual orientation. Researchers who document sexual multidimensionality typically critique dichotomous constructions of sexuality, a deconstructionist approach that rejects the notion of a "core" homo- or heterosexuality. As Spitzer notes, even other researchers who study reparative therapy stop short of claiming changes in core sexual orientation. The real challenge Spitzer poses, therefore, is not the assertion that changes in sexual identity, feelings, and behavior occur, but the assertion of a core sexual orientation that is, although core, amenable to change. If a core orientation can change, what defining characteristic renders it "core"? The proposition that a malleable core sexual orientation exists is untestable. Its function is not scientific, but psychological; it allows individuals undergoing reparative therapy to hope that they will, ultimately, be able to live without fear that their same-sex desires will resurface.

Spitzer acknowledges his respondents' high motivation to demonstrate the efficacy of "reparative therapy," but asserts that he found their claims credible. He points out that his respondents did not report rapid or complete change, that some admitted using gay pornography, and that findings for women and men differed. I agree that these findings would be unlikely if respondents were lying, but I find them entirely consistent with the argument that subjects were deceiving themselves or, as I believe, reconstructing themselves. Both self-deceptive processes and reconstructive processes can be lengthy, and reconstructive processes can be gendered. The change must be credible to the respondent as well as to observers; otherwise, the self-deception, or reconstruction, cannot be successful.

Spitzer notes the possibility of interviewer bias, but underestimates other methodological biases. Recruitment via ex-gay ministries and the National Association for Research and Therapy of Homosexuality ensured respondents with personal interests in the success of reparative therapy. Given the impossibility of randomly assigning individuals to treatment and control groups, this bias is probably unavoidable. Many had obvious vested interests. Spitzer reports that 78 percent had spoken publicly in favor of reparative therapy. More important, however, is that subjects self-selected in response to "repeated notices of the study" sent to them by organizations upon which they relied for their "recovery." Endorsement of the research by these organizations would have suggested to potential respondents an organizational interest in the study's outcome, thus heightening both self-selection and response biases.

Spitzer's lack of criticism for the term "reparative therapy" and his equation of sexual addiction with homosexuality are disturbing. In all fairness, Spitzer does not advocate the use of reparative therapy to treat homosexuality in general. Spitzer's respondents underwent therapy because they desired to function heterosexually. These desires undoubtedly stem from social disapproval of homosexuality, and I would prefer to change the attitudes, not the individual; however, this choice belongs to the individual. Although Spitzer does not explicitly advocate reparative therapy in general, his failure to critique it speaks loudly. As social scientists, we cannot be held responsible for others' use of our findings, but I do believe we have a responsibility to consider the political circumstances within which we choose our research questions and present our findings. Social responsibility is particularly important when our research touches on areas of sexuality in which social prejudices have caused so much suffering for so many for so long.

REFERENCES

Blumstein, P.W. & Schwartz, P. (1976a), Bisexuality in women. *Archives Sexual Behavior,* 5:171-181.

Blumstein, P.W. & Schwartz, P. (1976b), Bisexuality in men. *Urban Life,* 5:339-358.

Blumstein, P.W. & Schwartz, P. (1977), Bisexuality: Some social psychological issues. *J. Social Issues,* 33(2):30-45.

Cass, V.C. (1996), Sexual orientation identity formation: A Western phenomenon. In: *Textbook of Homosexuality and Mental Health,* eds. R.P. Cabaj & T.S. Stein. Washington, DC: American Psychiatric Press, pp. 227-251.

Coleman, E. (1982), Developmental stages of the coming-out process. *J. Homosexuality,* 7(3):41-43.

Diamond, L.M. (2000), Sexual identity, attractions, and behavior among young sexual-minority women over a 2-year period. *Developmental Psychology,* 36:241-250.

Dixon, J.K. (1984), The commencement of bisexual activity in swinging married women over age thirty. *J. Sex Research,* 20:71-90.

Ekstrand, M.L., Coates, T.J., Guydish, J.R., Hauck, W.W., Collette, L., & Hulley, S.B. (1994), Are bisexually identified men in San Francisco a common vector for spreading HIV infection to women? *American J. Public Health,* 84:915-919.

Giallombardo, R. (1966), *Society of Women: A Study of a Women's Prison.* New York: Wiley.

Laumann, E.O., Gagnon, J.H., Michael, R.T., & Michaels, S. (1994), *The Social Organization of Sexuality: Sexual Practices in the United States.* Chicago: University of Chicago Press.

McCaghy, C.H. & Skipper, J.K. Jr. (1969), Lesbian behavior as an adaptation to the occupation of stripping. *Social Problems,* 17:262- 270.

Pillard, R.C. (1990), The Kinsey scale: Is it familial? In: *Homosexuality/Heterosexuality: Concepts of Sexual Orientation,* eds. D.P.M. McWhirter, S.A. Sanders, & J.M. Reinisch. New York: Oxford University Press, pp. 88-100.

Rosario, M., Meyer-Bahlburg, H.F.L., Hunter, J., Exner, T.M., Gwadz, M., & Keller, A.M. (1996), The psychosexual development of urban lesbian, gay, and bisexual youths. *J. Sex Research,* 33:113-126.

Rust, P.C. (1992), The politics of sexual identity: Sexual attraction and behavior among lesbian and bisexual women. *Social Problems,* 39:366-386.

Rust, P.C. (1993), 'Coming out' in the age of social constructionism: Sexual identity formation among lesbian and bisexual women. *Gender & Society,* 7:50-77.

Rust, P.C. (1996a), Finding a sexual identity and community: Therapeutic implications and cultural assumptions in scientific models of coming out. In: *Preventing Heterosexism and Homophobia,* eds. E.D. Rothblum & L.A. Bond. Thousand Oaks, CA: Sage, pp. 87-123.

Rust, P.C. (1996b), Sexual identity and bisexual identities: The struggle for self-description in a changing sexual landscape. In: *Queer Studies: A Lesbian, Gay, Bisexual, and Transgender Anthology,* eds. B. Beemyn & M. Eliason. New York: New York University Press, pp. 64-86.

Rust, P.C. (2001), Make me a map: Bisexual men's images of bisexual community. *J. Bisexuality,* 1(2/3):47-108.

Rust, P.C.R. (2000a), *Bisexuality in the United States: A Social Science Reader.* New York: Columbia University Press.

Rust, P.C.R. (2000b), Bisexuality: A contemporary paradox for women. *J. Social Issues,* 56:205-221.

Savin-Williams, R.C. (1995), An exploratory study of pubertal maturation timing and self-esteem among gay and bisexual male youths. *Developmental Psychology,* 31:56-64.

Schwartz, P. & Blumstein, P. (1998), The acquisition of sexual identity: Bisexuality. In: *Bisexualities: The Ideology and Practice of Sexual Contact with Both Men and Women,* eds. E.J. Haeberle & R. Gindorf. New York: Continuum, pp. 182-212.

Ward, D.A. & Kassebaum, G.G. (1965), *Women's Prison: Sex and Social Structure.* Chicago: Aldine.

Weinberg, M.S., Williams, C.J., & Pryor, D.W. (1994), *Dual Attraction: Understanding Bisexuality.* New York: Oxford University Press.

Weinberg, M.S., Williams, C.J., & Pryor, D.W. (2001), Bisexuals at midlife: Commitment, salience, and identity. *J. Contemporary Ethnography,* 30:180-208.

Wooden, W.S. & Parker, J. (1982), *Men Behind Bars: Sexual Exploitation in Prison.* New York: Plenum.

24

A Candle in the Wind:
Spitzer's Study of Reparative Therapy

Donald S. Strassberg

Spitzer is to be congratulated on tackling a difficult research question in a manner that, in some ways, is superior to many of the previous research efforts in this important area. He asked more, and often better, questions of more people who have "successfully" undergone reparative therapy than anyone else. However, his study has some serious methodological limitations. Although he acknowledges most of these limitations, he may be too willing to minimize or deny their impact on the meaningfulness of his results.

The acknowledged major limitations of this study are the manner in which participants were recruited and its reliance on self-report measures of change. Beyond the fact that there was no control group and no random assignment to treatment, interviewees were self- and therapist-selected because they believed that they had changed as a result of reparative therapy. This, obviously, creates several important limits. For example, we have no idea how typical these self-reported changes are. Spitzer admits that these are likely exceptional cases, but how exceptional? Do they represent the top 25 percent, 10 percent, 1 percent? This is not a trivial matter, especially as one is trying to weigh the relative benefits and risks associated with reparative therapy. Of course, a related limit to this recruitment strategy is that we have absolutely no idea about how many reparative therapy patients might have been harmed by their participation, or in what ways.

This chapter appeared originally under the same title in *Archives of Sexual Behavior* 32(5):451-452. Copyright 2003 Kluwer Academic/Plenum Publishers. Reprinted with permission.

doi:10.1300/5503_24

The sole reliance on self-reports of this select group is also problematic. I agree with Spitzer's belief that few of his participants consciously misrepresented themselves on the pre- and post-measures. However, it seems likely to me that he may have underestimated the degree to which, for religious and self-esteem reasons, his participants may have been highly motivated to see themselves as having changed more than was really the case. Furthermore, we have the cognitive dissonance that would have been created had these men and women seen their years of work as unsuccessful and ineffective. Spitzer is more convinced than I by the "evidence" of the reality of these reports (i.e., that most reported less than complete change on all dimensions). These were educated people who, as a result of their own experiences and the experiences of others similar to them, knew that absolute change in orientation was unlikely, even for those "successful" in treatment. They could have been easily unrealistically positive in their appraisals while reporting less than complete "cures."

Where does that leave us? It is unlikely that many practitioners or theorists currently believe that sexual orientation is completely fixed and unalterable for all people, in all ways, throughout the life span. A number of qualitative studies document individuals, particularly women, who experienced significant transitions in many aspects of sexual orientation without the benefit of formal, or even informal, reparative therapy (e.g., Blumstein and Schwartz, 1976a, 1993; Charboneau and Lander, 1991; Diamond, 2000; Kinnish and Strassberg, 2002; Kitzinger and Wilkinson, 1995). If change in many aspects of sexual orientation is possible without therapy, sometimes without even intention, than certainly such change is possible for some of those who will invest years of concentrated effort toward bringing about such change.

Then what does this study tell us beyond that some people in reparative therapy can and do significantly change, or at least believe that they do, in some aspects of orientation? It tells us that among such self-identified changers, most were not exclusively same-sexed oriented before treatment and most, perhaps all, were not exclusively other-sexed oriented after treatment. Does this surprise anyone? Perhaps more change was reported by more people here than many of us would have expected, but this is a highly select group of men and women. These are among the "best" the reparative therapy movement could offer—they are the poster adults for this movement. Even if we accept their self-reports as fact, what these data say is that some un-known (but likely small, perhaps very small) fraction of those who are motivated to spend years trying, were able to move, often to a sub-stantial degree, along most dimensions of the sexual orientation con-tinuum. This is not trivial, but not terribly surprising either.

Although Spitzer made some laudable methodological improve-ments in his approach to an important research question, the design of his survey does not really put it into the category of "scientific evi-dence supporting the efficacy of reparative therapy" for which so many seem to be looking. We need to know a lot more about those who may benefit and those who may be harmed by an approach that labels gay/lesbian/bisexuals as pathological and in need of repair (an issue, by the way, that Spitzer avoids discussing). I doubt any of us has yet to see, let alone conduct, the perfect study on virtually any psychological issue, and certainly not one as complex as sexual ori-entation. Spitzer is to be congratulated on trying to "light a candle" rather than continuing to "curse the darkness" when it comes to trying to understand what happens as a result of reparative therapy. How-ever, the amount of illumination provided by this particular candle does not strike me as quite as bright as Spitzer seems to believe. More important, it does not tell of nearly as much about reparative therapy as the media or the religious right is likely to want to make of it.

REFERENCES

Blumstein, P.W. & Schwartz, P. (1976a), Bisexuality in women. *Archives Sexual Behavior,* 5:171-181.

Blumstein, P.W. & Schwartz, P. (1993), Bisexuality: Some social psychological is-sues. In: *Psychological Perspectives on Lesbian and Gay Male Experiences,* eds. L.D. Garnets & G.C. Kimmel. New York: Columbia University Press, pp. 168-183.

Charboneau, C. & Lander, P.S. (1991), Redefining sexuality: Women becoming lesbian in midlife. In: *Lesbians at Midlife: The Creative Transition,* eds. B. Sang, J. Warsaw, & A. Smith. San Francisco: Spinsters Book, pp. 35-43.

Diamond, L.M. (2000), Sexual identity, attractions, and behavior among young sex-ual-minority women over a 2-year period. *Developmental Psychology,* 36:241-250.

Kinnish, K.K. & Strassberg, D.S. (2002, June), *Gender Differences in the Flexibil-ity of Sexual Orientation: A Multidimensional Retrospective Assessment.* Poster session presented at the meeting of the International Academy of Sex Research, Hamburg, Germany.

Kitzinger, C. & Wilkinson, S. (1995), Transitions from heterosexuality to lesbianism: The discursive production of lesbian identities. *Developmental Psychology*, 31:95-104.

25

Spitzer's Oversight: Ethical-Philosophical Underpinnings of "Reparative Therapy"

Marcus C. Tye

Spitzer introduces data from a self-selected sample who responded to requests for those who had "sustained some change in homosexual orientation" and concludes that "there was no evidence of harm" to these participants. Although Spitzer does not claim that this study provides any evidence that such interventions are harmless for all individuals who seek them, he suggests that further research be conducted. Although Spitzer presents an ostensibly scientific call for further inquiry, the justification for changing sexual orientation is ultimately an ethical-philosophical one: "In fact, the ability to make such a choice should be considered fundamental to client autonomy and self-determination."

Although I do not question Spitzer's science, a glaring oversight occurs in his article: a failure to examine the ethical and philosophical underpinnings of sexual orientation modification (SOM). I will refer to this as SOM instead of "reparative therapy," because the latter phrase suggests a clinically indicated treatment for a disorder, a method of repairing something that is broken. Although heterosexuality may be normative, it is no longer argued in the clinical literature that heterosexuality is inherently healthier than a nonheterosexual orientation nor that its absence is a defect in need of fixing. Even though sexual orientation is no longer thought of as a preference, the desire to change it most clearly *is* a preference, one that is deeply in-

This chapter appeared originally under the same title in *Archives of Sexual Behavior* 32(5):452-453. Copyright 2003 Kluwer Academic/Plenum Publishers. Reprinted with permission.

doi:10.1300/5503_25

fluenced by culture. Furthermore, SOM is a directionally neutral term, whereas reparative therapy inherently suggests a unidirectional modality. If Spitzer or other advocates of SOM were really value-neutral and supportive of client autonomy, they would also be calling for research into changing heterosexual orientation to bisexual or homosexual.

The ultimate issues regarding SOM are ethical-philosophical ones and not empirical. It is not whether sexual orientation *can* be changed, but whether it *should* be changed. To the extent that we are organic and have an ever-greater command and control over our biology, a great many changes to our biologically influenced makeup will one day be possible. The implication of Spitzer's position is that on the basis of client autonomy and self-determination, any such change that is desired should be granted if it can be safely effected, but it is a glaring oversight to state this without examining the ramifications of such a position.

Since this is an ethical issue, I will follow the conventions of the philosophy of ethics and, rather than cite empirical research, will suggest three hypothetical cases that illustrate problems and inconsistencies with Spitzer's position. First, assume that in the near future a sequence of genes will be identified that contributes significantly to an individual's sexual orientation. Preimplantation genetic diagnosis (PGD) presently offers physicians and their patients the ability to screen embryos with certain sequences of DNA, such as those identified with genetically linked diseases. The same technology that already exists could easily be adapted to selectively decide which genetically influenced traits will be allowed to continue in future generations, as soon as specific genetic sequences are identified for such traits or predispositions. Thus, in this hypothetical example in which a sequence of genes has been identified, a much more effective SOM would be using PGD to screen out those embryos whose genetic inheritance predisposes them to a heightened probability of having a parentally unwanted sexual orientation. Spitzer's assumption about individual autonomy—do not deny the patient any available effective treatment for modifying sexual orientation—would surely extend to our hypothetical case, and this new, more efficacious method of SOM would be the free choice of prospective parents, perhaps even more for those living in a free market economy, where treatment providers insist on unrestricted trade in therapeutic interventions. A second example: consider the parallel with

race. If an individual experiences discomfort because of racial prejudice, would one encourage the development of interventions that successfully altered skin tone if patients requested it, or would one abandon such "treatments" and instead undertake the harder work of
changing societal attitudes and laws? A third example illustrates an inconsistency within Spitzer's position. Many primarily heterosexual individuals occasionally have same-sex attractions, and so one could
suggest that SOM be pursued to aggressively encourage bisexuality
and thus double the opportunity for finding a soul mate. Advocates of
SOM generally assume without question that heterosexuality is the
only change that should be pursued.

It could be argued that Spitzer's SOM does not involve such hypothetical cases, but is designed to deal with the reality of clients who
are distressed by their nonheterosexuality and who genuinely wish to
change themselves. Yet, consider this equally true reality: the mental
health professions accept that healthy, happy sexual orientation is not
confined to heterosexuality. It is furthermore a reality that the desire
for nonheterosexuals to change is not an inherent property of a nonheterosexual orientation, but a discomfort contributed to by certain
cultural, religious, and social norms. Spitzer's response to this reality
is to turn aside from the sources of the discomfort, to treat the proxi-
mate rather than the ultimate cause of the distress.

If one strips away the empirical veneer, there are chiefly three ethical-philosophical underpinnings of reparative therapy:

1. Proponents of SOM are interested in taking individuals whose
   naturally occurring, potentially nondysfunctional sexual orientation causes them discomfort because of the social and cultural
   norms of *others,* and they wish to "help" these individuals conform to these norms rather than address the dysfunctional norms
   themselves.
2. For individuals who themselves have intensely unsatisfactory
   adjustment to their own sexual orientation, advocates of SOM
   are unwilling to recommend techniques such as gay-affirmative
   therapy that may question or change aspects of self that are very
   clearly a matter of belief rather than biology, deciding instead
   that clients' dysfunctional beliefs about sexual orientation enjoy
   a privileged status that should not be challenged—despite the
   fact that many forms of empirically supported psychotherapy are

based on the ability to modify cognitive distortions and change irrational beliefs.

3. Whether called "reparative therapy" or something else, by offering such "treatments" therapists implicitly deny that nonheterosexual orientation can be healthy, and they instead reinforce the cognitive distortion that nonheterosexual orientation is defective, inferior, and/or immoral. For all three possibilities, it is not really client autonomy that is the basis of reparative therapy, but therapist autonomy to change clients, based chiefly on a therapist preference for heterosexuality. This is ultimately a value judgment and not something that can be fruitfully addressed through further empirical research.

26

Sexual Diversity and Change Along a Continuum of Bisexual Desire

Paul L. Vasey
Drew Rendall

Despite the unusual care with which this study was undertaken, we are not entirely convinced that most, if any, of Spitzer's subjects experienced a change in sexual orientation from homosexual to heterosexual. The overarching problems are twofold: one methodological, pertaining to sample selection, and the other conceptual. The manner in which Spitzer's sample was composed suggests that many of his subjects were apt to experience cognitive dissonance around issues pertaining to their sexual orientation and this may have prompted them to lie or engage in elaborate self-deceptive narratives when reporting change in sexual orientation. As Spitzer notes, the vast majority (93 percent) of his subjects stated that religion was "very" or "extremely" important in their lives. We question whether it is reasonable to expect that "extremely" religious individuals will honestly answer explicit questions about details of their sexuality, let alone details that they find deeply reprehensible and that they are actively attempting to repress. The role of religion in fostering an atmosphere of lies and enabling the production of self-deceptive narratives has been well documented in the form of many first-person narratives from "ex-ex-gays" (Duberman, 1991; Maniaci and Rzeznik, 1993). These narratives demonstrate how gay men and lesbians can be motivated to believe what they *want* to believe or are *told* to believe in matters of

---

This chapter appeared originally under the same title in *Archives of Sexual Behavior* 32(5):453-455. Copyright 2003 Kluwer Academic/Plenum Publishers. Reprinted with permission.

doi:10.1300/5503_26

sexual orientation that they find morally distasteful. Perhaps more of a concern, however, is the fact that 19 percent of Spitzer's subjects were mental health professionals who espouse reparative therapy and directors of ex-gay ministries. In light of their personal and professional investment in such enterprises, it seems reasonable to assume that such individuals would be highly motivated to communicate the message that change in sexual orientation is not only possible, but desirable.

There are additional important conceptual problems with this study. Prior to "reparative" therapy, most of Spitzer's subjects reported that they were predominantly attracted to same-sex individuals and experienced some attraction to opposite-sex individuals. Post-therapy, most subjects reported the opposite pattern. Spitzer points out that reports of complete change from homosexual to heterosexual were uncommon. Unfortunately, he does not elaborate on this point, so it is impossible to say how many of his homosexual subjects, if any, experienced such change. As such, we believe that the title of this paper is misleading because most of Spitzer's subjects were bisexual, not homosexual. For such individuals, change, if it occurred, was on a continuum of bisexuality, and did not entail a binary shift from homosexual to heterosexual orientation. Spitzer obviously chose to categorize such individuals as gay or lesbian because they were predominantly attracted to same-sex sexual partners, but this relects subjective decision-making processes on his part that ultimately mask the extent of bisexual variation that exists in the real world.

The existence of sexual diversity, or variation, is quickly becoming a growing area of inquiry in the biological and behavioral sciences. Humans are, if anything, a behaviorally diverse species and this diversity extends to sexual interactions. Given the extent to which behavioral diversity characterizes the expression of human sexuality, it does not seem particularly surprising to us that change in sexual orientation might be possible in *some* individuals without harmful effects on the individual. Such change seems particularly plausible along a continuum of bisexuality, as appears to be the case for most of Spitzer's subjects. In fact, a similar phenomenon has been observed among Japanese macaques *(Macaca fuscata),* a species of monkey endemic to Japan. In some populations of these monkeys, females engage in varying proportions of heterosexual and homosexual mounting, courtship, and sexual relationships from one annual mating season to the next (Vasey, 2002).

Thus, perhaps the most robust result of Spitzer's study is that some individuals can change along a continuum of bisexuality. However, it is equally, if not more, important to point out that sexual orientation is unlikely to be amenable to change in many, if not most, individuals, and that attempts to bring about such change are likely to cause harm to the individual (American Psychiatric Association, 2000; Haldeman, 2001; Friedman and Downey, 2002). Indeed, Spitzer's study seems to support this conclusion. He noted that most of his subjects spent years, even decades, in therapy, attempting to change their sexual orientation. This time frame alone suggests that sexual orientation is, even in the most highly motivated individuals, remarkably resistant to change.

Some readers may interpret Spitzer's study as evidence that homosexual and bisexual orientations are chosen. We believe that such an interpretation is unfounded. Spitzer's study demonstrates individuals can choose to foster their latent heterosexual tendencies while repressing their overt homosexual tendencies. It does not provide evidence that individuals choose or learn to be homosexual. Change in sexual orientation over the lifespan does not indicate that one's primary sexual orientation (i.e., that which is first expressed) is a learned choice. A left-handed individual might choose to use only their right hand because of social restrictions (Dawson, 1977; Payne, 1987) and may, with practice, become adept at doing so, but this does not imply that the initial use of their left hand for daily tasks reflected any sort of conscious choice.

We believe that the next steps in this program of research (if any) are to, first, identify what parameters differentiate individuals that *can* change their sexual orientation in the *absence* of harmful effects, from those that either cannot or will not. Second, the nature of change must be clarified. Is the change truly from homosexual to heterosexual or vice-versa? Is the change from homosexual or heterosexual to bisexual, or vice-versa? Or, is the change merely along some continuum of bisexual desire? Third, the relation between reparative therapy and change in sexual orientation may simply be spurious and reflect a correlation between either of these variables with religiosity. As such, future research should employ appropriate control groups to identify whether change in sexual orientation is contingent on participation in some form of reparative therapy. We should not assume, a priori, however, that participation in such therapy is a necessary prerequisite for change. Finally, if change is contingent on therapy, the next question is which types of reparative therapy facilitate change and which do not.

In conclusion, there seems to be a basic contradiction in the overall message of this work. The emphasis on the efficacy of reparative therapy in changing sexual orientation seems to hinge on the notion that sexual orientation is flexible to begin with. If not, change would be impossible. Clearly, in the minds of some, sexual flexibility is real and is a good thing, but only insofar as it operates in the service of promoting sexual inflexibility in the form of a heterosexual endpoint. Strangely lost in this line of reasoning is the potential normativeness of the original variability to begin with. Acknowledging this contradiction might shift the focus of attention to the arguably more relevant issue of why there is any perceived need for change. To this end, the foundational assumption inherent in much reparative therapy that same-sex attraction reflects a developmental disorder needs to be critically addressed, particularly in light of the American Psychiatric Association's (2000) formal position that homosexuality is not a disordered outcome.

REFERENCES

American Psychiatric Association (2000), Commission on Psychotherapy by Psychiatrists (COPP): Position statement on therapies focused on attempts to change sexual orientation (Reparative or conversion therapies). *American J. Psychiatry,* 157:1719-1721.

Dawson, J.L.M.B. (1977), Alaskan Eskimo hand, eye, auditory dominance and cognitive style. *Psychologia,* 20:121-135.

Duberman, M. (1991), *Cures: A Gay Man's Odyssey.* New York: Dutton.

Friedman, R.C. & Downey, J.I. (2002), *Sexual Orientation and Psychoanalysis: Sexual Science and Clinical Practice.* New York: Columbia University Press.

Haldeman, D.C. (2001), Therapeutic antidotes: Helping gay and bisexual men recover from conversion therapies. *J. Gay & Lesbian Psychotherapy,* 5(3/4):117-130. Reprinted in: *Sexual Conversion Therapy: Ethical, Clinical and Research Perspectives,* eds. A. Shidlo, M. Schroeder, & J. Drescher. Binghamton, NY: The Haworth Press, 2001, pp. 117-130.

Maniaci, T. & Rzeznik, F.M. (1993), *One Nation Under God* [Motion picture]. (Available from 3Z/Hourglass Productions, Inc. New York, NY).

Payne, M.A. (1987), Impact of cultural pressures on self-reports of actual and approved hand use. *Neuropsychologia,* 25:247-258.

Vasey, P.L. (2002), Sexual partner preference in female Japanese macaques. *Archives Sexual Behavior,* 31:51-62.

27

Science and the Nuremberg Code:
A Question of Ethics and Harm

Milton L. Wainberg
Donald Bux
Alex Carballo-Dieguez
Gary W. Dowsett
Terry Dugan
Marshall Forstein
Karl Goodkin
Joyce Hunter
Thomas Irwin
Paulo Mattos
Karen McKinnon
Ann O'Leary
Jeffrey Parsons
Edward Stein

This comment combines the perspectives of 14 researchers in the social and behavioral sciences from diverse backgrounds who have serious concerns about Spitzer's study on sexual orientation change through "reparative interventions." In his article, he reviewed research on sexual orientation change through reparative interventions, noting policies and position statements of key institutions, and deficiencies in previous studies. Spitzer recruited 143 men and 57 women based on their assertions that they had changed their homosexual orientation to

This chapter appeared originally under the same title in *Archives of Sexual Behavior* 32(5):455-457. Copyright 2003 Kluwer Academic/Plenum Publishers. Reprinted with permission.

a predominantly heterosexual orientation. Subjects were recruited through their therapists, pro-change religious ministries, and targeted advertising. He then assessed these individuals about their pre- and post-reparative intervention sexual interests using a structured telephone interview. The main study finding is self-fulfilling: Participants selected through this sampling strategy reported changes that were the basis of their recruitment into the study.

Designing a study using as a conceptual framework the assumption that the heterosexual/homosexual binary provides an accurate description of the organization of human sexual desire and expression is out of step with the field of sexuality research (Stein, 1999). Studies over the past 50 years have shown cross-cultural variations in sexual expression and relationships (Kumar and Ross, 1991; Naz Foundation, 2000), which suggest that the binary is not evidence of nature at work; rather, it is evidence of the historical forces that continue to shape our concept of relationships (Crawford et al., 1998).

In addition to conceptualizing sexual expression in a way that is inconsistent with the scientific literature, this study suffers from bias introduced via the recruitment strategy and other serious methodological flaws, rendering it problematic from a scientific point of view. Spitzer acknowledged some methodological limitations of his study, including involvement of an unblinded research interviewer and the potential fallibility of participants' self-reports that were not corroborated with any objective measures. However, Spitzer did not make use of other systematic, well-established scientific procedures that are crucial to obtaining valid scientific results nor addressed how his results may have been affected by the many design flaws in his study. Therefore, it is important to underscore scientific problems in the study, including

1. a recruitment strategy resulting in not only a sample of convenience but a sample invested in demonstrating change, potentially building in a strong bias;
2. lack of a comparison or control group, leaving the study unable to demonstrate the effects of a reparative intervention or determine that a reparative intervention is responsible for any reported changes;
3. many measurement problems, including lack of operational definitions of "homosexuality," "heterosexuality," or "bisexuality,"

use of nonneutral language in the measures, and noncomparable measurement of "heterosexuality" and "homosexuality";
4. use of a telephone interview with an unvalidated instrument;
5. lack of interviewer selection and training to reduce reactivity and social desirability pressures;
6. statistical analysis that did not address any of the research questions, since all statistical tests concerned gender differences in the responses. These tests lend an appearance of scientific weight to the study, which is misleading because gender differences were not the point of the study; and
7. lack of expertise or experience on the part of the investigator in sexuality outcome studies.

Although veracity from research participants is a concern in any interview study, here the problem is greater than the typical wish to please the interviewer; these participants want or need to please *themselves,* to believe their self-assertions of heterosexuality. Spitzer declared that "the key question is judging the credibility of the[ir] self-reports." Desire to avoid stigmatization by one's community can be a source of motivation for reporting treatment success. Contrary to Spitzer's contentions, studies whose outcomes depend on socially desirable responding never obtain absolute denial of undesirable behavior (Turner, et al., 1998). It is an error to assume that a participant's potential *under*reporting of unwanted and socially undesirable feelings represents veracity (Turner et al., 1998).

Spitzer failed to provide evidence for his assertion that "changing sexual orientation can be a rational, self-directed goal." In fact, he did not design a study that tests this hypothesis. Furthermore, his statement that "change in sexual orientation seems plausible (again, at least to the author) as the participants used change strategies commonly effective in psychotherapy" is an unsupported inference. Referring to unmeasured psychotherapeutic techniques does not attest to change.

Our concerns go beyond the lack of rigor in this study's scientific methodology—the scientific problems lead to serious ethical problems as well. According to the *Nuremberg Code* (Directive 4; Nuremberg Code, 1949), "The experiment should be so conducted as to avoid all unnecessary physical and mental suffering and injury." Research ethics dictate that the harm associated with any treatment be the first thing to be evaluated. If substantial harm is found, then any degree of "change" is irrelevant. Spitzer asserted that his study "questions the current conventional view that desire for therapy to change sexual orientation is always succumbing to societal pressure and irrational internalized homophobia," and that his findings demonstrated "no obvious harm." Both assertions are unsupported by his work. There was no objective measurement of harm to participants in this study; moreover, there was no attempt to assess the harm accruing to individuals who attempted but failed "reorientation." Harm from reparative interventions has been demonstrated (Shidlo and Schroeder, 2002) and a body of work on homophobia shows that health care providers' attitudes can be hazardous to their patients (Baker, 1993; Brotman, et al., 2002; Garofalo and Katz, 2001; Plummer, 1995). When doing research, scientists have the responsibility not only to ensure protection of the research subjects but also to minimize the negative impact that the research may have on the community the subjects represent. To disregard the potential for harm exposes populations that experience discrimination to additional risks. If the publication of this study makes psychotherapists more comfortable (perhaps in subtle ways) encouraging their homosexual patients to "change," then the study will have done further harm.

To imply that "change" in sexual orientation is possible, without indicating how likely it is for a given individual to achieve any degree of "change," suggests that most or all homosexuals can "change" orientation if sufficiently motivated and serves only to reinforce the false notion that homosexuality is a choice. Thus, creating an unsupported impression that reparative interventions are effective is unethical. There are social and cultural disincentives to being attracted to people of the same sex: violence, discrimination, marginalization, illegal status and imprisonment, individual and social abuse, and less than equal status in relation to public services (Bedard and Gertz, 2001; Hart, 2001; Ragins and Cornwell, 2001; Yomtoob, 2001). Being gay or lesbian is stigmatized in many workplaces, families, communities, and institutions (e.g., high schools), whereas significant social, cultural, and economic benefits are available to those with a heterosexual orientation. Therefore, to be a gay man or a lesbian involves more than simply solving a question of sexual attraction or identity. Researchers conducting studies on sexual orientation have a responsibility to evaluate the potential implications of those studies. Feasibility does not justify poor science.

In hypothesizing that "same-sex attractions . . . can be significantly diminished through development of stronger and more confident gender identification, possibly demystifying males and maleness," reparative interventions confuse gender role, sexual orientation, and sexual identity (Stein, 1999). Reparative interventions assume homosexuality is sinful, wrong, and, as quoted by Spitzer, "reflect[s] a developmental disorder," making homosexuality pathological in the service of an agenda that aims at reinstitutionalizing homosexuality as a mental disorder. Harm will be done if this study is used to justify any attempt to relabel homosexuality as a mental disorder. Spitzer asserted that he began the study with a skeptical view of the outcome. This point is worth noting, as Spitzer (1981) has written: "If there were a 'treatment' for homosexuality . . . that was available and effective in most cases, it is likely that there would be little objection to classifying it as a disorder" (p. 213).

We are troubled by the publication of work filled with scientific flaws that disregards harm and conveys a number of false impressions. It is likely that this study will attract considerable attention in the media, and that lay audiences will not appreciate its lack of scientific rigor. Homophobic and heterosexist audiences will use it to further their agendas. Documented consequences of homophobia include suicide among young homosexual men and women (Cochran and Mays, 2000; Fergusson, Horwood, and Beautrais, 1999; Garofalo et al., 1999; Herrel et al., 1999; Hershberger and D'Augelli, 1995; McDaniel et al., 2001; Remafedi, 1998, 1999a, 1999b, 2002; Remafedi, et al., 1998). We fear the repercussions of this study, including an increase in suffering, prejudice, and discrimination (Stein, 1998; Suppe, 1984).

REFERENCES

Baker, J.A. (1993), Is homophobia hazardous to lesbian and gay health? *American J. Health Promotion,* 7:255-256, 262.

Bedard, L.E. & Gertz, M.G. (2001), Differences in community standards for the viewing of heterosexual and homosexual pornography. *International J. Public Opinion Research,* 12:324-332.

Brotman, S., Ryan, B., Jalbert, Y., & Rowe, B. (2002), The impact of coming out on health and health care access: The experiences of gay, lesbian, bisexual and two-spirit people. *J. Health & Social Policy,* 15:1-29.

Cochran, S.D. & Mays, V.M. (2000), Lifetime prevalence of suicide symptoms and affective disorders among men reporting same-sex sexual partners: Results from NHANES III. *American J. Public Health,* 90:573-578.

Crawford, J., Kippax, S., Rodden, P., Donohoe, S., & Van de Ven, P. (1998), *Malecall 96: National Telephone Survey of Men who Have Sex with Men.* Sydney: National Centre in HIV Social Research.

Fergusson, D.M., Horwood, L.J., & Beautrais, A.L. (1999), Is sexual orientation related to mental health problems and suicidality in young people? *Archives General Psychiatry,* 56:876-880.

Garofalo, R. & Katz, E. (2001), Health care issues of gay and lesbian youth. *Current Opinion in Pediatrics,* 13:298-302.

Garofalo, R., Wolf, R.C., Wissow, L.S., Woods, E.R., & Goodman, E. (1999), Sexual orientation and risk of suicide attempts among a representative sample of youth. *Archives Pediatrics & Adolescent Medicine,* 153:487-493.

Hart, J. E. (2001), Gay men: Grieving the effects of homophobia. In: *Men Coping with Grief,* ed. D.A. Lund. Amityville, NY: Baywood Publishing, pp. 65s-84s.

Herrell, R., Goldberg, J., True, W.R., Ramakrishnan, V., Lyons, M., Eisen, S., et al. (1999), Sexual orientation and suicidality: A co-twin control study in adult men. *Archives General Psychiatry,* 56:867-874.

Hershberger, S.L. & D'Augelli, A.R. (1995), The impact of victimization on the mental health and suicidality of lesbian, gay, and bisexual youths. *Developmental Psychology,* 31:65-74.

Kumar, B. & Ross, M.W. (1991), Sexual behaviour and HIV infection risks in Indian homosexual men: A cross-cultural comparison. *International J. STD & AIDS,* 2:442-444.

McDaniel, J.S., Purcell, D., & D'Augelli, A.R. (2001), The relationship between sexual orientation and risk for suicide: Research findings and future directions for research and prevention. *Suicide & Life-Threatening Behavior,* 31(Suppl.): 84-105.

Naz Foundation (2000), *Sexual Health of Males in South Asia Who Have Sex with Other Males: Results of Situational Assessments in Four Cities in India and Bangladesh.* London: Author.

Nuremberg Code (1949), *Trials of War Criminals Before the Nuremburg Military Tribunals under Control Council Law.* Washington, DC: U.S. Government Printing Office.

Plummer, D. (1995), Homophobia and health: Unjust, anti-social, harmful and endemic. *Health Care Analysis,* 3:150-156.

Ragins, B.R. & Cornwell, J.M. (2001), Pink triangles: Antecedents and consequences of perceived workplace discrimination against gay and lesbian employees. *J. Applied Psychology,* 86:1244-1261.

Remafedi, G. (1999a), Sexual orientation and youth suicide. *J. American Medical Association,* 282:1291-1292.

Remafedi, G. (1999b), Suicide and sexual orientation: Nearing the end of controversy? *Archives General Psychiatry,* 56:885-886.

Remafedi, G. (2002), Suicidality in a venue-based sample of young men who have sex with men. *J. Adolescent Health,* 31:305-310.

Remafedi, G., French, S., Story, M., Resnick, M.D. & Blum, R. (1998), The relationship between suicide risk and sexual orientation: Results of a population-based study. *American J. Public Health,* 88:57-60.

Shidlo, A. & Schroeder, M. (2002), Changing sexual orientation: A consumers' report. *Professional Psychology: Research & Practice,* 33:249-259.

Spitzer, R.L. (1981), The diagnostic status of homosexuality in DSM-III: A reformulation of the issues. *American J. Psychiatry,* 138:210-215.

Stein, E. (1998), Choosing the sexual orientation of children. *Bioethics,* 12:1-24.

Stein, E. (1999), *The Mismeasure of Desire: The Science, Theory, and Ethics of Sexual Orientation.* New York: Oxford University Press.

Suppe, F. (1984), Curing homosexuality. In: *Philosophy and Sex,* Revised edition, eds. R. Baker & F. Elliston. Amherst, NY: Prometheus Books, pp. 394-420.

Turner, C.F., Ku, L., Rogers, S.M., Lindberg, L.D., Pleck, J.H., & Sonenstein, F.L. (1998), Adolescent sexual behavior, drug use, and violence: Increased reporting with computer survey technology. *Science,* 280:867-873.

Yomtoob, E.J. (2001), A comparison of psychologists' identification, conceptualization, and treatment of domestic violence in heterosexual, gay, and lesbian couples. *Dissertation Abstracts International:* Section B: *The Sciences & Engineering,* 62(2-B):1105.

28

Sexual Reorientation Therapy: Is It Ever Ethical? Can It Ever Change Sexual Orientation?

Jerome C. Wakefield

I address four questions—methodological, ethical, and conceptual/ theoretical—raised by Spitzer's courageous report on 200 subjects claiming post-therapy changes in sexual orientation from homosexuality toward heterosexuality:

1. Are subjects' responses dismissable as lies or self-deceptions, as some critics claim?
2. Is the study's design too weak to show anything of scientific interest, as critics also claim?
3. Does the study imply that reorientation therapy is sometimes ethically allowable, contrary to recent professional association edicts?
4. Do the data demonstrate change in core sexual orientation itself, as Spitzer claims?

CAN SUBJECTS' REPORTS BE DISMISSED AS DECEPTIONS?

Given the subjects' personal and political motivations to represent therapy as successfully changing sexual orientation or related vari-

This chapter appeared originally under the same title in *Archives of Sexual Behavior* 32(5):457-459. Copyright 2003 Kluwer Academic/Plenum Publishers. Reprinted with permission.

doi:10.1300/5503_28

ables (I use "sexual reorientation" for convenience throughout, but only later consider whether sexual orientation itself really changed), it remains possible that subjects massively lied or deceived themselves, as critics suggest. However, to assume without evidence that reports of changes must be deceptions begs the question of whether change sometimes occurs. Moreover, for reasons somewhat different from Spitzer's, I believe the data suggest that lies and self-deceptions are probably not the major source of reported changes.

First, some changes are publicly verifiable and thus presumably not as subject to lies or self-deception, such as the enormous increase in the percentage of subjects in ongoing heterosexual relationships (for males, from 26 percent PRE to 87 percent POST). Although this variable indicates sexual orientation less directly than others, changes in relationship behavior are important in themselves and tend to corroborate reports of psychological changes that may facilitate relationship changes.

Second, regarding crucial subjective experience indicators of sexual orientation, if subjects were massively prevaricating or self-deceiving to support evidence of change, why would so many males report POST continuing significant same-sex masturbatory fantasies (45 percent) and significant same-sex attraction (50 percent)? It might be argued that subjects were sophisticated enough deceivers to avoid extreme claims. However, subjects were highly motivated to deny *any* continued homosexual interest. Moreover, in usual social desirability responses, moderation may be exercised because extremes are uncommon and sometimes even of questionable desirability (e.g., always honest). In contrast, complete and exclusive heterosexuality is considered both common and socially desirable (within subjects' communities), so the "moderate lie" hypothesis lacks motivation.

Third, the Dyadic Adjustment Scale (DAS) was independently completed by the subjects' partners POST, and their scores corroborated the subjects' positive relationship reports. Spitzer also pertinently observes that both the subjects' and their partners' DAS scores were not inflated from norms. Again, one might argue that spouses also lied. However, such increasingly elaborate ad hoc hypotheses, although not impossible, demand independent evidence to be taken seriously.

Fourth, when asked to explain changes, subjects generally cited standard cognitive, psychodynamic, and behavioral therapy techniques that have face validity as causes of such changes. Indeed, the suggestion that standard therapeutic techniques can sometimes influence sexual object choice is a fascinating aspect of Spitzer's study.

Taken together, these considerations, plus the current lack of any evidence of massive deception, suggest the data should be taken to have some prima facie credibility.

IS THE STUDY METHODOLOGICALLY TOO WEAK TO SHOW ANYTHING OF SCIENTIFIC IMPORTANCE?

Many critics set up straw men by misinterpreting the study's purpose, then criticizing the study for not achieving that purpose. Certainly, given the study's retrospective nature, subject self-selection, and lack of controls, the study cannot *prove* anything about the general or even occasional effectiveness of sexual reorientation therapy. Rather, it offers inconclusive prima facie evidence that a few severely conflicted and highly motivated patients may be enabled by this kind of therapy to change their behavior and experiences in ways they believe are helpful.

Why would such a weak conclusion be of any interest? A study's scientific importance is a function of the claims it addresses. The current scientific context contains explicit or implicit universal claims that sexual reorientation therapy is unhelpful and/or harmful. Spitzer's study offers prima facie exceptions that cast doubt on these generalizations; thus, it is scientifically useful.

Comparably weak studies have influenced other areas subject to universal hypotheses. For example, when some alcoholism researchers maintained that alcoholism is a universal disease with a predictable course of deterioration, methodologically weak studies using newspaper ads to find people who self-reported having recovered from alcoholism without treatment had substantial impact. Despite their inconclusiveness, the studies raised prima facie doubts regarding the universal disease entity hypothesis and thus challenged attitudes about treatment derived from it.

WHAT ARE THE STUDY'S IMPLICATIONS
FOR THE ETHICS OF REORIENTATION THERAPY?

Given the historical and ongoing oppression of homosexual individuals, it is understandable that therapeutic attempts to change homosexual orientation have been looked upon with suspicion, often justifiably so. However, in the absence of evidence that subjects' self-reports lack credibility, Spitzer's study offers prima facie support for the ethical acceptability of reorientation therapy in some cases of severe ego-dystonic homosexuality. Subjects' symptoms (depression, bothered by homosexual feelings) declined precipitously from PRE to POST. Even if reorientation therapy only rarely offers substantial benefits, it is potentially unethical to ignore evidence of such substantial reduction of suffering in some highly motivated, deeply conflicted patients when considering treatment options, especially given the lack of any proven alternative. Under such conditions, a difficult decision regarding possible benefits versus possible harms must sometimes be made, and the ethical focus should be on informed consent and sensitivity to patient preferences rather than on a general ethical judgment applying to all patients. The study thus implies that recent professional association statements declaring such therapy unethical are potentially oppressive to some clients and should be rescinded or revised.

The study alerts us to two clinical circumstances in which attempts to change sexual orientation in severely ego-dystonic homosexual individuals may be ethically justified by patient self-determination and need: (1) The patient strongly wants to save or improve a marriage he or she considers more important than satisfying homosexual desires. For many patients, marital dissolution may be the best choice, but any rule about treatment goals that ignores individual circumstances and preferences is ethically unacceptable. (2) The patient's deeply held religious, social (wanting to remain part of a community), or moral convictions cause severe conflict with homosexual desires, and the patient strongly considers the convictions more important than the desires.

Spitzer's study particularly supports the occasional power of therapy to improve marital heterosexual functioning of ego-dystonic homosexual individuals. Spitzer demandingly defines "good heterosexual functioning" (GHF) as requiring a loving, ongoing heterosexual relationship with sex at least several times monthly, high emotional and physical satisfaction, and at most rare same-sex fantasies during heterosexual sex. Of 55 subjects in continuing PRE-to-POST marital relationships with regular sex, only 5 percent displayed GHF PRE versus 84 percent POST. In the overall male sample, just 3 (2.1 percent) displayed GHF PRE versus 94 (65.7 percent) POST (Spitzer, personal communication, March 15, 2003). It would be unethical to preclude such help for homosexual patients' marriages or marital aspirations.

The ethics of sexual reorientation therapy must be distinguished from other issues. Many therapists practicing sexual reorientation therapy unethically impose an antigay bias on clients; but therapists need not do so, and it is also unethical to impose an antichange bias. Most of Spitzer's subjects almost certainly had negative attitudes toward the gay rights movement; nonetheless, they have a right to help that is not politically constrained. Many critics of reorientation therapy assume its acceptance implies the repathologization of homosexuality (i.e., that homosexuality is considered a disorder), but no such implication is made, and it is generally recognized that individuals with nondisorders may benefit from treatment (even the DSM-IV contains a section coding nondisorder problems that are often the focus of treatment). Spitzer's subjects clearly needed help with their intense conflicts whether or not they had a disorder.

What about the objection that the patient's desire to change homosexuality is always due to internalized homophobia; thus, sexual reorientation therapy is always collaboration with social oppression? This interesting but unproven hypothesis is a one-size-fits-all etiological speculation that ignores the diversity of clients' meaning systems and should not take priority over client self-determination. Giving homoerotic sexual desires higher priority than relationship commitments and religious meanings with which they are in conflict is a value judgment that is itself a product of one internalized socially constructed meaning system among many. Imposing this approach on all clients unethically sacrifices individual clients' possible relief from suffering on the altar of sexual politics. It is all too easy for the oppressed in this way to inadvertently rationalize becoming the oppressor.

DID REORIENTATION THERAPY
CHANGE CORE SEXUAL ORIENTATION?

Granting that reorientation therapy likely benefited some subjects and is sometimes ethically defensible, did at least incremental changes in core sexual orientation also occur, as Spitzer claims? Impressively, Spitzer goes beyond reporting changes in subjects' orientational self-labeling, symptoms, and behavior, which changed dramatically but do not necessarily indicate orientation change. He also reported changes in experiential variables that are generally more valid indicators of sexual orientation (e.g., fantasies during masturbation and intercourse, attraction, lustful looking), and these changed substantially, although not as much as self-labeling, symptoms, and behavior.

One common objection to claims of orientation change is that subjects were bisexual PRE and simply suppressed homosexual responses and focused on heterosexual responses POST. Even if true, this objection would only cast doubt on whether core sexual orientation changed. It would not vitiate the importance of the changes subjects reported. In any event, this objection is countered by Spitzer's report that even those most extreme and exclusive on homosexual measures and history prior to treatment changed in ways and at rates similar to others. If, as some claim, everyone is inherently bisexual and just selecting from a menu of sexual object choice options, then the whole notion of sexual orientation has to be rethought.

Nonetheless, uncertainties about orientation change remain because of subtleties in the relation of the orientation construct to the study's measures. The measures (e.g., spontaneous masturbation fantasies) are excellent indicators of sexual orientation in the general population, but have unknown validity in subjects consciously attempting to influence their "spontaneous" desires. Sexual orientation is a dispositional/theoretical construct referring to a hypothesized internal structure that disposes one to respond with desire to males or females or both. Such a disposition is consistent with the desires not actually being experienced (i.e., remaining "latent").

Blocking a disposition's expression is not the same as changing it. Salt remains water-soluble even when stored away from water and even though it fails to dissolve when placed in water under high pressure, because water solubility refers to a disposition to dissolve in water under certain standard circumstances. Correspondingly, potential desires and fantasies that under standard circumstances would be generated by one's sexual orientation may be habitually blocked from conscious development with minimal effort or awareness through techniques such as redirection of attention, thought-stopping, or placing experiences within narratives portraying them as irrational expressions of unresolved family-of-origin problems. Such efforts may or may not solidify into enduring structural changes in core dispositions.

Consider an analogy: A married male patient, troubled by a low-threshold disposition to intensely sexually desire attractive women strangers, cultivated a counterfantasy that the woman would be horrifically difficult in a relationship, bursting the erotic fantasy bubble. The counterfantasy became so automatic and effective that the patient stopped experiencing substantial longing and claimed to be cured. However, when he subsequently became casually acquainted with one such woman, his counterfantasy became implausible, his defense crumbled, and his disposition expressed itself in desire, leading to an affair. The conceptual moral is that to restrain experiential expression of a desire-disposition is not necessarily to change the core disposition.

Of course, habitual inattention or reframing may eventually solidify into new psychic structures and dispositions that endure across environments and constitute true change in core sexual orientation. However, 21 percent of Spitzer's subjects were still in treatment POST, presumably needing continued intervention to maintain new experiences. Others reported actively counteracting spontaneous homoerotic desires. Remaining subjects may have developed habitualized strategies for influencing desire and fantasy, but these strategies' stability and effectiveness across situations remains unknown.

Uncertainties about orientation change notwithstanding, the findings that subjects report impressive changes toward more satisfying lives, including major changes in sexual behavior and experiences and reduction in symptoms, stand as prima facie arguments for reorientation therapy's acceptability in carefully selected cases fitting the profile of Spitzer's subjects, with due awareness of and informed consent regarding the likelihood of failure and possible negative effects. Moreover, Spitzer's provocative report usefully moves questions about orientation change from the political to the scientific domain and opens them to fresh critical scrutiny, hopefully inaugurating overdue scientific examination of issues currently highly politicized.

29

Heterosexual Identities, Sexual Reorientation Therapies, and Science

Roger L. Worthington

Despite overwhelming opposition by the most respected scientific and professional mental health organizations (e.g., American Academy of Pediatrics, 1983; American Psychiatric Association, 1999, 2000; American Psychological Association, 1998a, pp. 934-935; National Association of Social Work, 1997), there appears to be increasing momentum behind attempts to sanction the credibility of sexual reorientation therapies (e.g., Nicolosi, 1991; Throckmorton, 2002; Yarhouse and Burkett, 2002). For the most part, these efforts are directed by a small number of vocal individuals associated with conservative political and religious movements (e.g., Exodus International, the Family Research Council, and the National Association for Research and Therapy of Homosexuality). One provocative aspect of Spitzer's article is that he has not been associated with these organizations, and instead was a central figure in the removal of homosexuality as a mental disorder in the *Diagnostic and Statistical Manual of Mental Disorders* (see Bayer, 1981). Thus, his research has fostered extensive fanfare among those who promote sexual reorientation therapies (e.g., Nicolosi, 2001). In this [chapter], I provide a critique of Spitzer's work, articulating a number of scientific and conceptual flaws that result in serious concerns about the validity of his conclusions.

This chapter appeared originally under the same title in *Archives of Sexual Behavior* 32(5):460-461. Copyright 2003 Kluwer Academic/Plenum Publishers. Reprinted with permission.

doi:10.1300/5503_29

IS THIS SCIENCE?

A host of flaws exist in the research methodology, drastically limiting the types of conclusions that can be drawn from the data. Yet, Spitzer extended his analysis far beyond the data and drew conclusions that result from faulty, nonscientific logic. The numerous flaws include but are not limited to

1. a sample intentionally selected to include only individuals who reported change in sexual attraction after participating in reorientation therapy, and were likely to have an investment in reporting positive outcomes of reorientation therapy;
2. a transparent, self-report, retrospective design that relied on subjective comparisons of pre- and post-therapy outcomes that provided no protection against participant biases;
3. failure to fully describe the wide-ranging types of reorientation therapy experiences that had occurred across decades, some of which was ongoing and others which had been terminated many years before the study;
4. demand characteristics inherent to the research procedure that were likely to prompt responses suggesting positive outcomes of reorientation therapy; and
5. lack of adequate operationalization of the variables and a high likelihood that measurement was both unreliable and invalid.

Although I could spend the remainder of the space allotted on a detailed explication of these points, instead I will attend primarily to additional conceptual issues that interact with these methodological flaws and seriously undermine the validity of the data and any conclusions drawn from it.

DEFINING AND MEASURING SEXUAL ORIENTATIONS AND IDENTITIES

Any researcher intending to address the potential for change in sexual orientation must first provide an accurate definition of the construct under study, and operationalize the construct within some method of measurement. Spitzer never effectively defined any of the variables under study, and never provided reliability and validity information about his measures. *Sexual orientation* refers to "an enduring emotional, romantic, sexual or affectional attraction to [(an)other person(s)] . . . that ranges from exclusive homosexuality to exclusive heterosexuality and includes various forms of bisexuality" (American Psychological Association, 1998b). Recognition, acceptance, and identification with one's sexual orientation can be collectively understood as *sexual orientation identity,* which is only one facet of a broad concept of *sexual identity* (Worthington et al., 2002).

Spitzer only implicitly acknowledged the distinction between sexual orientation and sexual identity, and expressed the belief that both were measured via the retrospective, self-report interviews conducted over the telephone with his participants. Measurement of the various constructs that converge on sexual orientation identity is a formidable task, and problems in measurement will frequently result in misleading research outcomes (Worthington and Navarro, 2003). It has long been known that it is extremely difficult to obtain accurate self-reports regarding sexual contact, arousal, attraction, and fantasy (Masters and Johnson, 1979), which therefore diminishes our ability to simply and easily disentangle sexual orientations from the sexual identities of research participants, in part due to the influence of personal and societal homonegativity. As Spitzer pointed out, physiological methods result in much more reliable and valid measurements for sexual arousal, one of the key elements of sexual orientation. Thus, irrespective of a participant's intent regarding deception, sexual orientations and sexual identities are inherently intertwined when self-report instruments are used. Since Spitzer did not adequately measure sexual orientation, he was unable to answer the central research question used in his title, "Can some gay men and lesbians change their sexual orientation?" In fact, an abundant literature demonstrates that sexual orientations are highly impenetrable to a wide variety of interventions, from the seemingly benign to the most distastefully heinous (for a thorough review, see Murphy, 1992). Even some proponents of sexual reorientation therapies have begun to acknowledge that research clearly demonstrates that sexual orientations are relatively immutable, and instead have begun to target sexual orientation identity as the object of change (e.g., M. Yarhouse, personal communication, December 2, 2002). On the basis of this conceptual analysis, we must reach the conclusion that Spitzer's data did not contain acceptable evidence of sexual orientation change. As such, we are left with the question, "Can some individuals with a history of same-sex attraction, arousal, and behavior change their sexual orientation *identity* and lead functional heterosexual lives?" Before attempting to address this question, we must further disentangle heterosexual identities from sexual orientation identities more broadly.

HETEROSEXUAL IDENTITY DEVELOPMENT

Worthington et al. (2002) described a model of heterosexual identity development that provides a framework by which Spitzer's conclusions can be further analyzed. We defined *heterosexual identity development* as the individual and social processes by which heterosexually identified persons acknowledge and define their sexual needs, values, sexual orientation, and preferences for sexual activities, modes of sexual expression, and characteristics of sexual partners. Careful reading of Spitzer's article demonstrates that he has confounded group membership identity, preferences for characteristics of sexual partners, preferred sexual activities, preferred modes of sexual expression, and sexual values with sexual orientation and sexual orientation identity. For example, few, if any, of these individuals were likely to have ever achieved a completely gay or lesbian group membership identity (e.g., Fassinger and Miller, 1996; McCarn and Fassinger, 1996), primarily because it is apparent that they did not desire to do so. Despite the fact that Spitzer labeled his participants as "gay men" and "lesbians" who became "heterosexuals," it is apparent that the participants in Spitzer's sample had probably always perceived their group membership as "heterosexual" despite recognizing and acknowledging their history of same-sex arousal, fantasy, and attraction (sexual orientation identity). Therefore, at best Spitzer's sample comprises a group of individuals of unknown sexual orientation, who probably always identified their group membership as heterosexual, and thus cannot be said to have changed their sexual orientations or sexual orientation identities in any verifiable way.

Furthermore, Worthington et al. theorized that the highest level of identity integration or *synthesis* entails congruence among all sexual identity dimensions, which requires active exploration of sexual needs, values, orientation, and preferences for characteristics of sexual partners, modes of sexual expression, and sexual activities. Spitzer implicitly acknowledged the importance of congruence in his selection of the variables of interest, yet he left this important variable uninvestigated. Instead, Spitzer relied heavily on self-reported dyadic adjustment in the context of a heterosexual relationship as evidence for "good heterosexual functioning," but he neglected to address two important issues: (1) that the data presented tell us nothing about the extent to which individual participants achieved congruence among various dimensions of sexual identity, and (2) that the process of reorientation therapies seemed to intensely *discourage* active exploration of important components of sexual identity, thus making synthesis highly unlikely among his participants. To the degree that individuals experience incongruence among various dimensions of sexual identity, there is little hope that they will truly achieve an undistorted sense of good heterosexual functioning. As such, Spitzer's claims for good heterosexual functioning among his participants were based on overly simplistic notions of what it means to be heterosexual in the face of tremendous complexity in human sexual functioning.

CONCLUSION

In this commentary, I have argued that a host of scientific and conceptual flaws are inherent to the work reported by Spitzer. From this analysis, I believe that the only valid conclusion we can draw from Spitzer's data is that it is possible to locate 200 individuals who are motivated to retrospectively report changes in their sexual functioning as a means of promoting the use of sexual reorientation therapies. Despite all of the numerous assertions that he believes the data to be useful and untainted, credible behavioral science cannot be based solely on the persuasive power or reputation of a single researcher. Substantial dangers are involved in the publication of Spitzer's article because of the politically charged atmosphere within which the findings and conclusions are presented. It is unfortunate that the provocative nature of the article might continue to result in widespread publicity and fanfare that ignores the lack of scientific rigor and conceptual flaws described herein.

REFERENCES

American Academy of Pediatrics (1983), Policy statement. Homosexuality and adolescence. *Pediatrics,* 92:631-634.

American Psychiatric Association (1998), Position statement on psychiatric treatment and sexual orientation. *American J. Psychiatry,* 1999; 156:1131.

American Psychiatric Association (2000), Commission on Psychotherapy by Psychiatrists (COPP): Position statement on therapies focused on attempts to change sexual orientation (Reparative or conversion therapies). *American J. Psychiatry,* 157:1719-1721.

American Psychological Association (1998a), Proceedings of the American Psychological Association, Incorporated, for the Legislative Year 1997. Minutes of the annual meeting of the Council of Representatives August 14 and 17, 1997, Chicago, IL, and Minutes of the June, August, and December 1997 meetings of the Board of Directors. *American Psychologist,* 53:882-939.

American Psychological Association (1998b), *Answers to Your Questions About Sexual Orientation and Homosexuality.* Washington, DC: Author.

Bayer, R. (1981), *Homosexuality and American Psychiatry: The Politics of Diagnosis.* New York: Basic Books.

Ellis, A.L. & Mitchell, R.W. (2000), Sexual orientation. In: *Psychological Perspectives on Human Sexuality,* eds. L.T. Szuchman & F. Muscarella. New York: Wiley, pp. 196-231.

Fassinger, R.E. & Miller, B.A. (1996), Validation of an inclusive model of sexual minority identity formation on a sample of gay men. *J. Homosexuality,* 32:53-78.

Masters, W.H. & Johnson, V.E. (1979), *Homosexuality in Perspective.* Boston: Little, Brown.

McCarn, S.R. & Fassinger, R.E. (1996), Revisioning sexual minority identity formation: A new model of lesbian identity and its implications for counseling and research. *The Counseling Psychologist,* 24:508-534.

Murphy, T.F. (1992), Redirecting sexual orientation: Techniques and justifications. *J. Sex Research,* 29:501-523.

National Association of Social Work. (1997), Social Work Speaks: National Association of Social Work Policy Statements. Washington, DC: NASW Press.

Nicolosi, J. (1991), *Reparative Therapy of Male Homosexuality: A New Clinical Approach.* Northvale, NJ: Jason Aronson.

Nicolosi, L.A. (2001), *Historic Gay Advocate Now Believes Change Is Possible.* Retrieved March 13, 2003, from National Association for Research and Treatment of Homosexuality, http://www.narth.com/docs/spitzer3.html.

Throckmorton, W. (2002), Initial empirical and clinical findings concerning the change process for ex-gays. *Professional Psychology: Research & Practice,* 33:242-248.

Worthington, R.L. & Navarro, R.L. (2003), Pathways to the future: Analyzing the content of a content analysis. *The Counseling Psychologist,* 31:85-92.

Worthington, R.L., Savoy, H., Dillon, F.R. & Vernaglia, E.R. (2002), Heterosexual identity development: A multidimensional model of individual and group identity. *The Counseling Psychologist,* 30:496-531.

Yarhouse, M.A. & Burkett, L.A. (2002), An inclusive response to LGB and conservative religious persons: The case of same-sex attraction and behavior. *Professional Psychology: Research & Practice,* 33:235-241.

30

How Spitzer's Study Gives a Voice to the Disenfranchised Within a Minority Group

Mark A. Yarhouse

There is no question today that people who identify as lesbian, gay, and bisexual (LGB) are a sexual minority group, but what is less clear to some is that LGB persons are part of a larger population of those who experience same-sex attraction. In other words, some people who experience same-sex attraction report a homosexual or bisexual orientation. Among those who report a homosexual or bisexual orientation, some integrate their experiences of attraction into an LGB identity. However, a disenfranchised group of persons exists who experience same-sex attraction but *dis*-identify with a gay identity. They have no voice in the community of persons who experience same-sex attraction, in part because that community is currently represented by those who have integrated their experiences of same-sex attraction into an LGB identity. This is one of the ways in which Spitzer's study has made a contribution: it has given a voice to the disenfranchised within a minority group.

A second contribution is that Spitzer's study supports the view that some people experience a change of sexual orientation. Spitzer's study is not a unique contribution in this sense. No, many studies of people who either claim to have experienced a change of sexual orientation are available. Treatment approaches of studies published between 1950 and the mid-1980s included behavioral interventions

This chapter appeared originally under the same title in *Archives of Sexual Behavior* 32(5):462-463. Copyright 2003 Kluwer Academic/Plenum Publishers. Reprinted with permission.

(e.g., Freeman and Meyer, 1975; Schwartz and Masters, 1984), aversion treatments (e.g., MacCulloch and Feldman, 1967; McConaghy, 1970), and psychoanalysis (e.g., Hatterer, 1970). Group therapy has also been found to be successful (e.g., Birk, 1974; Munzer, 1965; Pittman and DeYoung, 1971; Truax and Tourney, 1971). The major methodological concerns with these studies were that the measures of "success" varied considerably from study to study (Haldeman, 1994). Some studies focused more on increasing heterosexual behavior, fantasy, or desire, while others focused on decreasing homosexual behavior, fantasy, or desire, but nearly every study ever conducted reported that some people experienced successful change of some kind. More recent surveys of people who say they experience change of orientation (e.g., Schaeffer et al., 199; Schaeffer et al., 2000) or who have worked with patients or clients who they believe changed their sexual orientation (e.g., MacIntosh, 1994) also support the view that some people can experience a change in their sexual orientation.

Even studies that are being mistakenly cited to suggest that reorientation therapies are *intrinsically* harmful point to the possibility of successful change of orientation (e.g., Shidlo and Schroeder, 2002). Shidlo and Schroeder reported the results from their study of 202 "consumers" of reorientation therapy. Their study was originally titled "Homophobic Therapies: Documenting the Damage," and was later changed to "Changing Sexual Orientation: Does Counseling Work?" (see pp. 251, 259) because they found that some people reported benefits to reorientation therapy, including, in a few instances, change of orientation. Although the percentage of success ("self-perceived success") was small ($n = 26$ or 13 percent), we cannot draw conclusions from their study as to the likelihood of successful change (or unsuccessful change or harm) because the study was of a convenience sample and not representative of the population of persons who have a homosexual orientation and seek change. This is in no way meant to detract from the possibility that some people may report harm from their experience in reorientation therapy, and this is an empirical question that should be explored further, but anyone familiar with the research in this area would have to acknowledge that the limitations discussed in these two studies sound familiar. The methodological limitations in the Shidlo and Schroeder study are, in some important ways, quite similar to those limitations found in the Spitzer study. To reject one study on methodological grounds means rejecting the other. Of course, the other option is to try to learn what we can from both studies while keeping in mind the methodological limitations of each.

To continue with the methodological limitations, Spitzer's study can also be criticized for relying upon client recall. Memory recall of this sort can be unreliable. To be fair, however, much of what we know about LGB experiences, including theories for the etiology of sexual orientation and studies of sexual identity development and synthesis, is based upon retrospective studies utilizing memory recall. Anytime proponents of the biological hypothesis for the etiology of homosexuality cite the Bell et al. (1981) study they are referencing a study that utilized retrospective memory recall. The Shidlo and Schroeder (2002) study also relied upon memory recall and is subject to the same criticism.

Some will perhaps say that what is needed is a controlled experiment—that researchers should solicit volunteers who want to change their sexual orientation and randomly assign half of the group to a wait-list control group while the other half pursues a course of reorientation therapy. Of course, this would be an ideal design, but it is impractical for many reasons. It would be hard to imagine that researchers could solicit a group of volunteers who were not participating to either prove or disprove claims of successful change. Another reason such a study is impractical is that, if Spitzer's study is any indication, it would mean having the control group wait for three to five years before having access to treatment. In Spitzer's study, he reports it took an average of two years for participants to begin to experience change, and an average of five years for 79 percent of participants to experience a change of orientation. This is far too long to ask a control group to wait for professional services.

These criticisms do point to a legitimate concern. There is a need for studies with improved methodology. This would include a prospective longitudinal design in which participants provide information on sexual behavior, attractions, fantasy, and so on, prior to or in the early stages of therapy, and then tracked over time, so that something as potentially unreliable as memory recall would not play so prominent a role in studies that touch on such a controversial topic.

How ought we, then, understand Spitzer's study? The key to understanding Spitzer's study is to understand what he intended to examine. His intention was to study whether *anyone* had *ever* experienced a change of sexual orientation. He was not studying how likely it is that someone will experience change of orientation. This is a crucial distinction. Spitzer's study is not a treatment efficacy study, and scientists should not criticize it for failing to provide evidence for that which it was never designed. Critics would do well to make a more accurate comparison of Spitzer's study to the famous studies by Hooker in the 1950s. When Hooker (1957) studied the topic of psychopathology among homosexuals, she asked the question of whether all homosexuals are manifestly disturbed to the extent that a panel of health professionals could distinguish them from heterosexuals. Her study did not prove that all homosexuals are healthy, just as Spitzer did not prove that all homosexuals can change their sexual orientation. But Hooker demonstrated that some homosexuals are as healthy as heterosexuals on various measures of mental health symptoms (Jones and Yarhouse, 2000). Spitzer's study accomplishes something akin to this: whether it is ever possible for a person with a homosexual orientation to report change in the direction of a heterosexual orientation. His study suggests that the answer to this question is "Yes." For those who experience same-sex attraction and do not wish to integrate their experiences of same-sex attraction into a gay identity, for those who have felt disenfranchised within a minority group, this may be a welcome finding. More research is needed to flesh out which variables are better predictors of the likelihood of change, and it would behoove researchers interested in the scientific study of sexuality to try to answer such complicated questions.

REFERENCES

Bell, A.P., Weinberg, M.S., & Hammersmith S.K. (1981), *Sexual Preference: Its Development in Men and Women.* Bloomington, IN: Indiana University Press.

Birk, L. (1974), Group psychotherapy for men who are homosexual. *J. Sex & Marital Therapy,* 1:29-52.

Freeman, W. & Meyer, R.G. (1975), A behavioral alteration of sexual preferences in the human male. *Behavior Therapy,* 6:206-212.

Haldeman, D.C. (1994), The practice and ethics of sexual orientation conversion therapy. *J. Consulting & Clinical Psychology,* 62(2):221-227.

Hatterer, L. (1970), *Changing Homosexuality in the Male: Treatment for Men Troubled by Homosexuality.* New York: McGraw-Hill.

Hooker, E. (1957), The adjustment of the male overt homosexual. *J. Projective Techniques,* 21:18-31.

Jones, S.L. & Yarhouse, M.A. (2000), *Homosexuality: The Use of Scientific Research in the Church's Moral Debate.* Downers Grove, IL: InterVarsity Press.

MacCulloch, M.J. & Feldman, M.P. (1967), Aversion therapy in the management of 43 homosexuals. *British Medical J.,* 2:594-597.

MacIntosh, H. (1994), Attitudes and experiences of psychoanalysts in analyzing homosexual patients. *J. American Psychoanalytic Association,* 42:1183-1207.

McConaghy, N. (1970), Subjective and penile plethysmograph responses to aversion therapy for homosexuality: A follow-up study. *British J. Psychiatry,* 117: 555-560.

Munzer, J. (1965), Treatment of the homosexual in group psychotherapy. *Topical Problems of Psychotherapy,* 5:164-169.

Pittman, F. & DeYoung, C. (1971), The treatment of homosexuals in heterogeneous groups. *International J. Group Psychotherapy,* 21:62-73.

Schaeffer, K.W., Hyde, R.A., Kroencke, T., McCormick, B. & Nottebaum, L. (2000), Religiously-motivated sexual orientation change. *J. Psychology & Christianity,* 19:61-70.

Schaeffer, K.W., Nottebaum, L., Smith, P., Dech, K., & Krawczyk, J. (1999), Religiously-motivated sexual orientation change: A follow-up study. *J. Psychology & Theology,* 27:329-337.

Schwartz, M.F. & Masters, W.H. (1984), The Masters and Johnson treatment program for dissatisfied homosexual men. *American J. Psychiatry,* 141:173-181.

Shidlo, A. & Schroeder, M. (2002), Changing sexual orientation: A consumers' report. *Professional Psychology: Research & Practice,* 33:249-259.

Truax, R.A. & Tourney, G. (1971), Male homosexuals in group psychotherapy. *Diseases of the Nervous System,* 32:707-711.

31

Study Results Should Not Be Dismissed and Justify Further Research on the Efficacy of Sexual Reorientation Therapy

Robert L. Spitzer

The reader of the commentaries will surely be impressed by the wide range of views expressed by the 26 different commentators as to the value of my study. On the one hand, Yarhouse says the study "has given a voice to the disenfranchised within a minority group," Wakefield says the study "usefully moves questions about orientation change from the political to the scientific domain and opens them to fresh critical scrutiny, hopefully inaugurating overdue scientific examination of issues currently highly politicized," and Klein says "Spitzer presents face valid evidence that changes in homosexual behavior and feelings of desire and satisfaction can be achieved by some, to varying degrees, via 'reparative therapy'." On the other hand, Cohen and Savin-Williams state that "As scientists, we must disbelieve Spitzer's data because they are so compromised by subject selection bias as to raise serious objections to any claims Spitzer might make about their meaning and generalizability." Wainberg et al. not only argue that the study was unscientific and harmful but in the title of their commentary ("Science and the Nuremberg Code")

This chapter appeared originally as "Reply: Study Results Should Not Be Dismissed and Justify Further Research on the Efficacy of Sexual Reorientation Therapy" in *Archives of Sexual Behavior* 32(5):469-472. Copyright 2003 Kluwer Academic/Plenum Publishers. Reprinted with permission.

imply that in conducting the study I violated the Nuremberg Code of medical ethics.

I enjoyed—and pretty much agree with—Strassberg's assessment:

> Spitzer is to be congratulated on trying to "light a candle" rather than continuing to "curse the darkness" when it comes to trying to understand what happens as a result of reparative therapy. . . . He asked more, and often better, questions of more people who have "successfully" undergone reparative therapy than anyone else. . . . However, the amount of illumination provided by this particular candle does not strike me as quite as bright as Spitzer seems to believe.

This verdict—that the study has value despite its limitations—is shared as well by several other commentators, such as Klein, Wakefield, and Yarhouse, who have made, at least to me, very cogent arguments in defense of the study. I now attempt to show that despite the study limitations, and my having to now qualify claims made in the paper, the study results are important and should not be dismissed.

TERMINOLOGY

Several commentators criticized me for using the term "reparative therapy" because of its derogatory assumptions. I used the term because the American Psychiatric Association (2000) position statement used it. I now will simply use the term "reorientation therapy."

I will use the term "ex-gay" to refer to any individual who reports that their sexual orientation was predominantly homosexual but who now considers himself or herself to be heterosexual and attributes this change to having had some kind of reorientation therapy. By definition, such an individual now has a heterosexual identity, but sexual orientation may or may not continue to be predominantly homosexual.

THE STUDY'S RESEARCH QUESTION

The impetus for the study was the American Psychiatric Association's (2000) "Position Statement on Therapies Focused on Attempts to Change Sexual Orientation," which stated "APA encourages and supports research . . . to further determine 'reparative' therapy's risks versus its benefits." The study attempted to contribute to that research by focusing on the possible benefits to some gays of reorientation therapy. The study did not attempt to study possible harm of reorientation therapy (hardly controversial) but I certainly did not "dismiss" the issue of harm (Drescher). In the introduction to the paper, I referenced seven articles that argued that reorientation therapy is frequently harmful.

In assessing the value of the study, it is essential that one understand that when it was initiated the conventional wisdom in the mental health professions was clear: reorientation therapy can get some gays to identify themselves as "heterosexual" and therefore "ex-gay," but few if any experience true changes in sexual orientation. This view has been supported by two important studies both authored by researchers critical of reorientation therapy (Beckstead, 2001; Shidlo and Schroeder, 2002). In both studies, ex-gays who claimed to have become "heterosexual" from reorientation therapy were interviewed about their sexual behavior and feelings before the therapy and at the time of the interview. Beckstead (2001) studied 20 ex-gays (18 men and 2 women). He concluded:

> Participants reported that their sense of peace and contentment did not indicate a change in sexual orientation but a change in self-acceptance, self-identity, focus, and behavioral patterns. No substantial or generalized heterosexual arousal was reported, and participants were not able to modify their tendency to be attracted to their same sex. (p. 103)

In other words, Beckstead claimed that these ex-gays reported that reorientation therapy helped them feel better identifying themselves as "heterosexual," but not a single one reported changes in sexual orientation. Shidlo and Schroeder (2002) reported that only 8 of their sample of 26 ex-gays gave answers consistent with a change in sexual orientation.

CLARIFYING THE RESEARCH QUESTION

When I started the study and told colleagues about it, I was greeted with anger and disbelief that I would be so foolish as to believe what ex-gays said about themselves. I therefore should have realized that, despite any methodological improvements in assessment of change that I could incorporate into the study (such as the use of a fully structured interview schedule with detailed questions assessing multiple components of sexual orientation), many critics would never accept the subject's self-reports as credible. In the Discussion section, I said, "There is no doubt about what the subjects in the study reported. The key question is judging the credibility of their self-reports." By my focusing on the issue of subject credibility, I made it easy for the critics to dismiss the study findings by their merely asserting—without proof—that the self-reports *could* be self-deception. I should have, like Beckstead (2001) and Shidlo and Schroeder (2002), focused on what the subjects *reported*. Instead of the research question "Can some gays change their sexual orientation?" the primary question should have been "Contrary to conventional wisdom, do some ex-gays describe changes in attraction, fantasy, and desire that are consistent with true changes in sexual orientation?" The credibility of the subjects' self-report, as it is in all treatment efficacy studies that use self-report, becomes an additional issue to be considered.

LISTENING TO WHAT EX-GAYS SAY

The basic assumption of the study is that research on the possible benefit of reorientation therapy must *begin* with listening to what ex-gays say about how they believe they have changed. Listening to what ex-gays say about how they have (or have not) changed is exactly what Beckstead (2001) and Shidlo and Schroeder (2002) did in their studies—the only difference being that, according to them, few if any of their subjects gave answers to their interview questions that indicated a change in sexual orientation, whereas the great majority of the subjects in my study did report major changes in multiple components of sexual orientation.

Critics of my study who question the credibility of my subjects' self-reports of change should be equally critical of Beckstead and of Shidlo and Schroeder for accepting their subject's self-reports of no change. It certainly makes no sense for ex-gays to be believed only when they acknowledge that they are still gay. Neither their studies nor mine are the last word, but they both represent reasonable first attempts to assess the possible benefit to some gays of reorientation therapy.

WAS SUBJECT RECRUITMENT BIASED TOWARD FINDING BENEFIT?

Most of the critics argued that the recruitment strategy and study design were biased toward positive findings: According to Herek, "It is difficult to imagine how his recruitment strategy would have yielded anything other than reports of substantial shifts to a heterosexual orientation." According to Beckstead, "It should not be surprising that individuals who identify as 'ex-gay' would report positive results when invited to participate in a study designed to support their position." What Beckstead apparently fails to realize is that my study design is the same as his: listening to ex-gays who believe that reorientation therapy works as they answer questions about their sexual feelings, both at the time of the interview and retrospectively. I fail to see how the study was designed to support the view that reorientation therapy actually changes sexual orientation. Nothing prevented large numbers of the ex-gays who wanted to be in my study from reporting no or only minimal change in various components of sexual orientation, as did all of Beckstead's (2001) 22 subjects and as did 18 of 26 subjects in Shidlo and Schroeder's (2002) study. With my design, I could have had equally negative results.

The astute reader might object to a comparison of my study results with theirs. The entry criteria for my study required at least some minimal report of change in sexual attraction whereas in their studies the only requirement was that the subject claimed to be an ex-gay. However, my actual referrals were the same as theirs: it asked for individuals who claimed to be ex-gays. As noted in the paper, only 18 such referrals were disqualified from the study because they did not meet the additional entry criterion of at least minimal change in sexual attraction. Even if the entry criteria for my study are made equivalent to their studies by *including* these 18 individuals, the majority of the total sample still reported changes in sexual attraction, fantasy, and desire consistent with a change in sexual orientation from predominantly homosexual to predominantly heterosexual.

Several commentators criticized the study design, but significantly, none offered an alternative design. According to Herek, "Recognizing that even subtle and unintentional biases can affect the data, researchers routinely adopt elaborate safeguards to prevent their own expectations and those of their research subjects from affecting a study's outcomes. Spitzer's study lacked such safeguards." However, as Klein and Yarhouse noted, study designs for treatment efficacy studies that have these safeguards, such as masked assessment of subjects randomly assigned to a treatment and to a control group, are clearly not possible when evaluating reorientation therapy (e.g., placing a subject on a waiting list or in a "sham" treatment condition group for several years' duration).

CREDIBILITY OF THE SUBJECTS' SELF-REPORTS

Perhaps the major critique of the study is that the critics found my arguments for subject credibility unconvincing. I must (painfully) admit that they are correct in noting that the absence of extreme responses does not insure the absence of self-report bias. Consider a man whose same-sex masturbation fantasies have actually not changed in frequency. He may be able to deceive himself that they are far less frequent now than before having reorientation therapy but be unable to deceive himself into believing that they are no longer present at all. Therefore, the critics are correct in claiming that significant response bias *could* have been present but they certainly have not proved that it was present. They also did not point to anything in the study results that suggests response bias. I acknowledge that some response bias could certainly have occurred, but I find it hard to believe that it can explain all of the reported changes.

None of the critics commented on the interesting finding that the mean score on the self-report measure of marital adjustment for the study subjects was not higher than the mean for the instrument's normative community reference group. Surely if bias were present, one would expect that the subjects (as well as their spouses) would be motivated to give particularly glowing accounts of marital functioning. They did not. Another finding (not reported in the article) that is not what would be expected if, as suggested by several critics, is that religious fervor was an important variable predisposing to response bias. The 186 subjects who claimed that religion was "very" or "extremely" important did not report more change in sexual attraction than did the 14 subjects who reported that religion was "not very" or only "somewhat" important.

This study had essentially the same design and a similar recruitment strategy of ex-gay subjects as in the Beckstead (2001) and Shidlo and Schroeder (2002) studies. This raises the question of why so very few of their subjects gave answers consistent with a change in sexual orientation whereas the majority of my subjects did? The possibility of researcher bias must be considered. A major advantage of my study is that the reader can know, by looking at the appendix in the paper, exactly what ten questions were asked to assess sexual orientation. In contrast, in the reports by Beckstead and by Shidlo and Schroeder, the reader has no way of knowing the specific questions that were asked of the subjects that led to the conclusions.

HISTORICAL PARALLELS

Yarhouse noted a historical parallel between my study and Hooker's famous studies conducted in the 1950s. Hooker (1957) studied the question of whether, contrary to conventional wisdom at that time, any homosexuals are without significant psychopathology. Her study did not attempt to find out how often homosexuals are without psychopathology, just that some homosexuals are (Jones and Yarhouse, 2000). My study asked a similar question: Are there some ex-gays that report changes in attraction, fantasy, and desire consistent with a change from a predominantly homosexual orientation to a predominantly heterosexual orientation following reorientation therapy?

Another historical parallel is that just as many of the study critics assert that my subjects have deceived themselves into believing that their sexual orientation has changed, so, too, in the 1970s the conventional wisdom was that when homosexuals said they were comfortable with their sexual orientation they were also deceiving themselves. An additional personal historical parallel—the anger that has been directed at me for doing this study reminds me of a similar reaction to me during my involvement in the removal of the diagnosis of homosexuality from DSM-II in 1973.

CONCLUSION

In the paper, I wrote, "The study provides evidence that change in sexual orientation following some form of reparative therapy does occur in some gay men and lesbians." With the benefit of time and the many thoughtful commentaries on my study, a more accurate assessment is the following: The conventional wisdom in the mental health profession is that reorientation therapy can get some gays to identify themselves as "heterosexual" and therefore "ex-gay," but few, if any, will report changes in sexual attraction, fantasy, and desire consistent with true changes in sexual orientation. The study findings call this view into question. In a sample of 200 ex-gays, the majority reported changes in sexual attraction, fantasy, and desire that are consistent with what would be expected if true changes from predominantly homosexual to predominantly heterosexual orientation had occurred. Although some response bias could have occurred, it is unlikely that it can explain all of the reported changes in sexual orientation.

The study provides the level of evidence appropriate to the initial stages of therapeutic evaluation with regard to an important and controversial issue. What is needed is a prospective outcome study in which a consecutive series of volunteer subjects are evaluated before starting reorientation therapy and after several years. Given the cost and complexity of such a study and the current view in the mental health professions of the benefits and risks of reorientation therapy, such a study is not going to happen in the near future. This is unfortunate because of the real questions raised, albeit admittedly not resolved, by this study.

REFERENCES

American Psychiatric Association (2000), Position statement on therapies focused on attempts to change sexual orientation (reparative or conversion therapies), *American J. Psychiatry,* 157:1719-1721.

Beckstead, A.L (2001), Cures versus choices: Agendas in sexual reorientation therapy. *J. Gay & Lesbian Psychotherapy,* 5:87-125. Reprinted in: *Sexual Conversion Therapy: Ethical, Clinical and Research Perspectives,* eds. A. Shidlo, M. Schroeder, & J. Drescher. Binghamton, NY: The Haworth Press, 2001, pp. 87-125.

Hooker, E. (1957), The adjustment of the male overt homosexual. *J. Projective Techniques,* 21:18-31.

Jones, S.L., & Yarhouse, M.A. (2000). *Homosexuality: The Use of Scientific Research in the Church's Moral Debate*. Downers Grove, IL: InterVarsity Press.

Shidlo, A. & Schroeder, M. (2002), Changing sexual orientation: A consumers' report. *Professional Psychology: Research & Practice*, 33(3):249-259.

Section IV:
Commentaries on the Spitzer Study
and an Interview with Dr. Spitzer
from the Journal of Gay & Lesbian
Psychotherapy

32

Studying Sexual Orientation Change: A Methodological Review of the Spitzer Study

Theodorus G. M. Sandfort

INTRODUCTION

If not hindered by serious ethical considerations and severe budgetary restraints, how would a researcher study whether therapeutic interventions can change an individual's sexual orientation? In one scenario, the researcher could set up an experiment by recruiting random samples of homosexual and heterosexual men and women, randomly assigning them to the experimental and control conditions, and extensively assessing them before and after the experiment as well as at several one-year follow-ups. This design would enable a researcher to draw the most valid conclusions about a therapeutic intervention's potential for changing someone's orientation.

Another, albeit questionably ethical alternative, would be to recruit people who are discontent with their homosexual orientation and to randomly assign them to two treatment conditions: one focused on changing their sexual orientation and the other one on dealing with their discontent and promoting a pleasurable homosexual lifestyle. One could then assess both the satisfactory and unsatisfactory outcomes of both strategies.

This chapter appeared originally as "Studying Sexual Orientation Change: A Methodological Review of the Spitzer Study, 'Can Some Gay Men and Lesbians Change Their Sexual Orientation?'" in the *Journal of Gay & Lesbian Psychotherapy* 7(3):15-29. Copyright 2003 The Haworth Press, Inc.

Robert L. Spitzer, MD, working with a very limited budget, adopted another, much less rigorous approach in his recently published report, "Can Some Gay Men and Lesbians Change Their Sexual Orientation?: 200 Participants Reporting a Change from Homosexual to Heterosexual Orientation" (Spitzer, 2003). He recruited men and women who reported to once have had a predominantly homosexual orientation—which they felt conflicted about—and who claimed, due to some kind of "therapy" to have sustained some change to a heterosexual orientation for at least five years. "Therapy" in this study included either seeing a mental health professional, attending an ex-gay or other religious support group, bibliotherapy, repeated meetings with a heterosexual role model, or, without any external support, changing one's relationship to God.[1] Spitzer interviewed his participants by telephone, asking 114 closed-ended and some open-ended questions, which were answered in about 45 minutes.

Spitzer acknowledges that this approach has numerous limitations and discusses several of them in the paper. These limitations, however, do not dissuade him from concluding that "some gay men and lesbians are able to change the core features of sexual orientation" (p. 415). He further claims that his study "provides evidence that reparative therapy is sometimes successful" (p. 414) and that there was "no evidence of harm" (p. 414).

However, a careful methodological assessment of how Spitzer's study was conducted leads to the conclusion that its author's claims are not warranted.[2] The major issue is how was *change* assessed. The study's assessment of change is problematic because of the following combination of reasons:

1. reliance on self-report;
2. biased selection of the sample;
3. retrospective design of the study;
4. use of a telephone interview as the data collection method;
5. the way "harm" was operationalized; and
6. insufficient reporting of the findings.[3]

Even if the respondents' reports were valid, the changes observed are not as large as the title of the report suggests. The paper's discussion suggests what Spitzer could have done to do a better study, and then concludes with suggestions about what Spitzer should have done.

RELIANCE ON SELF-REPORT

A major problem in Spitzer's study is its exclusive reliance on self-report. This is a problematic method, as people may not respond accurately to questions about themselves (Moss and Goldstein, 1985; Stone et al., 2000; Wiederman, 2002). For instance, research participants have a tendency to give answers that put them in a favorable light, otherwise known as socially desirable responses (Nicholas, Durrheim, and Tredoux, 1994; Wiederman, 2002). Even when they are motivated to tell the truth, people may give inaccurate reports due to imperfect recall or poor memory (Loftus et al., 1992). The latter is especially problematic when surveying past experience (Pearson, Ross, and Dawes, 1992). Finally, people might fall into response sets, such as the tendency to endorse a statement rather than disagreeing with its opposite (the acquiescence response set), or the preference for strong statements versus moderate or indecisive ones (Greenleaf, 1992).

That these processes affect research participants' self-reports has been demonstrated extensively. It is very unlikely that these processes would not have influenced the outcomes of Spitzer's study. Consider the tendency to prefer black and white answers above more subtle gray responses. This could have encouraged study participants to present themselves as "more homosexual" than they actually were before "therapy" started and as "more heterosexual" than they currently are.

Regardless of its drawbacks, many researchers rely almost exclusively on self-report in their work. In Spitzer's case, however, the problem of self-report is further exacerbated by the other methodological problems cited below.[4]

SAMPLE SELECTION

A second serious problem with the study is the method Spitzer used to recruit his participants. He provides only sparse information about the recruitment process, an omission that is crucial in judging the validity of the participants' reports. The majority of the study's participants were recruited via ex-gay religious ministries and the National Association for Research and Therapy of Homosexuality

(NARTH). Spitzer describes NARTH as a group "of mental health professionals and lay people who defend the right of gay men and lesbians to receive sexual reorientation therapy" (p. 406).[5] These organizations had sent "repeated notices of the study" (p. 406) to their members.

It is not clear how the study was presented in these notices to potential participants. With what kind of information were potential respondents encouraged to participate in the study? What role did ex-gay organizations and NARTH play in convincing the study's respondents to participate? If it can at least be assumed that the selection criteria were described in these notices, how were the objectives of the study explained to the participants?[6] What were recruited participants expected to do? Were they called upon as witnesses who had to prove that reparative therapy "works?"[7] How many of the study's participants were paid spokespersons of the ex-gay movement (Besen, 2003)?[8]

Regardless of what was said in efforts to recruit participants, the presented goal of the study will have induced self-selection among respondents, potentially biasing the outcomes in a specific direction. Furthermore, the recruitment procedure will have affected the way participants entered the interview situation as well as the answers participants they gave in response to its questions. Consequently, not having provided this crucial aspect of the recruitment process in the published study is an important omission.

In general, it has been demonstrated that people's awareness of being a subject in a study forces "a specialized selection from among the many 'true' selves or 'proper' behaviors available in any respondent" (Webb et al., 2000, p. 16). This Role Selection sometimes even *creates* data, that is, data that are not related to any actual reality other than the research situation (Orne and Evans, 1965). In this specific context, and given the information about the study that the participants probably received, it is rather likely that some participants presented themselves as successfully converted gay and lesbian people—even if they were not. It does not necessarily mean that participants consciously and purposely fabricated stories, but what they knew about the goals of the study would have influenced their reports.[9]

Although it is difficult to demonstrate to what extent these distorting effects were present in Spitzer's study, it is reasonably plausible to assume that they were there. Unfortunately, we can only speculate about the pervasiveness of these effects. Spitzer himself frames this issue as *either* it is true what the people report *or* what they say are self-deceptive narratives (he does entertain the possibility that some of his participants actually did lie). The issue, however, is not black or white. Various processes might be at work at the same time, differently affecting people's self-reports.

Regardless of the information provided about the study to the participants, Spitzer's recruitment procedures were likely to result in a sample of "true believers" (Besen, 2003). Significantly, he reports that 78 percent of his participants had publicly spoken in favor of efforts to change one's homosexual orientation, often at their church. How would such a public commitment affect their self-reports? It could likely result in overstating the positive outcomes and downplaying the limitations and negative effects of "therapy." A researcher who studies such a "biased" sample would like to find ways to challenge his participants and to prevent participants' tendencies to distort the study's outcome (see the following section). Spitzer, however, did not do that.

RETROSPECTIVE DESIGN

The aforementioned problem of self-report in Spitzer's study is further amplified by the fact that crucial variables—various aspects of sexual orientation prior to starting "therapy"—are retrospectively assessed (Pearson, Ross, and Dawes, 1992). In other words, the participants were asked to provide information about their past selves. Among the retrospective information they were asked to provide regarding the year before starting conversion therapy were: (1) feelings of attraction; (2) the frequency of homosexual sex; (3) the frequency of looking with lust at a partner of the same sex or daydreaming about having sex with someone of the same sex, etc.[10] Although it was a study requirement that all of the participants had to have been at least five years post-"treatment," some of them were reporting about a period that occurred ever further in the past. On average, the participants were reporting about a period that ended twelve years prior to the time they were surveyed. Such a time frame would raise questions about the accuracy of any individual's retrospective reports, regardless of their sexual orientation (Hindley, 1979; Moss and Goldstein,

1985). For those troubled by their homosexual feelings and who experienced major life events related to sexuality and relationships—they underwent some kind of conversion therapy; they made public statements about their conversion; at least 48 percent of the sample married in that period[11]—retrospective questions are unlikely to lead to accurate answers.

Retrospective assessment of sexual orientation would have been less of a problem had it not been such a central focus of the research question: Retrospective answers to the study's questions are used to compute the magnitude of the change. If the initial situation has not been accurately assessed, the calculated change becomes meaningless.

Even if change had been assessed in a valid manner, the retrospective design would not allow causal interpretations. So, it would have been unclear whether conversion therapy (or which specific aspect of the intervention) caused observed changes or whether such changes were a consequence of other factors.

TELEPHONE INTERVIEWS
AS THE DATA-COLLECTION TECHNIQUE

Another troubling aspect of the Spitzer study is its use of the telephone interview as the method of data collection. Telephone interviews limit not only the number of questions a researcher can pose, but also the kind of questions (Sudman and Bradburn, 1982; Lavrakas, 1998). Questions have to be short and the number of answering categories have to be limited in order to adjust to the peculiarities of this way of communicating—for example, not being able to utilize visual cues and limited opportunities to establish and maintain rapport.

Spitzer's study took these limitations into account in regard to the questions that it posed, by developing short questions with a limited number of answering categories. The consequence of this approach is, however, that various issues were only assessed superficially and that other crucial issues had to be skipped. To assess participants' pre-"therapy" stage, more information about their sexual life could, for instance, have resulted in a more valid assessment of their former sexual orientation. Although it has been calculated that 20 to 28 percent of the sample was married before "therapy,"[12] little is known about participants' heterosexual activity before then. It is reported that 50 percent of the men and 56 percent of the women reported homosexual sex at least a few times a year before "therapy," but it is not known what they actually did. What was meant when participants were asked about "homosexual sex" and how was this concept understood by the participants? Is this anal intercourse (for men), mutual mastur-bation, watching gay pornography, or physically even less intimate forms of sexual involvement? One of the crucial issues Spitzer's study did not systematically address in its telephone questions to par-ticipants was harm resulting from the "therapy." Despite this omis-sion, Spitzer explicitly claims that there was no evidence of such harm.

MEASUREMENT OF HARM

The fact that the data were collected via telephone may be the most important reason that some crucial variables were operationalized poorly. The most significant of them is the concept of "harm" as a po-tential consequence of reparative therapies.[13] Although Spitzer con-cludes that there is no evidence of harm, the basis of this conclusion is not clear. The methods section of the study doesn't mention anything about how harm was assessed and Spitzer also did not indicate that he had considered in advance what kind of harm could be expected and how it should be assessed. It seems that people were asked to answer only one specific question about how depressed they were. This hardly seems a valid basis for concluding that no harm was done.

Even if the issue of harm had been addressed in a more in-depth way, it is unlikely that given the way the sample was collected that these participants would have volunteered any experience of harm. To objectively establish whether and how reparative therapies are harmful, a sample of convinced ex-gays and lesbians is not adequate. It might be impossible to study this in a random sample of people who seek reparative therapy.[14] It should be possible, though, to create a less selective group than the one put together for this study. Study-ing this topic in a longitudinal way, starting with people before they enter this kind of "therapy," would have resulted in more valid way of addressing harm.

INSUFFICIENT REPORTING OF THE FINDINGS

A final issue is the incomplete reporting of the findings. This applies to what Spitzer's study called the homosexual measures and the measures assessing heterosexual sex with one's spouse.[15] Most of the study's outcomes are presented in a dichotomized way, which means that only percentages of participants that score below or above a certain point of the scale are reported. It is reported that 52 percent of the sample had homosexual sex at least a few times a month before "therapy." It is not reported how many had no homosexual sex or how many had homosexual sex daily, even though the study's author has that information. It is not made clear why the data is not presented more extensively. Presenting the data in a dichotomized way makes it impossible to assess the size of various changes.

The author also doesn't report whether he conceptually constructed the various dichotomies before or after he started the study, although it is likely that he did so after he had collected (and inspected) the data. That would have been less of a problem if the published study also had given a fuller account of the data. Consequently, one is not sure now to what extent the choice of cutoff points is opportunistic.

For some variables, the study also presents PRE and POST percentages calculated on different n's. For instance, it is reported that 92 percent of 50 women (the total number of women in the study was 57) had same sex fantasies on 20 percent or more masturbatory occasions before the "therapy," while 18 percent out of 39 reported that for the year preceding the interview. Obviously, 11 women stopped masturbating. To be able to assess the extent of change, the study should not have included these eleven women in the PRE report and presented these findings only for women who masturbated both before and after the "therapy."

THE MAGNITUDE OF CHANGE ASSESSED

The previous methodological arguments are sufficient reason to dismiss the Spitzer study's findings. Even if one were to assume that the participants' reports were valid, is there as much change as the study suggests?[16] As mentioned, *change* is assessed in this study by comparing the situation in the year before "therapy" with the year preceding the interview (which took place at least five years after the start of the "therapy").

How "homosexual" were the people according to their reports before they started "therapy?" Spitzer's study presents the data in terms of the glass being half full. The opposite approach gives a more qualified picture of the participants' homosexuality and heterosexuality. Forty-four percent of the participants reported that as teenagers they had opposite sex attraction more frequent than "only rarely." More than half of the participants had experienced consensual heterosexual sex before "therapy" and a quarter of the sample was married before the beginning of "therapy." Over 50 percent of the participants had not had homosexual sex in the year before "therapy" more frequently than "at least a few times per month." Ten percent of the participants had never had any homosexual involvement. A majority of the participants (59 percent) had not been "openly gay."

In addition, for over a third of the participants (37 percent), homosexuality was a conflicted experience, inducing serious thoughts of suicide. An even bigger group (73 percent) reports to have been extremely or markedly bothered by unwanted homosexual feelings. So how typically *homosexual* were these people actually before they started "therapy?" As a group, they do not resemble the picture one usually gets from studies among gay men and lesbian women (see, for instance, Bell and Weinberg, 1978; Nardi and Sherrod, 1994; Weeks, Heaphy and Donovan, 2001).

How *heterosexual* had the participants become? For various reasons, this is difficult to assess. Participants' sexuality is predominantly described in terms of its degree of homosexuality; 68 percent of the participants are still at least somewhat bothered by unwanted homosexual feelings. In addition, 71 percent reported having had heterosexual sex in the preceding year. No specific statement is given about the sexual behavior of the 64 men and women (32 percent) who, after "therapy," did not get married—although a few of them may have had heterosexual sex and a few others had masturbated.[17] They had not engaged in any (hetero)sexual behavior? This, of course, qualifies the claim of being converted. It remains unclear whether the participants truly had a heterosexual orientation, which would imply predominant sexual attraction to the other sex in general (other than what the participants themselves state about this).

The obvious conclusion for the total group of participants is that their homosexuality before and their heterosexuality after "therapy" is rather diffuse. So even if one were to take the participants' self-reports as valid data, the conclusion that they changed from homosexual to heterosexual is lacking solidity.

DISCUSSION

It is clear from the discussion section of his paper that Spitzer is aware he could have done a better methodological job. As previously stated, he discusses several of the limitations to his study.[18] The discussion of the study's limitations is guided, however, by the author's strong belief in the validity of the findings and not by a careful assessment of relevant arguments.

It is obvious that the study's data would have been a lot stronger if its author had adopted a longitudinal study design, in which people were assessed before they started the "therapy" and followed over time. Although still not an experimental design, seeing people change after they started "therapy" would have been more convincing.

Instead of telephone interviews, face-to-face interviews could have been conducted. This would have been a much more suitable instrument to collect the kind of data necessary to answer the research question the study tried to answer. It would have created the opportunity to pose longer and more open questions, which are better when dealing with threatening issues (Sudman and Bradburn, 1982). It would also have had created the opportunity to assess more relevant variables, because face-to-face interviews offer the opportunity to maintain rapport over a much longer period than telephone interviews. There would have been more opportunities to probe after participants answered questions, making sure that the correct answers were reported. In-person interviews would also have given the researcher the opportunity to assess and make use of physical expressions, which could have offered the researcher clues about the validity of the data.

Having chosen self-report, the study could have adopted directions to improve the quality of answers participants gave to interviewer questions. There is an extensive body of literature not only about the problems of retrospective data, but also about the way to counteract some of these problems (Baddeley, 1985; Belli, 1998; Brewer and

Garrett, 2001; Fowler, 1998; Spanier, 1976). One way would have been to stimulate recall activities on the part of the participants to help them place their experiences in time before posing the crucial questions (Fowler, 1998). Another would have been to carefully consider what kind of questions would have been reasonable to ask and which questions would likely result in more reliable answers. One might wonder, though, whether such approaches would have been helpful in this specific situation.

Instead of exclusively relying on self-report, a variety of ways could have been used to collect additional information to triangulate its findings. One possibility would have been to interview people who knew the participants before, during, and after the "therapy."[19] Some standardized tests could have been administered. Furthermore, psycho-physiological measures could have been applied, such as penile and vaginal plethysmography (Janssen, 2002). The latter offer a more valid assessment of people's sexual responsiveness than what participants are willing to volunteer. Such measures would really have put the respondents' claims of changing sexual orientation to the test.

So much for the question of what could have been done to improve the quality of the study. What *should* Spitzer have done? The published account does not mention the author's motives to do the study, other than concern for "the truth" about the possibility to change one's sexual orientation.[20] As a consequence, one can only speculate about Spitzer's motives and the situation that gave rise to this study. Did he start this project completely on his own, out of personal interest, or was he invited by fundamental Christian organizations to take up the issue? Was he offered an interesting opportunity to study something in which he was truly interested?

Whatever the answer to these questions is, it was obvious that limited resources were available to carry out the study and that these limited resources made it impossible for the study to address the issue using a sophisticated research design. Spitzer should therefore have realized beforehand that the validity of his data would turn out to be highly questionable. Given the delicacy of the topic and considering how charged this issue is in the cultural debates surrounding homosexuality, the serious limitations of the study design should have made Spitzer decide not to do the study at all.[21]

NOTES

1. Spitzer reports, however, that 21 percent of his sample is still "involved in some kind of reparative therapy." It is not clear why he did not remove those subjects who did not meet the inclusion criteria of having completed "therapy" from his sample, and how their inclusion affected the study outcomes.

2. To his credit, Spitzer quite elaborately describes how he actually conducted the study. This makes it possible to judge what he did and to assess the validity of his conclusions. He even makes the data set available for review. Even though someone should inspect this data set once to arrive at an assessment of the study based on an examination of the original data, that was not done for this paper.

3. Spitzer's study has been criticized for a variety of invalid reasons, such that he used a nonrandom sample and had no control group. Although a random sample or control group would have strengthened the design of the study, they are not indispensable given the aims of the study.

4. An additional problem besides those discussed in the text of this [chapter] is that of the data analysis. Spitzer's study reports that the interviews of 43 participants were coded by Spitzer himself and a research assistant. Because the agreement between both coders was high, it is concluded that there was no bias in interviewing coding. This is, of course, only the case if both coders didn't share the same bias. In this reasoning, reliability is incorrectly equated with validity.

5. NARTH does more than defend people's right to conversion therapy. Its members also consider homosexuality to be a mental disorder. In addition, prior to the 2003 Supreme Court decision outlawing sodomy laws, some NARTH members testified to keep laws criminalizing homosexual behavior on the book (see Drescher, 2001).

6. It is unlikely that this was done in terms of the concrete operationalizations described in the study.

7. Given the ideological belief systems of the ex-gay movement, this is not an unreasonable assumption.

8. Also see Wayne Besen's chapter, "*Political* Science," which [was] reprinted in the *Journal of Gay & Lesbian Psychotherapy* [2003, 7(3)] [and in this book].

9. Presenting themselves as successfully converted gays and lesbians would also not necessarily imply that the participants would now claim 100 percent heterosexuality (although some seemed to have done so). Some would have realized the importance of coming across as credible. In that case it is more convincing, at least for some, to present some traces of their homosexuality.

10. Although Spitzer writes throughout the paper that he used retrospective accounts, when he uncritically states "At PRE [therapy], 46 percent of the males and 42 percent of the females reported exclusively same-sex attraction (p. 409)," he gives the impression that he collected this information before the start of conversion therapy.

11. This percentage is deduced from the information the study presents about the participants' marital status. Before "therapy," 21 percent of the men and 18 percent of the women were married (30 men and 10 women, respectively); at the moment of the interview 76 percent of the men and 47 percent of the women were married (108 and 27, respectively). These findings are in contrast with the reported figure of 55

men and women who are said to have had sex with their spouse both currently and before treatment. It is not clear from where these additional 15 persons come.

12. See previous note.

13. Anecdotal reports of harm done to patients by conversion therapies led the American Psychiatric Association to call for a moratorium on such interventions (American Psychiatric Association, 2000). For reports of harm done to patients in conversion therapy, see Shidlo, Schroeder and Drescher (2001).

14. See Shidlo and Schroeder (2002).

15. The study only reports about current heterosexual sex of the people who were married. Laumann et al.'s (1994) findings show that a substantial part of heterosexual activity does not occur between married partners.

16. Although Spitzer's study is very precise in the amount of change it assessed, the exactness in the paper itself is not in line with its sweeping subtitle implying that all 200 subjects changed from a homosexual to a heterosexual orientation.

17. Table 1 in Spitzer's study (p. 411) suggests that 25 percent of the participants had not masturbated in the year preceding the interview and 29 percent had not had heterosexual sex in the same period. This is a little less than the 33 percent participants that were not married. Since all married people seemed to have had sex with their spouse, this implies that about eight of the 65 unmarried participants had had heterosexual sex.

18. Spitzer discusses whether the subjects' "self-report of change" are credible. The subjects were, however, not asked to report on *change*. One of the good things about the study is that PRE and POST states were assessed independently and that the issue of whether change had occurred was established by comparing PRE and POST measures. This is the best way to assess change, if only the validity of both measures would have been more secure. If the study had based its conclusions on change as reported by the subjects, there even would had been more grounds to disqualify them.

19. Spitzer actually reports in the method section of his study that he did include the spouses of the study's subjects: He sent two copies of Spanier's Dyadic Adjustment Scale to 130 study subjects and their spouses with the instruction to complete the forms independently and mail them back to him. It is not clear from the data how often both partners returned the questionnaire. All he reports to have are mean scale scores for "94 subjects or their spouses" (p. 412). It would not only have been interesting to know how many complete sets were returned, but also whether the scores of the spouses corresponded. The latter would have added credibility to the subjects' reports about marital adjustment. The limited way in which Spitzer reports about this scale makes it hard to evaluate the findings.

20. In contrast to quantitative research, investigators involved in qualitative research customarily make explicit what made them study a specific topic (Creswell, 2003), to give the reader the opportunity to assess how his engagement with the issue might affect the study design and outcome.

21. It is more than likely that this study will be abused by some sectors of society to convince unsuspecting people—either potential clients or their families—that, if they want to, gay men and lesbian women can change their homosexual orientation. Even if this was proven by the study, the study also shows that some participants did not succeed. One should further realize that while change happened in some of the study's participants, the outcomes would not necessarily apply to all gay men and

lesbian women. This study deals with a very specific sample, people who didn't want to be gay or lesbian, and who were highly motivated not to be gay or lesbian.

The *Archives of Sexual Behavior,* which published Spitzer's study, is not directly responsible for any misrepresentation or abuse of the study's claimed outcomes. The journal's editor should nevertheless have realized that publishing it would contribute to such misuse by giving the study an unwarranted status as objective scientific research. The journal could at least have made sure that the study's published title did not suggest that 200 subjects *had* changed from a homosexual to a heterosexual orientation.

REFERENCES

American Psychiatric Association (2000), Commission on Psychotherapy by Psychiatrists (COPP): Position statement on therapies focused on attempts to change sexual orientation (Reparative or conversion therapies). *Amer. J. Psychiat.,* (157):1719-1721.

Baddeley, A. (1985), The limitations of human memory: Implications for the design of retrospective surveys. In: *The Recall Method in Social Surveys,* eds. L. Moss & H. Goldstein. London: University of London Institute of Education, pp. 13-30.

Bell, A.P. & Weinberg, M.S. (1978), *Homosexualities: A Study of Diversity Among Men and Women.* New York: Simon and Schuster.

Belli, R.F. (1998), The structure of autobiographical memory and the event history calendar: Potential improvements in the quality of retrospective reports in surveys. *Memory,* 6(4):383-406.

Besen, W.R. (2003), *Anything but Straight: Unmasking the Scandals and Lies Behind the Ex-Gay Myth.* Binghamton, NY: Harrington Park Press.

Brewer, D.D. & Garrett, S.B. (2001), Evaluation of interviewing techniques to enhance recall of sexual and drug injection partners. *Sexually Transmitted Diseases,* 28(11):666-677.

Creswell, J.W. (2003), *Research Design: Qualitative, Quantitative, and Mixed Methods Approaches,* Second edition. Thousand Oaks, CA: Sage.

Drescher, J. (2001), Ethical concerns raised when patients seek to change same-sex attractions. *J. Gay & Lesbian Psychother.,* 5(3/4):181-210. Reprinted in: *Sexual Conversion Therapy: Ethical, Clinical and Research Perspectives,* eds. A. Shidlo, M. Schroeder & J. Drescher. Binghamton, NY: The Haworth Press, 2001, pp. 181-210.

Fowler, F.J. (1998), Design and evaluation of survey questions. In: *Handbook of Applied Social Research Methods,* eds. L. Bickman & D.J. Rog. Thousand Oaks, CA: Sage, pp. 343-374.

Greenleaf, E.A. (1992), Measuring extreme response style. *Public Opinion Quarterly,* 56:328-351.

Hindley, C.B. (1985), Problems of interviewing in obtaining retrospective information. In: *The Recall Method in Social Surveys*, eds. L. Moss & H. Goldstein. London: University of London Institute of Education, pp. 100-114.

Janssen, E. (2002), Psychophysiological measurement of sexual arousal. In: *Handbook for Conducting Research on Human Sexuality*, eds., M.W. Wiederman & B.E. Whitley. Mahwah, NJ: Lawrence Erlbaum, pp. 139-171.

Laumann, E.O., Gagnon, J.H., Michael, R.T. & Michaels, S. (1994), *The Social Organization of Sexuality: Sexual Practices in the United States*. Chicago: University of Chicago Press.

Lavrakas, P.J. (1998), Methods for sampling and interviewing in telephone surveys. In: *Handbook of Applied Social Research Methods*, eds. L. Bickman & D.J. Rog. Thousand Oaks, CA: Sage, pp. 429-472.

Loftus, E.F., Smith, K.D., Klinger, M.R., & Fiedler, J. (1992), Memory and mismemory for health events. In: *Questions About Questions: Inquiries into the Cognitive Bases of Surveys*, ed. J.M. Tanur. New York: Russell Sage Foundation, pp. 102-137.

Moss, L. & Goldstein, H., eds. (1985), *The Recall Method in Social Surveys*. London: University of London Institute of Education.

Nardi, P.M. & Sherrod, D. (1994), Friendship in the lives of gay men and lesbians. *J. Social & Personal Relationships,* 11:185-199.

Nicholas, L.J., Durrheim, K., & Tredoux, C.G. (1994), Lying as a factor in research on sexuality. *J. Personality & Social Psychology,* 56:950-957.

Orne, M.T. & Evans, F.J. (1965), The nature of hypnosis: Artifact and essence. *J. Abnormal & Social Psychology,* 58:277-299.

Pearson, R.W., Ross, M. & Dawes, R.M. (1992), Personal recall and the limits of retrospective questions in surveys. In: *Questions About Questions: Inquiries into the Cognitive Bases of Surveys*, ed. J.M. Tanur. New York: Russell Sage Foundation, pp. 65-94.

Shidlo, A. & Schroeder, M. (2002), Changing sexual orientation: A consumers' report. *Professional Psychology: Research & Practice,* 33(3):249-259.

Shidlo, A., Schroeder, M. & Drescher, J., eds. (2001), *Sexual Conversion Therapy: Ethical, Clinical and Research Perspectives*. Binghamton, NY: The Haworth Press.

Spanier, G.B. (1976), Use of recall data in survey research on human sexual behavior. *Social Biology,* 23(3):244-253.

Spitzer, R.L. (2003), Can some gay men and lesbians change their sexual orientation? 200 participants reporting a change from homosexual to heterosexual orientation. *Arch. Sexual Behavior,* 32(5):403-417.

Stone, A.A., Turkkan, J.S., Bachrach, C.A., Jobe, J.B., Kurtzman, H.S. & Cain, V. S., eds. (2000), *The Science of Self-Report: Implications for Research and Practice*. Mahwah, NJ: Lawrence Erlbaum.

Sudman, S. & Bradburn, N.M. (1982), *Asking Questions: A Practical Guide to Questionnaire Design*. San Francisco: Jossey-Bass.

Webb, E.J., Campbell, D.T., Schwartz, R.D., & Sechrest, L. (2000), *Unobtrusive Measures,* Revised edition. Thousand Oaks, CA: Sage.

Weeks, J., Heaphy, B., & Donovan, C. (2001), *Same Sex Intimacies. Families of Choice and Other Life Experiments.* London: Routledge.

Wiederman, M.W. (2002), Reliability and validity of measurement. In: *Handbook for Conducting Research on Human Sexuality,* eds. M.W. Wiederman & B.E. Whitley. Mahwah, NJ: Lawrence Erlbaum, pp. 25-50.

33

The Religious Conversion
of Homosexuals: Subject Selection
Is the Voir Dire of Psychological Research

Charles Silverstein

INTRODUCTION

At the annual meeting of the American Psychiatric Association (APA) in May 2001, Robert Spitzer of Columbia University presented a paper that generated a great deal of heat and publicity (Spitzer, 2003). Spitzer is well known for his help, in 1973, in removing homosexuality as a mental disorder from the APA's *Diagnostic and Statistical Manual* (DSM) (Bayer, 1981; Silverstein, 1976/ 1977). All the greater wonder then the Associated Press' headline that Spitzer was presenting, "An explosive new study that says that some gays can go straight if they really want to" (Lund and Renna, 2003).

There was extensive media coverage of the paper and the subsequent conflict between gay activists, and antigay Christian groups who claimed that gay people could "change" their sexual orientation through prayer and religious experience. Gay spokesmen claimed a lack of efficacy in the attempts to change sexual orientation and its insidious influence in the battle for gay civil rights, while "ex-gays," as they called themselves, argued the immorality of homosexuality and the potential for salvation through Jesus.

The attack by the religious right against gay people was stimulated by two previous events in the mental health community. The first was

This chapter appeared originally under the same title in the *Journal of Gay & Lesbian Psychotherapy* 7(3):31-53. Copyright 2003 The Haworth Press, Inc.

Published by The Haworth Press, Inc., 2006. All rights reserved.
doi:10.1300/5503_33

the 1973 APA decision to remove homosexuality as an official pathology, and an accompanying call from virtually all professional organizations to support civil rights legislation for gay people. The second was the official statements of the American Psychological Association and the American Psychiatric Association that the attempt to "cure" homosexuals by "reparative" therapy was intrinsically unethical, ineffective as a treatment, and ultimately harmful to the patient (Haldeman, 2001; Drescher, 2002). It was recommended to members of these two APAs not to attempt sexual orientation conversions. This second event was an especially painful rebuke to the Christian "ex-gay" movement.

The Spitzer study is now being used as the spearhead for a third wave attempt by the Christian religious right to repathologize homosexuality. They would have psychiatry put homosexuality back into APA's DSM. Furthermore, recriminalizing homosexuality would support their national campaign against civil rights for gay people (Drescher, 2001). They have interpreted Spitzer's study as support for their religious belief that all behavior (especially sexual behavior) is a question of "choice," and therefore, voluntary.

HISTORICAL ANTECEDENTS OF THE EX-GAY MOVEMENT

The twentieth century concept of "choice" currently favored by the conservative Christian right is a regression to an earlier religious belief in "free will."[1] The present day "ex-gay" movement and their Christian supporters (e.g., Exodus International, Focus on the Family, and Homosexuals Anonymous) are heirs to nineteenth century organizations such as the Society for the Suppression of Vice. Founded in 1873, the Society's charter claimed responsibility for "the enforcement of laws for the suppression of the trade in and circulation of obscene literature and illustrations, advertisement, and articles of indecent or immoral use" (Gilfoyle, 1992, p. 187). They saw sexual dangers lurking in everyday activities: reading novels, looking at artwork, dancing, singing, drinking alcohol, sleeping on feather beds, and especially masturbation.[2] Even nocturnal emissions were believed to result in the "leprosy of desire" (Stall, 1897, p. 98).[3] The nineteenth century purity movement intended to regulate the behavior of people through religious doctrine and the passage of laws against whatever behavior they condemned; so does the purity movement of the twenty-first century.[4]

With the foundation of conservative religion to support the window out of which one looks upon the development of lust, mental health professionals worked hard to quiet the leprosy of desire called homosexuality. Their techniques included the following:

1. Surgically transplanting testicular cells from a heterosexual man into the testes of a gay man (Schmidt, 1984; Wolff, 1986)
2. Castration of gay men (Bremer, 1959)[5]
3. Implanting stereotaxic leads into the brain of a gay man (Heath, 1972)[6]
4. Cerebral ablation of "sexual deviants" (Schmidt and Schorsch, 1981; Rieber and Sigusch, 1979)
5. Androgen replacement (Tennent, Bancroft, and Cass, 1974)[7]
6. Aversive conditioning, including electrical, chemical, and covert (McConaghy, 1969; Bancroft, 1974; Cautela, 1967)[8]
7. Hypnosis (Freund, 1977)
8. Psychoanalysis (Bergler, 1956)

It bears noting that in almost all of the studies cited, gay men "volunteered" to be treated by these often sadistic means. As a rule, society convinces people that their behavior is immoral. This is guilt-producing and leads them to accept whatever treatment is offered to reduce it (Davison, 1976, 1978; Silverstein, 1972). The belief that "sexual deviants," and mental inmates are less than human created an environment in which they were treated with extreme cruelty (Schmidt and Schorsch, 1981; Sigusch et al., 1982). By internalizing guilt and shame, people have agreed to be "treated" by hydrotherapy, insulin shock, sexual sterilization, and lobotomies (Braslow, 1997).

What follows is a comparison between the Spitzer study and that of Ariel Shidlo and Michael Schroeder. The purpose is to learn what both pieces of research teach about the religious conversion of gay men and women. I will do this with a low "Quibble Quotient," methodological nuances (large and small), and concentrate on the major problems and weaknesses of the research. The reader is referred to the original papers for further detail of their procedures and results (Spitzer, 2003; Schroeder and Shidlo, 2001; Shidlo and Schroeder, 2002).

THE SPITZER STUDY

Spitzer asked the following question: can he find a man or a woman who, after some form of religious intervention, has changed his/her sexual orientation from homosexual to heterosexual? From a logical point of view, he need only find one person in order to answer, "yes." But that must be a person who has been certified/proven to have been totally gay—six on the Kinsey scale (Kinsey, Pomeroy and Martin, 1948; Kinsey et al., 1953)—at some time in the past, and after undergoing an identifiable procedure/treatment for a specified period of time, can now be certified/proven to be totally heterosexual (zero on the Kinsey scale). Finding two people would be even better, but he does not need to find many who can be authenticated as having crossed the Rubicon from homosexual to heterosexual. The most convincing way he could have demonstrated sexual orientation change would be through the use of phallometric testing for men (Blanchard et al., 2001) and vaginal photoplethysmograph testing for women (Laan et al., 1994) in a before/after treatment design. The study would be similar to this: physiological testing, followed by an identifiable and replicable treatment, and then a final physiological test.[9]

But this standard is very difficult (and expensive) to meet, so Spitzer did the next best thing he could think of: he asked them. Therefore, what he found was not sexual orientation change but people *who claimed* their sexual orientation was changed. Spitzer didn't use a control group in his study.

Enlisting the Subjects

There were exactly 200 subjects in the Spitzer study. Forty-three percent were enrolled by appealing to "ex-gay" ministries—religious groups established with the intent of converting homosexuals into heterosexuals through the use of prayer. Exodus International, founded in 1976, is one such often-quoted group. Twenty-three percent were recruited through the National Association for Research and Therapy of Homosexuality (NARTH), an organization whose members believe homosexuality to be an illness and who support efforts at sexual reorientation.[10] Another 25 percent of the subjects were referred by "therapists" who provide sexual reorientation therapy.[11] The remaining 9 percent were referred by their former therapists. There was no way of knowing how many subjects participated in more than one form of sexual orientation change. Nineteeen percent of the subjects, however, claimed to be themselves either mental health professionals involved in the treatment of gays or directors of ex-gay ministries.[12] Lund and Renna (2003) state that Dr. Laura Schlesinger had also been soliciting subjects for the Spitzer study on her nationally syndicated talk show. The subjects were clearly not a random group of people, nor did Spitzer claim they were. Although they were not tested for their attitude toward homosexuality, it is clear that it would not be affirmative.

Characteristics of the Subjects

Of the 200 subjects, about 70 percent were men and 30 percent were women. Three-quarters of the male subjects were married at the time of the interview, whereas only half of the women were married. Ninety-five percent of the subjects were Caucasian. Geographically, most of the subjects came from either the western or southern United States. Religiously, 81 percent were Protestant, while Catholics represented 8 percent, Mormon, 7 percent, and Jewish, 3 percent. The mean ages of the subjects were 42 for men and 44 for women.

It would be useful to know what percentage of these subjects came from rural areas, as opposed to cities. Knowing how many came from cities with large gay populations would be a check upon the availability of gay alternatives in their lives.

Ninety-three percent of the subjects said that religion was either extremely or very important in their lives, and of the 200 subjects, 79 percent said they wanted to change their sexual orientation because it conflicted with the tenets of their religion. Seventy-eight percent had spoken publicly in favor of changing their sexual orientation, often in church. Only 41 percent said that they had been openly gay *at some time* [13] in their lives prior to their attempt to change their sexual orientation.[14] More than one-third of both men and women had had serious thoughts of committing suicide because of their homosexuality, but no figures were reported on how many actually attempted it.

Method of Data Collection

Spitzer's method of data collection was very clever. He wanted to avoid some of the typical methodological problems in conducting homosexual conversion research. In the first place, he made no assumptions regarding the mental health of gay people. Therefore, he would have a right to claim that his data do not conflict with his earlier contribution in removing homosexuality as a mental illness from DSM (although the same could not be said for the study's effect upon civil rights issues). He also avoided the "bean counting" definition of homosexuality, that who one chooses to bed with and how often is a valid measure of homosexuality and heterosexuality (especially since almost 60 percent of his subjects appear not to have engaged in homosexual behavior).

By doing this, Spitzer ignores the problem of *the definition of homosexuality,* a much argued variable in the professional literature (Sell, 1997). Consequently, there is no reliability between his subjects on whether one is or is not a homosexual. In the place of bean counting, Spitzer attempted to investigate the internal fantasy production of his subjects both before and after the "treatment."[15] Third, to avoid the criticism that any change of sexual orientation was only temporary, he required that subjects have made a minimal change on all scales for at least five years. He also collected data on the extent to which a previously gay man, for instance, became sexually and romantically interested in a number of women, instead of only his own spouse.

The subjects were interviewed through a structured phone interview. They were asked to report their same sex attraction, overt sexual behavior, sexual fantasies, and yearning[16] while in their homosexual period and after "treatment" in their heterosexual lives. The questions appear to be unbiased.

There were 114 questions asked in 13 categories that included homosexual and heterosexual attraction and sex, fantasies, masturbation fantasies, use of pornography, and physical and emotional satisfaction. Spitzer mailed a marital satisfaction questionnaire after the telephone interview to those who were married.

RESULTS OF THE STUDY

The results of the study are reported by Spitzer as the difference between each subject before therapy (called "PRE"), and after therapy (called "POST"). A subject was required to claim a move of at least 10 percent from PRE to POST measures in order for him/her to be counted as making a change.

Motivation—The most common motivation to change was emotional unhappiness, followed by conflicts between gay feelings and religious beliefs, and to get or remain married.

Sexual attraction—At PRE, the overwhelming majority of subjects had had homosexual attractions as teenagers, and no heterosexual interest. One-third of the men (negligible for women) had more than fifty same-sex partners in their lives.

At POST, 17 percent of men and 54 percent of women report *exclusive* heterosexual attraction. That means that 83 percent of men and 46 percent of women failed to change their sexual orientation. Spitzer says, "Reparative therapy rarely, if ever, results in heterosexual arousal that is as intense as a person who never had same-sex attractions. However, advocates of reparative therapy do not make that claim" (p. 414). He goes on to say that reparative therapy is sometimes successful.

Therapy—Spitzer found that almost half his subjects saw a licensed professional at some time with the intention of changing his/her sexual orientation. Most of the remaining subjects attended an ex-gay or other religious group. But 90 percent of the total sample went to both. Twenty-one percent of his subjects were still attending some form of treatment and had been for an average of 15 years.

Homosexual behavior went from 50 percent to virtually zero. However, there were "slips" from time to time, but Spitzer does not clarify what they signify.

Gay daydreaming went from 99 percent to 31 percent in men and a greater drop in women.

Other changes included: a reduction in same sex masturbatory fantasies (but more than two-thirds of men are still masturbating to same sex imagery), use of gay pornography, and an increase in opposite sex fantasies (but no more than 31 percent in men and 72 percent in women).

Heterosexual sex—28 percent of the sample that was married had sex with their spouses, and they reported a greater frequency and satisfaction with their spouses at POST than PRE.

Heterosexual arousal—Spitzer reports that 72 percent of men and 76 percent of women report arousal to more than one opposite-sex person, demonstrating, he states, that sexual orientation change can be generalized to opposite-sex individuals, not just to one's spouse.

Spitzer claims that his study:

> questions the current conventional view that desire for therapy to change sexual orientation change is always succumbing to societal pressure and irrational homophobia. Second, it suggests that the mental health professions should stop moving in the direction of banning sexual reorientation therapy. (p. 414)

It is difficult to assess why Spitzer does not believe that religion (and its inevitable accusations of sin) is not a powerful stressor. Since his sample consists of people in their forties, they remember when sodomy[17] was a criminal offense in fifty states. In the last half-century, gay people were arrested after entrapment by police, fired from their jobs, rejected by their families, and had their names and addresses printed in the tabloids. One wonders what factors Spitzer would list as societal pressures and homophobia, if not those?

Spitzer goes on to say that prohibiting clinicians from practicing sexual conversion therapy because there is not yet enough evidence of its effectiveness reflects a bias in both APAs. He maintains that what is known as gay affirmative therapy is approved by members of both APAs, even though it too lacks empirical evidence of its effectiveness.

SHIDLO AND SCHROEDER

There have been many studies over the years looking at the effects of sexual orientation change. At this point, it would be instructive to look at a recent one that also examines the effects of attempting to change sexual orientation from homosexual to heterosexual, especially since the authors used similar subject pools and testing procedures. Shidlo and Schroeder (2002) examined the effects of sexual orientation conversion, but in contrast to Spitzer, they intended to track the harmfulness of the practice. Subjects were required to have had at least six sessions in any form of conversion intervention, and a Kinsey rating of predominantly homosexual. They did not have a control group.

Subjects

Subjects were recruited via the gay media, Web sites, unnamed organizations, and mailings to ex-gay ministries. Two hundred and two subjects were finally enrolled in the study, of which 90 percent were men. The mean age of their subjects was 40 years, and 86 percent of them were Caucasian. Sixty-six percent of their subjects considered themselves religious, but almost 50 percent refused to identify their religion. Of those that did, 38 percent were protestant, with other religions being negligible.

Method

Subjects were interviewed via a 90-minute telephone interview using a semistructured questionnaire. Shidlo and Schroeder, similar to Spitzer, commingled treatment (called an "intervention") offered by both professionals and nonprofessionals. However, they did make a count of each group. Two-thirds of the interventions were from licensed mental health counselors (mainly psychologists), and one-third were from peer and ex-gay counselors. While Shidlo and Schroeder made every attempt to identify the specific type of therapy offered, 52 percent of the treatment modality of licensed counselors was "unspecified."

Subjects were told that the experimenters were gay and that the study had been funded by two gay organizations. The authors protest that this did not bias the procedure because the subjects reported (to them) that they did not think it influenced their responses.[18]

The goal of the telephone interview was to assess a number of effects of the interventions, the most significant for this discussion are

(1) perceived help or harm; and (2) effects of the intervention on sexual desire, behavior, and romantic relationships. Harm was assessed by asking the subjects, "Do you feel that this counseling harmed you or had a negative effect on you?" (p. 254).[19]

The authors, similar to Spitzer, asked their subjects about time frames: before the first conversion intervention, after the intervention, and at the time of the interview.

Results

Subjects were asked what prompted them to attempt sexual conversion. Although no specific data is reported, the most common answers included feeling rejected by other gays, religious guilt, lack of exposure to the gay community, coercion, and help with other psychological problems such as depression, anxiety and guilt. Seventy-four percent of the subjects initiated treatment themselves; the others were the result of coercion or therapist request.[20]

The authors found that their subjects' evaluation of therapy depended upon when treatment began. Early in therapy (in what Shidlo and Schroeder call the "honeymoon period"), patients have a high degree of confidence that it will be effective, but they become discouraged over time when the expected change remains elusive. They feel like failures, reinforcing feelings of guilt.

After the honeymoon period, continued treatment leads to either success or failure in sexual conversion.[21] The authors state that 87 percent ($N = 176$) of their subjects failed in their attempt to convert to heterosexuality, while 13 percent ($N = 26$) succeeded. They divided their "successes" into three groups:

1. Successful and struggling—$N = 12$
2. Successful and not struggling—$N = 6$
3. Successful heterosexual shift—$N = 8$

The distinction between groups two and three is far from clear. Furthermore, while Shidlo and Schroeder say that only group three ($N = 8$) represents successes (4 percent of the sample), it seems to this reviewer that there are really 14 successes, and therefore, 7 percent of their sample reported a successful change of sexual orientation. Although I don't think this is quibbling, in one respect it is irrelevant.

The fact is that some subjects claimed a successful conversion from gay to straight.

The authors write, "conversion therapy provided help in shifting their sexual orientation" (p. 257). They go on to say that of the eight successful subjects, "These participants appeared well-adjusted and content with living as heterosexuals" (p. 253). This is similar to Spitzer's statement that, "Although initially skeptical, in the course of the study, the author became convinced of the possibility of change in some gay men and lesbians" (p. 412).

For argument sake, one could accept the 4 percent conversions in authors' group three as correct. Who are these people? Seven out of the eight subjects in this group provided ex-gay counseling to other people who requested sexual orientation change, and four out of those seven held paid jobs in their ex-gay ministries. Is it possible that these eight individuals are from the same subject pool as Spitzer's sample of ex-gays? Some of them might even have volunteered for both studies. Could their joining the Shidlo and Schroeder study be an attempt to bias it? The problem in understanding these subjects is their personal investment in the results. It would have been acceptable for the authors to reject any subject with an identifiable investment in the results, including gays holding paid jobs in gay centers.

The authors were obviously uncomfortable with their finding that some of their subjects claimed successful sexual conversion. (Their study was published over a year before Spitzer's.) Therefore, they administered follow-up interviews, but only of this group of subjects who claimed successful conversion through religion. They did not conduct follow-up interviews of the much larger failure-to-convert group. They rationalize this procedure saying that while some of the successes may change to failures over time, that failures could not change to successes. This is a dubious rationale with no evidence to support it. They go on to give examples of some (we do not know how many) successes turning into failures, but it is not known how many failures might have turned into successes. It would have been very significant for them to demonstrate that failures do not "go back."

Assessment of Harm

Shidlo and Schroeder provide a great deal of anecdotal evidence for the psychological and social harm done to their subjects when under the treatment of licensed professionals and peer counselors with the goal of "curing" their homosexuality. The authors found significant harm to their respondents in three broad areas: Psychological, social/interpersonal, and spiritual. They state, "Our research suggests a likelihood of harmful side-effects of conversion therapy for those who fail to change" (p. 258). Their work is consistent with the findings of Haldeman (1999, 2001). They suggest that clinicians educate clients about the harm done by religious conversion, and that they be given positive information about resources in the gay community.

However, they found (and this is really interesting) that those who failed to convert were not universally harmed by the attempt. Of the failures, while one group was harmed, another group was not. Unfortunately the number of subjects in each of these two groups is not known. Future research might identify the variables that control the harmfulness of the procedures. However, three possibilities come to mind:

1. The premorbid personality of the subject might lay down so toxic a feeling about oneself that the failure of treatment would only reinforce feelings of shame;
2. The potential harmfulness of the specific treatment used, e.g., aversion therapy;
3. The degree to which the subject initiated treatment (and exit) or was coerced.

In a companion paper, Schroeder and Shidlo (2001) address the question of ethical treatment. They define as unethical any treatment that violates the rulings of the American Psychological and American Psychiatric Associations' statement about conversion therapy. (The reader is referred to their paper and to Drescher, 1998, 2001 for a good summary of those statements.) The authors recognize, however, that professionals who are not members of these two organizations are not required to conform to their ethical code, nor are ex-gay and other peer counselors.

They asked respondents whether their therapists informed them that both APAs did not consider homosexuality a mental illness, and that conversion is unlikely. Only 26 percent said yes. The ethical codes also prohibit the misrepresentation of scientific data.[22]

The authors cite the opposing ethics of NARTH. On its Web site[23] is the following 1999 statement by Stern: "It should be the client's right, totally and completely, to choose a therapy which is consistent with his goals and values." Some respondents also told the authors that their therapists said that religious-based therapy supersedes secular attitudes, such as an APA code of ethics.

Schroeder and Shidlo next mention the American Psychological Association's ethical requirement to keep abreast of the latest research on homosexuality. It is at this point that ethics, politics, and science become hopelessly entangled. If the requirement is to tell potential patients about the latest research on homosexuality, are Schroeder and Shidlo suggesting that clinicians should tell patients how Spitzer found 17 percent of men and 54 percent of women of his subjects successfully converted, and that Shidlo and Schroeder themselves found 4 percent (or 7 percent) successfully converted—and that all the converts claim to be happy in their newfound heterosexual life? I do not mean to denigrate their work. They had the character to address these exceedingly difficult questions, and if they come out with some inconsistencies, it does not mean that any of us could do better.

A CRITIQUE OF THE PROBLEMS

It is time to reflect upon the implications of studies based upon religious conversions. One can try to separate the empirical, ethical, and political questions raised by Spitzer's work. This will be somewhat artificial since these variables are not orthogonal, rather a gestalt of factors that influence one another.

Empirical Questions

There will be many criticisms of Spitzer's methodology (see Sandfort, 2003). A few are offered below. Some will argue that his method is deeply flawed and that he didn't control for this or that. Others will say that his respondents were lying. These criticisms miss the point. Suppose that ten other researchers build upon the Spitzer study by correcting his errors, and that using ten other ex-gay populations find gay men and women who claim to successfully convert from gay to straight. Would his critics change their minds then? While methodology is directly related to validity, considered alone it will not explain the results of the Spitzer study. The problem is the character of the subjects who volunteered, not the reliability and validity of his scales. More on this later. Yet there are a few methodological problems that do bear mentioning:

1. The problem of an intervening variable. It is not certain what effected change in these people (if any change occurred at all). What is required is an identifiable and replicable procedure that can be independently verified and replicated.
2. There is no cause/effect relationship established. Although it is known what the respondents told Spitzer, he has no right to claim that the reported changes were due to prayer. For the same reason, Shidlo and Schroeder cannot claim that their subjects were harmed by religious conversions.
3. What is the proper definition and measure of homosexuality (Sell, 1997)? Spitzer avoided using the Kinsey Scale. It might have provided a problem for him since 60 percent of the men never had a homosexual experience, and about the same percentage had heterosexual attraction. Might some of his subjects be bisexual rather than homosexual?
4. All the studies noted here combine the work of licensed professionals with that of ex-gay peer counselors. No comparison was made between these two classes of people in order to learn if one was more or less effective than the other in changing sexual orientation.

Another interesting question (not methodological) is the number of successful conversions. At POST, 17 percent of the men and 54 percent of the women claimed conversion to heterosexuality. It is obligatory for a researcher to discuss the significant gender difference found, but Spitzer ignores it.

If 17 percent of the men and 54 percent of the women converted, then 83 percent of the men and 46 percent of the women didn't. What is to become of them? They begin by believing themselves sinners, and end up by failing to please God. "If I worked hard enough and trusted God enough . . ." one person said to Schroeder and Shidlo (2001, p. 147). He wasn't cured. He or she will certainly sink deeper into depression and feel that he's a hopeless sinner (even though he does not have sex).

Would it not be logical to say that attempts at religious conversion result in two different groups of men and women, one composed of a relatively small group of people who claim to be heterosexual, and the much larger group of dyed-in-the-wool homosexuals? If the heterosexuals are allowed to live their happy life, shouldn't something be done to bring about a measure of happiness to the greater number of homosexuals who are left? For instance, one might help them leave the church that makes them feel miserable about themselves in the first place, and introduce them to the gay community and its opportunities for love and sex. No doubt Spitzer would claim that he was not examining that question, but should he be let off the hook so easily?

But that still leaves the question of efficacy. Do changes in sexual orientation last over time? Freund (1977) wrote the following:

> Almost 20 years ago I started a therapeutic experiment, employing aversion therapy combined with positive conditioning toward females. Approximately 20 percent of the homosexual males, who came of their own accord to ask for help, married and founded families. However, this was a long-term study, and these marriages were followed up for many years. Virtually not one "cure" remained a cure. (p. 238)[24]

Freund went on to say:

> I am not happy about my therapeutic experiment which, if it has "helped" at all, has helped clients to enter into marriages that later became unbearable or almost unbearable. (p. 239)

It is possible that if Spitzer followed his subjects over time, as Freund did, that they too would fall back upon homosexual desire. But for many people, the question of efficacy is irrelevant when compared to the morality of sexual orientation change (Davison, 1974). As Popper (1959) noted, no amount of scientific information can prove or disprove a moral position.

Ethical Questions

The ethical challenge to "curing" homosexuals began in the early 1970s. I then argued (Silverstein, 1972) that no person "volunteers" for treatment in an environment of discrimination. I later proposed (Silverstein, 1977) that the only ethical act for a therapist was to turn away any request to change sexual orientation. My position was based upon the belief that no person can make a free choice in a world of criminalization, accusations of sin, and rejection by peers and family. I argued that there was no evidence that any gay people were cured by treatment, an empirical standard. I believed that patients had the right to ask for whatever treatment they wanted, but that I had the right to respect my own personal ethical standards. I still believe this.

Davison (1976, 1978) made the next ethical step. In a presidential speech to the Association for the Advancement of Behavior Therapy, he opposed any attempt to convert homosexuals into heterosexuals on moral rather than empirical grounds. He maintained that we have no right to treat a person for a behavior that is not abnormal. "Therapists should stop engaging in change-of-orientation programs, whether the client makes the request or someone else does" (Davison, 2001, p. 349). Davison then joined me in the successful political battle to end the use of aversion therapy (as well as any other therapeutic attempt) to cure gay men on ethical and humanitarian grounds.

What of a patient's right to choose his/her therapy? This writer agrees with NARTH's Stern: they have the right to make decisions based upon their goals and values. If a patient chooses to be imprisoned by a puritanical and slavish sexual system, rather than to smell the fresh air of freedom—well, that is his decision. It will not work, and he will be all the more unhappy for it, but it is his/her choice. I will not participate in it, and I will tell him/her my reasons.

Those of us fighting for gay and lesbian civil rights and dignity won the ethical and treatment battle of the 1970s. Why has it reappeared in the twenty-first century? More important, why are we letting the Christian right define our agenda, rather than charting our own course? What are the ethical issues for today?

1. By far the most important is the possibility of changing sexual orientation in the fetus. This idea is not new; Dörner made this suggestion two decades ago (Dörner, 1983). Professionals who

believe that homosexuality is socially constructed after birth will belittle the possibility (Gagnon, 1990), but those who suggest that sexual orientation is either biological or biosocial will be worried (Pillard and Weinrich, 1986).[25] There is already a professional debate about the right of parents to select sexual orientation (as well as other characteristics) in the fetus (Greenberg and Bailey, 2001; West, 2001). The implications are mind-boggling.

2. Homosexuality is no longer listed in the *Diagnostic and Statistical Manual,* but have we rid DSM of other sexual disorders that are also morally based? Might we address the question of why the paraphilias are still regarded as a disorder, even when played out between two consenting adults (Suppe, 1984)? Any experienced clinician knows that there are kinky sexual behaviors in the world, but what is the empirical foundation for calling them mental disorders?

3. While not in DSM, many clinicians accuse patients of suffering from "compulsive sex," because of its frequency or other socially disapproved criteria (Quadland, 1985). Compulsive is exactly the word used against homosexuals in the last century. Some of us believe that moral unacceptability is the only criterion governing the contrived diagnosis of compulsive or addictive sexuality, and its treatment a means of social control (Levine and Troiden, 1988).

4. Gender Identity Disorder is still listed in the DSM. It seems as if children are diagnosed and treated because other children (or their parents) beat them up for being different. Most of these children will grow up to be gay (Green, 1987); should we come to their defense?

5. "Don't ask, don't tell," although well-intentioned, results in over a thousand discharges from the armed services each year (Osburn, 2003).

These ethical concerns are intertwined with the political consequences of the actions of those who would have us declared a threat to society. If we sometimes integrate (or confuse) science and politics, it is due to the need to protect ourselves. The religious right wants the reinstitution of shame in gay people. If they have their way, we will all be attending ex-gay meetings and Sunday church, and will be jailed if we do not! Spitzer attempts to rise above the fray; he implicitly rejects the political implications of his work and its effects upon the unfinished battle for gay civil rights. This may be one of the reasons why gay professionals are so angry with him; he has confused the boundary between professional practice and religion. There is a mischievousness in his refusal to understand how potentially harmful the work is, and how much solace it provides to the conservative religious institutions that would squash our right to a gay identity, and especially our sexual freedom.[26]

Many on the religious right (and some professionals) claim that homosexuality was removed from DSM due to political pressures. They argue that a raise of hands is not science. They are right on both counts; political pressure helped the process along, and a raise of hands is not science. Yet, how do these critics think homosexuality got on the list in the first place? Every diagnostic category gets there by a raise of hands. Diagnoses change over time because they reflect changes in society (Silverstein, 1991). For better or for worse, there is no such thing as diagnosis or treatment unaffected by political meaning (Halleck, 1971; Bayer, 1981). Still, the diagnosis of homosexuality as a mental disorder was unable to withstand scientific scrutiny. This is anathema to the religious right who believe in the revealed word.

One might note that not every religious group condemns homosexuality. Kosnik et al. (1977) is a good example of enlightened Catholic thought about sexuality in general, and homosexuality specifically.

The Question of Religious Conversions

Ex-gays hold regular meetings and retreats. Many anecdotal reports exist of men slipping off the sexual wagon at these meetings (Besen, 2003; Haldeman, 1991; Lawson, 1987). One cannot, however, accuse all of Spitzer's subjects who claimed a heterosexual shift (or Shidlo and Schroeder's 4 or 7 percent) of lying. Lying is also a sin. How do we make sense of their claims, yet feel justified in saying that homosexuals cannot change to heterosexuals?

I believe the answer lies in the power of the religious beliefs of the respondents. Treatment is irrelevant. Science and conservative religion march to different tunes. Science is empirical; religion is revealed. Science has no overall authority; religion has God. Science has the concept of evidence; religion does not. Scientific beliefs are changeable; religious beliefs are static. Professionals are licensed by the state; peers are approved by God. Professionals are required to conform to a code of ethics; peers are answerable only to God. Whereas we believe in individual rights, they believe in conformity.

Spitzer avoids the issue of religion completely. The basic question in these studies is not about obedience to a professional association's rules; it is about obedience to God. For many Americans, it is God (or Jesus or Mary) who cures the ailing, not a professional with a state license. For them, the license comes from God, and it gives them the right to preach. And the way to God's love and compassion is through prayer, which, to them, is the intervening variable between homosexuality and heterosexuality. That is the treatment. They drink the waters of Lourdes, both metaphorically and literally. On TV, for instance, one can watch faith healers cure cancer, blindness, deafness and other physical ailments. Can the blind person see after praying to God? No. But is he lying? I think not. It is not a willing attempt to deceive. What is a change in sexual orientation next to that?

It is a terrible mistake to accept the work of licensed professionals and religious healers as comparable data. Apples are not oranges. They work from a different set of cognitive beliefs regarding the cause of the problem, how one treats it, and most important, different concepts of evidence. If a penitent fails to convert, or regresses afterward, it's not because he or she is homosexual; it is because he or she hasn't prayed enough or loved God enough. Therefore, failure means the failure to please God, and one is going to Hell as a result. These fears are strong motivators to believe that they have defeated the Devil and will end up in Heaven.

The testimonial is the stuff of which Spitzer's successful subjects are made. It is the same testimonial they give at ex-gay meetings and in church. I do not mean to suggest that all the successes were lying, although I suspect that some of them were. The majority, however, may believe they are no longer gay because the alternative is terrifying. This is why claims of successful conversions come only from the religious right (mainly protestant) community, as did Spitzer's subjects and the few successes from the Shidlo and Schroeder study. Religious gays are cognitively different than nonreligious ones. Therefore, one can choose subjects based upon the conclusion one wants to draw. Just as criminal lawyers know that the voir dire (the selection of a jury) may decide the guilt or innocence of their clients even before the presentation of evidence, so too can subject selection in psychological research determine its conclusion even before the data is collected. Spitzer knows that, too.

The Question of Strategies

What would be the best response by gay professionals to the ex-gay movement? My thought is that we have done some things wrong.

1. Many papers published in the gay professional press repeatedly attack the ex-gay movement and reparative therapy. Why give them so much publicity? Attacking them provides them a wider audience than they would have if we ignored them. Publicity (even if negative) provides the opportunity for them to enlist particularly vulnerable people to their side.
2. We have created a "hit list" of enemies that we attack at every opportunity. They respond with press notices about the cabal of homosexuals controlling the media and professional associations. We should stop mentioning them by name. Even a casual reader of this [chapter] will have noticed that I have tried to practice what I preach. In the place of a hit list, we might publicize a "heroes" list, a group of people who have made the lives of gay people better because of their professional work. I'll make the first nomination: Greg Herek at the University of California, Davis, for his work on heterosexism.
3. There is no reason why we must adopt the terminology of the people who hate us.[27] We should deny the word "therapy" to the religious right. If religion is their bailiwick, let them (and us) talk about "religious conversions," not therapy. Of course we cannot stop them from using any terms they want, but we should reserve "psychotherapy" for professional use. Shidlo and Schroeder made an attempt to follow this approach by using the term "intervention" rather than therapy. It will come as no surprise to learn that I would also reject "reparative" as a descriptive term. With few exceptions, the people who use the term are religiously based. We should keep them there. Religion-based conversions should be identified as such; psychotherapy, on the other hand, is defined by state (i.e., secular) law. They do not

practice therapy, reparative, or any other kind. If we want to discuss religious conversions, let us call it that.

4. We do a poor job at publicity. Some of the ex-gay ministries have produced very sophisticated Web sites. I am not sure we have done as well. A religious gay person in conflict is welcomed to their sites, but we do not have equivalent Web sites. Perhaps there should be a site specifically devoted toward religious gay people in conflict about coming out. All the other gay Web sites might have links to it.

5. The subjects in the cited studies were mainly protestant. Why are they so overrepresented? We might consider fine-tuning our community services to appeal to the religious gays most in need of help.

NOTES

1. Nature/nurture arguments actually go back as far as Aristotle, who believed that Catamites had an extra nerve that ran down the spine to the anus.

2. It was said that feathers made the body too hot, which increased feelings of desire. Many masturbation devices were patented, including some for horses.

3. For fifty cents, one could buy a device that prevented you from sleeping on your back, which would decrease the probability of a wet dream, or so they believed.

4. One can argue that the controversy between inheritance and the social construction of homosexuality is irrelevant because the bigot's hate is independent of causation.

5. Castration as a medical treatment was outlawed only in 1950.

6. Electrical leads were implanted in his brain. He was put into a room containing a naked prostitute. The leads were stimulated by electricity, in the belief that it would be associated with having sex with a women. It did not work.

7. Androgen replacement was based upon the belief that homosexuality represented failed masculinity. By giving gay men testosterone, a male hormone, they believed it would lead to heterosexual behavior. Since the effect of testosterone is highly correlated with libido, its only effect was to create a particularly horny group of gay men.

8. All forms of aversive conditioning used a paradigm of showing sexy pictures to a gay man. Electrical aversive gave him a shock if the picture aroused him. In chemical aversion, he was given a drug (usually anectine) that made him vomit. In covert conditioning, the subject was asked to imagine himself vomiting to the picture.

9. Physiological testing is not without problems but a discussion of them is beyond the scope of this review.

10. In 1995, I tried to join NARTH by filling out their application and paying dues. In a letter from its then-Secretary Joseph Nicolosi, dated November 8, 1995, I

was rejected for membership because, "We consider your professional views and objectives as too radically opposed to ours." They returned my check.

11. The word "therapist" was used to mean anyone who claimed to be one, not a state licensed professional.

12. We do not know if they were paid directors. This seemingly trivial question becomes relevant when we review the other studies.

13. We do not know what "at some time" means. Did they actually have gay sex or only fantasize about it or masturbate to it?

14. This tells us that almost 60 percent had not come out sexually yet.

15. "Treatment" is in quotes because its nature is never specified in the study. It includes religious counselors, converts in the ex-gay movement, and in some cases (but an unknown number) of licensed professionals.

16. "Yearning" seems redundant in the list and likely to skew the results in the direction of change.

17. Sodomy was defined as any nonreproductive act, oral, anal, or masturbatory. While it also applied to heterosexuals, it was virtually only used against gay people.

18. This is an important bias.

19. This is another biased question. A better question would be something to the effect of, "Please tell me in what ways this counseling both helped and/or harmed you"; in a counterbalanced design— _ help/harm, harm/help.

20. We should be thankful to Shidlo and Schroeder for informing us that religious school officials coerce some gays into treatment. Students are given the choice of treatment or expulsion.

21. It is never really clear what "success" means, nor do they operationalize "struggling."

22. The authors could have cited the case of Paul Cameron who was expelled from the American Psychological Association on December 2, 1983 for misrepresenting data about homosexuality. He made a number of outrageous and incorrect statements in the United States District Court of Dallas, saying that research proved that homosexuals sexually abuse children more than do straights, and that gays are forty-three percent more likely to commit crimes than straights. These and other equally egregious claims caused Judge Buckmeyer to accuse him of fraud. One can read more about Cameron on Greg Herek's Web site at http://psychology.ucdavis. edu/rainbow/index.html.

23. http://www.narth.com.

24. The reader should note the similarity between Spitzer's 17 percent cure and Freund's 20 percent.

25. While social constructionists reject the notion that we can genetically design gay or straight babies, they will be particularly cognizant of the psychological damage it will create in a family, and the insidious effects it will have on society—successful or not.

26. With keener perception than Spitzer, Drescher (1998, 2001) speaks to the manner in which the ex-gay movement politics for laws against gay people. He presents convincing evidence that they want to deny adoption rights for gay people by claiming that gay couples are unstable. He cites some of their threadworn stereotypes about youngsters, such as that boys are hunters, but girls are born to be mothers.

27. I know that the Christian right says that they hate the sin, not the sinner. If they would only practice what they preach. At a call-in radio program, after callers mentioned that they were Christians, they said to me, "We should do with you like Hitler did with the Jews"; "I hope you all die of AIDS"; "We should lock you all up in a barn and burn it down."

REFERENCES

Bancroft, J. (1974), *Deviant Sexual Behavior: Modifications and Assessment*. London: Oxford University Press.

Bayer, R. (1981), *Homosexuality and American Psychiatry: The Politics of Diagnosis*. New York: Basic Books.

Bergler, E. (1956), *Homosexuality: Disease or Way of Life*. New York: Ballantine.

Besen, W. (2003), *Anything but Straight: Unmaking the Scandals and Lies Behind the Ex-Gay Myth*. Binghamton, NY: Harrington Park Press.

Blanchard, R., Klassen, P., Dickey, R., Kuban, M. E., & Blak, T. (2001), Sensitivity and specificity of the phallometric test for pedophilia in nonadmitting sex offenders. *Psychological Assessment*, 13:118-126.

Braslow, J. (1997), *Mental Ills and Bodily Cures: Psychiatric Treatment in the First Half of the Twentieth Century*. Berkeley: University of California Press.

Bremer, J. (1959), *Asexualization, a Follow-Up Study of 244 Cases*. New York: McMillan.

Cautela, J. (1967), Covert sensitization. *Psychological Republic*, 20:459-468.

Davison, G. (1974), Presidential Address to the Eighth Annual Convention of the Association for Advancement of Behavior Therapy, Chicago, November 2.

Davison, G. (1976), Homosexuality: The ethical challenge. *J. Consulting & Clinical Psychology*, 44:157-162.

Davison, G. (1978), Not can but ought: The treatment of homosexuality. *J. Consulting & Clinical Psychology*, 46:170-172.

Davison, G. (2001), Values and constructionism in clinical assessment: Some historical and personal perspectives on behavior therapy. In: *A History of the Behavior Therapies: Founders' Personal Histories*, eds. W. T. O'Donohue, D.A. Henderson, S. C. Hayes, J. E. Fisher, & L. J. Hayes. Reno: Context Press, pp. 337-357.

Dörner, G. (1983), Letter to the editor. *Archives of Sexual Behavior*, 12:577-582.

Drescher, J. (1998), I'm your handyman: A history of reparative therapies. *J. Homosexual.*, 36(1):19-42. Reprinted in: *Sexual Conversion Therapy: Ethical, Clinical and Research Perspectives*, eds. A. Shidlo, M. Schroeder, & J. Drescher. Binghamton, NY: The Haworth Press, 2001, pp. 5-24.

Drescher, J. (2001), Ethical concerns raised when patients seek to change same-sex attractions. *J. Gay & Lesbian Psychother.*, 5(3/4):181-210. Reprinted in: *Sexual Conversion Therapy: Ethical, Clinical and Research Perspectives*, eds. A.

Shidlo, M. Schroeder, & J. Drescher. Binghamton, NY: The Haworth Press, 2001, pp. 181-210.

Drescher, J. (2002), Ethical issues in treating gay and lesbian patients. *Psychiatric Clinics of North America*, 25(3):605-621.

Freund, K. (1977), Should homosexuality arouse therapeutic concern. *J. Homosexuality*, 2:235-240.

Gagnon, J. H. (1990), Gender preference in erotic relations: The Kinsey Scale and sexual scripts. In: *Homosexuality/Heterosexuality: Concepts of Sexual Orientation*, eds. D. McWhirter, S. Sanders, & J. Reinisch. New York: Oxford University Press, pp. 177-207.

Gilfoyle, T. J. (1992), *City of Eros*. New York: W.W. Norton.

Green, R. (1987), *The "Sissy Boy Syndrome" and the Development of Homosexuality*. New Haven, CT: Yale University Press.

Greenberg, A. S. & Bailey, J. M. (2001), Parental selection of children's sexual orientation. *Archives of Sexual Behavior*, 30:423-438.

Haldeman, D. (1991), Sexual orientation conversion therapy for gay men and lesbians: A scientific examination. In: *Homosexuality: Research Implications for Public Policy*, eds. J. C. Gonsiorek & J. D. Weinrich. Newbury Park, CA: Sage Publications, pp. 149-161.

Haldeman, D. (1999), The pseudo-science of sexual orientation conversion therapy. *Angles: The Policy Journal of the Institute for Gay and Lesbian Strategic Studies*, 4:1-4.

Haldeman, D. (2001), Therapeutic antidotes: Helping gay and bisexual men recover from conversion therapies. *J. Gay & Lesb. Psychother.*, 5(3/4):117-130. Reprinted in: *Sexual Conversion Therapy: Ethical, Clinical and Research Perspectives*, eds. A. Shidlo, M. Schroeder, & J. Drescher. Binghamton, NY: The Haworth Press, 2001, pp. 117-130.

Halleck, S. L. (1971), *The Politics of Therapy*. New York: Science House.

Heath, R. G. (1972), Pleasure and brain activity in man. *J. Nervous & Mental Diseases*, 154:3-18.

Kinsey, A., Pomeroy, W., & Martin, C. (1948), *Sexual Behavior in the Human Male*. Philadelphia, PA: Saunders.

Kinsey, A., Pomeroy, W., Martin, C., & Gebhard, P. (1953), *Sexual Behavior in the Human Female*. Philadelphia, PA: Saunders.

Kosnik, A., Carroll, W., Cunningham, A., Modras, R., & Schulte, J. (1977), *Human Sexuality: New Directions in American Catholic Thought*. New York: Paulist Press.

Laan, E., Everaerd, W., Bellen, G., & Hanewalk, G. (1994), Women's sexual and emotional responses to male- and female-produced erotica. *Archives of Sexual Behavior*, 23:153-169.

Lawson, R. (1987), *Scandal in the Adventist-funded program to "heal" homosexuals: Failure, sexual exploitation, official silence, and attempts to rehabilitate the exploiter and his methods.* Paper given at the American Sociological Association, Chicago.

Levine, M. P. & Troiden, R. R. (1988), The myth of sexual compulsivity. *J. Sex Research,* 25:347-364.

Lund, S. & Renna, C. (2003), An analysis of the media response to the Spitzer study. *J. Gay & Lesb. Psychother.,* 7(3):55-67.

McConaghy, N. (1969), Subjective and penile plethysmography responses following aversion-relief and apomorphine aversion therapy for homosexual impulses. *Brit. J. Psychiat.,* 115:723-730.

Osburn, C. D. (2003), Colleges cave to Pentagon threat. *The Gay & Lesbian Review Worldwide,* 10:28-29.

Pillard, R. C. & Weinrich, J. D. (1986), Evidence of familial nature of male homosexuality. *Archives General Psychiatry,* 43:808-812.

Popper, K. P. (1959), *The Logic of Scientific Discovery.* Toronto: University of Toronto Press.

Quadland, M. C. (1985), Compulsive sexual behavior: Definition of a problem and an approach to treatment. *J. Sex & Marital Therapy,* 11:121-132.

Rieber, I. & Sigusch, V. (1979), Guest editorial: Psychosurgery on sex offenders and sexual "deviants" in West Germany. *Archives of Sexual Behavior,* 8:523-527.

Sandfort, T. (2003), Studying sexual orientation change: A methodological reveiw of the Spitzer study. "Can some gay men and lesbians change their sexual orientation?" *J. Gay & Lesb. Psychother.,* 7(3):15-29.

Schmidt, G. (1984), Allies and persecutors: Science and medicine in the homosexual issue. *J. Homosexuality,* 10:127-140.

Schmidt, G. & Schorsch, E. (1981), Psychosurgery of sexually deviant patients: Review and analysis of new empirical findings. *Archives of Sexual Behavior,* 10: 301-323.

Schroeder, M. & Shidlo, A. (2001), Ethical issues in sexual orientation conversion therapies: An empirical study of consumers. *J. Gay & Lesb. Psychother.,* 5(3/4): 131:166. Reprinted in: *Sexual Conversion Therapy: Ethical, Clinical and Research Perspectives,* eds. A. Shidlo, M. Schroeder, & J. Drescher. Binghamton, NY: The Haworth Press, 2001, pp. 131-166.

Sell, R. L. (1997), Defining and measuring sexual orientation: A review. *Archives of Sexual Behavior,* 26:643-658.

Sigusch, V., Schorsch, E., Dannecker, M., & Schmidt, G. (1982), Guest Editorial: Official statement by the German Society for Sex Research (*Duetsche Gesellschaft fur Sexualforschung e. V.*) on the research of Prof. Dr. Gunter Dörner on the subject of homosexuality. *Archives of Sexual Behavior,* 11:445-449.

Shidlo, A. & Schroeder, M. (2002), Changing sexual orientation; A consumers' report. *Professional Psychology: Research & Practice,* 33(3):249-259.

Silverstein, C. (1972), *Behavior Modification and the Gay Community*. Paper Presented at the Annual Convention of the Association for Advancement of Behavior Therapy, New York City, October.

Silverstein, C. (1976/1977), "Even psychiatry can profit from its past mistakes." *J. Homosexuality*, 2:153-158.

Silverstein, C. (1977), Homosexuality: The ethical challenge, Paper 2. *J. Homosexuality*, 2:205-211.

Silverstein, C. (1991), Psychological and medical treatments of homosexuality. In: *Homosexuality: Research Implications for Public Policy*, eds. J. C. Gonsiorek & J. D. Weinrich. Newbury Park: Sage Publications, pp. 101-114.

Spitzer, R. L. (2003), Can some gay men and lesbians change their sexual orientation? 200 participants reporting a change from homosexual to heterosexual orientation. *Archives of Sexual Behavior*, 32(5):403-417.

Stall, S. (1897), *What a Young Man Ought to Know*. Toronto: The Vir Publishing Company.

Suppe, F. (1984), Classifying sexual disorders: The diagnostic and statistical manual of the American Psychiatric Association. *J. Homosexuality*, 9: 9-28.

Tennent, G., Bancroft, J., & Cass, J. (1974), The control of deviant sexual behavior by drugs: A double-blind controlled study of benperidol, chlorpromazine and placebo. *Archives of Sexual Behavior*, 3: 261-271.

West, D. J. (2001), Parental selection of children's sexual orientation: A commentary. *Archives of Sexual Behavior*, 30:439-441.

Wolff, C. (1986), *Magnus Hirschfeld: A Portrait of a Pioneer in Sexology*. New York: Quartet Books.

An Analysis of the Media Response to the Spitzer Study

Sean Lund
Cathy Renna

This study is an attempt to "connect the dots" between the political, cultural, and psychotherapeutic worlds that collide when the issue of "ex-gays" and "reparative therapies and ministries" become part of public discourse.

In May 2001, one of the authors of this analysis (Sean Lund) received an e-mail regarding a study he had been tracking for the previous two years. Robert L. Spitzer, MD, a researcher and psychiatrist who had participated in the removal of homosexuality from the American Psychiatric Association's (APA) DSM-II list of mental disorders in 1973[1] had been conducting a study on sexual orientation. The study's thesis was that some highly motivated individuals, employing religious or psychotherapeutic means, could make substantial changes in more than one indicator of sexual orientation. Spitzer made some disclaimers about his study's results: such changes were not likely among more than a small fraction of the population; the selection of subjects was largely guided by (and the sample consisted mostly of) professional "ex-gays," and that radio host Laura Schlesinger had been actively and publicly soliciting subjects for this study on her nationally syndicated talk-show, "The Dr. Laura Program." Spitzer also later publicly stated that his results did not constitute a representative sample.

This chapter appeared originally under the same title in *Journal of Gay & Lesbian Psychotherapy* 7(3):55-67. Copyright 2003 The Haworth Press.

Two days before Dr. Spitzer's findings were to be presented at the 2001 annual gathering of the APA in New Orleans, the study and its conclusions—which had not yet been peer reviewed or even published—were leaked to the Associated Press. Simultaneously, nearly a half-dozen press releases from organizational opponents of gay and lesbian civil rights and promoters of so-called "conversion therapies" materialized. They claimed that Spitzer's study validated what they had been saying all along: that gays and lesbians "choose" homosexuality and that they can be "cured." And on their heels, a chorus of voices in the gay and lesbian community criticized the study's author, methodology, and conclusions, and focused attention on the exploitation of the study by antigay political groups.

For the week after the story broke, the news coverage focused on Spitzer's study as the latest development in the ongoing struggle for and against gay and lesbian civil rights. Pro-gay and antigay spokespeople debated the issues on television, print outlets printed news and feature articles on the issue, and opinion columnists declared their support for their skepticism of Spitzer's results (and, usually, for or against gay people themselves). For weeks afterward, letters to the editor poured into newspapers across the country on the subject of anything and everything gay.

THE EX-GAY MOVEMENT

On October 7, 1998, one of this paper's authors (Cathy Renna) was in between press conferences at the National Press Club in Washington, DC. She had just witnessed a press conference, sponsored by the Family Research Council (FRC) but joined by other groups—the American Family Association, the Center for Reclaiming America, Concerned Women for America, Focus on the Family, the National Association for the Research and Therapy of Homosexuality (NARTH), and a host of others—whose principal political activities involve opposing lesbian and gay civil equality. The topic: a new series of ads to be broadcast in Washington, DC, claiming that, through prayer and religious experience, gays and lesbians could "change" their sexual orientation.

These ads, following on the heels of a previous series of print ads that had run in major national newspapers in July 1998, concluded with the slogan, "It's not about hate. . . . It's about hope." Those ads had generated a year-long firestorm of media coverage of the emerging "ex-gay" movement and the debate over whether a homosexual orientation is a choice—and whether it is changeable.

The notion that homosexuality is a "choice" has long been one of the two tent pole arguments (the other being biblical proscriptions) in a coordinated religious/political campaign orchestrated by those opposed to full civil equality for lesbians, gay men, bisexuals, and transgender (GLBT) people. The argument is that, if civil rights are based on inherent, immutable differences that provoke discrimination (as in the case of race), and if gays and lesbians can choose not to be gay or lesbian, then there is no need for laws to codify their equality. As a result, the success or failure of attempts to change sexual orientation from gay to straight has become a litmus test for whether gays and lesbians should be allowed to exist at all.

Thus, one speaker at the October 1998 FRC press conference was their policy analyst Yvette Cantu, a self-professed "ex-gay." She was, at the time, paid by FRC to speak as a living testimonial to the ability of religion and/or therapy to "cure" and "prevent" homosexuality. As she put it, "If someone had told me seven years ago that I would be speaking at a National Coming Out of Homosexuality Day press conference, I would have thought they were crazy. Fortunately, I met people who were not afraid to tell me the truth about my lifestyle—not only about its damaging effects, but that I could be free from it."

This organized ex-gay movement consists of a mix of secular and religious organizations that promote or market "sexual conversion" therapy experiences for gays and lesbians. Prominent among them are the National Association for Research and Therapy of Homosexuality (NARTH), an organization of mental health professionals, some of whom are ex-gays themselves,[2] and Exodus International, a lay group whose members claim to be or who aspire to become ex-gays. Professional and lay groups work in concert with political groups such as the Family Research Council, Concerned Women for America, American Family Association, Center for Reclaiming America, etc., in efforts to persuade the general public that a homosexual orientation is mutable. This coordinated effort attempts to undermine a growing public awareness, understanding, and acceptance of gay and lesbian lives, and to reverse continuing advances in GLBT civil rights. On one front, overtly political conservative groups such as FRC directly challenge legislative and cultural advances through lobbying, media appearances, and fund-raising materials designed to warn the general public of a "homosexual lobby" that "threatens to destroy the family." On another front, "ex-gay" groups and "reparative therapists" use testimonials, publish inflammatory tracts, and—as in the case of Spitzer's study—tout and selectively interpret research of questionable validity to marginalize the very notion of gay identity.

The "ex-gay" movement appears to have several broad goals:

- To work in coordination with other institutional opponents of gay and lesbian civil equality in efforts to persuade policy-makers and the general public that sexual orientation is both abnormal and mutable. From this perspective, civil rights and protections for GLBT people as vulnerable sexual minorities would be deemed unnecessary.
- To create a perception in the minds of vulnerable gays and lesbians struggling with private/public disapprobation of their sexual identities that there is a need to undergo a procedure that will ostensibly solve many of life's problems by making them heterosexual.
- To promote ex-gay movement leaders as legitimate spokespeople on gay cultural/political issues.
- To change the public perception that homosexuality is a normal variant of human sexuality.
- To destigmatize therapeutic attempts to change sexual orientation in an effort to undermine the APA's long-standing position that homosexuality is not a mental disorder.

This final goal is particularly worth underscoring. The pejorative labeling of gay and lesbian identities is important to an antigay movement that argues homosexuality is intrinsically disordered (in the religious sense) and that gay and lesbian people are psychologically disordered. Antigay extremists believe that a return to the pre-1973 position of the mental health professions regarding sexual orientation would tilt public opinion in their favor. The reclaiming of the illness label is equally important to the ex-gay movement, whose members hold a unique status as the only interest group that actively demonstrates at APA meetings for the right to be declared psychiatrically disordered! The shared goals of these two groups is not coincidental.

Today, many ex-gay ministries have financial and/or programmatic ties to an assortment of organizations. In addition, the opinions of reparative therapists are frequently cited by antigay political groups as "evidence" that ostensibly nonpolitical "mental health experts" still acknowledge the "pathology" of homosexuality. In this way, social conservatives have tried to back their "moral" claims about the social unsuitability of homosexuality with whatever selectively chosen "scientific evidence" they believe substantiates their moral viewpoint.[3]

Despite its current ability to grab headlines, the ex-gay movement as it operates today did not come into existence until recently. Mental health professionals advocating in favor of reparative therapy and ex-gay groups such as Exodus did exist, but they were not part of an orchestrated political campaign. However, in 1998, the antigay religious political movement—having suffered a number of setbacks on the cultural front and a legal one in President Clinton's signing of an executive order banning discrimination based on sexual orientation in federal jobs—launched print and TV ads proclaiming that "freedom from homosexuality is possible" and moved the ex-gay movement to the front and center of the culture wars.

THE EX-GAY ADS

The first wave of print ads—which ran between July 13 to 15, 1998—varied considerably in terms of content and message. The first ad ran on July 13 in *The New York Times* (Figure 34.1). It featured a series of quotes from Anne Paulk, identified in the caption superimposed on her photo as "wife, mother, former lesbian." Below the headline ("I'm living proof that Truth can set you free"), was a testimonial from Paulk detailing her abuse as a four-year-old by a teenage boy, her attraction to women, her decision to "forsake homosexuality," and her eventual "road to healing." At the bottom of the ad was the closing tagline that appeared in all five ads—"If you really love someone, you'll tell them the truth"—and a list of phone numbers to get in touch with the ad's sponsors.

The second ad (Figure 34.2) ran the next day (July 14) in *The Washington Post,* and also appeared on July 27, 1998, in *The Los Angeles Times*. It centered on a photo of a group of people identified

FIGURE 34.1. Ex-gay ad in *The New York Times,* July 13, 1998.

with a vague caption suggesting that they were part of an Exodus gathering. The photo was accompanied by a headline stating, "We're standing for the truth that homosexuals can change." The text of the ad focused on "Christian" objections to homosexuality. Homosexuality was included in a list of "sexual sins" that included premarital sex, adultery, and prostitution. The ad's text also asserted a number of causes of homosexuality, including "rejection from early childhood and lack of bonding to same-sex parents, sexual violence and rape, or mental and emotional abuse."

The third ad (July 15, 1998, in *USA Today*) shifted the focus away from ex-gays (Figure 34.3). Instead, it focused on a free-speech argument that defended former football player Reggie White, who had made public statements against gays and lesbians earlier in the year. The ad was titled "Toward an open debate on homosexual behavior." It employed such rhetorical statements as "Tyranny flourishes where

FIGURE 34.2. Ex-gay ad in *The Washington Post,* July 14, 1998.

free speech is forbidden," saying, "That's why all Americans should shudder when homosexual activists routinely use the tactics of threats, intimidation, blackmail, and deception to strangle a free and open exchange on homosexual behavior."

The broadcast ads—announced at the October 8, 1998, press conference but which did not run until mid-1999 due to the public outcry over the murder of Matthew Shepard in October 1998—featured ex-gay leader Michael Johnston. In the ad, Johnston details how his homosexuality drove him to drug abuse, promiscuity, and to contracting HIV. The ad also included comments from his mother about his "conversion."[4]

From a public relations standpoint, the intention of the ads is clear. They were not intended to reach or persuade gays and lesbians struggling with their sexual orientation. Instead, they were placed strategically in *The Washington Post, USA Today, The New York Times, The*

FIGURE 34.3. Ex-gay ad in *USA Today,* July 15, 1998.

Los Angeles Times, and Washington, DC's UPN station. Why? According to Bill Carter, spokesman for the Center for Reclaiming America, it was because "that's where the policymakers are."

But there was another reason for these calculated placements: it was not just the ads that were designed to convey the ex-gay movement's messages, it was the story of the ads themselves.

EARNED MEDIA

Much of the focus on "ex-gay" campaigns revolves around the concept of earned media, or what used to be called "free media." Earned media is essentially any media coverage that is not paid for, such as a news article or an op-ed piece. It is the most effective way to build credibility for an organization, cause, or ideological position. Earned media can take the form of coverage in either uncontrolled media (news articles in which a reporter is the ultimate arbiter of the organization's message) or controlled media (op-eds in which, aside from limited editorial discretion on the part of the outlet, the organization's message is under the control of the organization itself).

In the case of the "ex-gay" ads (and the rebuttal ads), the sponsoring organizations used a standard technique in public relations: they purchased ads in a limited number of high-profile venues with the expectation that the content of the ads would result in earned media visibility (or "hits"). Social issues advertising has long employed a variety of tactics, such as inclusion of celebrities in ads, use of inflammatory language and arguments, or attacks on public figures, to create newsworthiness and generate earned media.

Earned media, especially that which is uncontrolled, conveys a tremendous amount of respectability and credibility. Media consumers look to their newspapers, magazines, and news broadcasts not only for news, but for what those outlets—in their function as gatekeepers—think is news. If a newspaper believes something is newsworthy, a sense of importance and legitimacy is conveyed to the reader simply by virtue of its presence in the pages of the paper. And if it is being reported on by a staff news writer (as opposed to a self-penned op-ed), the impact, prominence, and perceived importance of the story or issue is heightened even further.

In the case of ex-gay ads, the ads on both sides were targeted at earning media at the national level (major newspapers, national news broadcasts) as the next phase of the ongoing "trend" story of the gay/antigay conflict. This was part of an attempt to lift the issue to national prominence and create a mass secondary audience for the messages in the ads of the general public. And this was also where the media's routines took a leading role in shaping the terms of the debate.

NEWS MEDIA ROUTINES AND FILTERS

- "An explosive new study says some gay people can turn straight if they really want to."
- "Furious gay-rights groups yesterday blasted an explosive new Columbia University study that suggests some homosexuals can turn straight—if they just try hard enough."

- "Can gay men and women become heterosexual? A controversial new study says yes—if they really want to. Critics, though, say the study's subjects may be deluding themselves and that the subject group was scientifically invalid because many of them were referred by anti-gay religious groups."
- "A study released on Wednesday concluded that many homosexuals can change their sexual orientation through counseling, but another said most attempts to counsel change fail and some are harmful."

These were but a handful of the news leads reporting the preliminary results of Spitzer's study on the efficacy of reparative therapy. Coverage of the Spitzer study was shaped by several internal and external influences, among them:

- the coverage of the ex-gay ads nearly three years earlier;
- journalistic emphasis on conflict and controversy; and
- an advance Associated Press story that misreported key aspects of Spitzer's work and set a sensationalistic tone that the other outlets had to struggle to overcome.

As a result, a highly complicated study—which its author has admitted has significant limitations and was conducted with questionable methodology—was reported in a manner that offered little in the way of true scientific insight but rather fed the existing conflict between pro-gay and antigay advocates.

Media themes often carry from story to story when the assumption is that the more recent incident is simply the latest installment in an ongoing trend. Coverage of the Spitzer study offers an opportunity to observe how the media's prior coverage of the ex-gay ads shaped and informed that coverage. Both stories were largely framed by antigay political groups and gay organizations that faced off in a series of televised debates (primarily on cable news outlets) and provided sets of dueling quotes for newspapers. Gay spokespeople argued against the efficacy and ethics of reparative therapy, while antigay religious groups argued the immorality of homosexuality and offered anecdotal evidence (or, in Spitzer's case, the support of a long-perceived ally of the gay community) for the proposition that gays could change.

An emphasis on conflict and controversy represents the foundation of most news coverage. Conflict is usually thought to be intrinsically more interesting to reporters and to media consumers than harmony and unity. Consequently, stories about advances in astronomy, economic theory, or psychotherapeutic techniques, for example, capture our collective attention less than stories about race relations, television violence, or drug abuse. Because media in the United States are usually commercial in nature, media outlets spend much of their time trying to figure out what their audiences want, working to strike a perfect balance between the information they have an obligation to deliver and a manner of delivery that appeals to the consumer. In most cases, conflict and controversy sell (and the media is, at its core, a commercial enterprise).

Journalistic values of conflict and controversy, however, tend to exert a dominant influence on media coverage of science that intersects with issues of cultural dispute. For examples, there are studies correlating images of violence on television with actual acts of violence committed by youth. However, discussion of such studies is usually reduced to a series of exchanged barbs by those who want television programmers to take responsibility for program content and by those who say that it is the parents' responsibility to monitor and regulate their children's media consumption. Why? Because the two warring factions have more of a stake in the outcome of the dispute than the researcher. Because it is easier for the media to frame an issue as one of social controversy than as one of scientific nuance. And because audiences are intimately familiar with—and likely want to see more of—the continuing sociocultural debate.

Similarly, the coverage of the Spitzer study was less about its scientific merit than it was about the ability of groups on one side of the debate to manipulate the science to their advantage and for groups on the other side to scrutinize the study's methods and limitations in an effort to counter the arguments of their opponents.

One of the most distressing aspects of this coverage was the near-complete absence of objective scientific voices from the discussion. Instead, the media relied on a firmly established rolodex of GLBT community leaders and allies (who approached the issue through a civil rights filter) and antigay representatives (who approached the issue largely through moral and religious filters) for commentary. And although gay organizations such as GLAAD spent much time calling attention to the deep methodological flaws in Spitzer's sampling technique and research question, those points were very likely lost on an audience that had a predetermined expectation of (and co-related level of receptiveness to) what a group called the Gay & Lesbian Alliance Against Defamation would have to say about the study.

Considering the role studies, surveys, and statistics play in quantifying newsworthy issues and opinions, objective analysts who can provide media professionals with sound appraisals and criticism of a study's reliability and validity are crucial. Without them, the science that touches on social issues will inevitably be employed solely to support or negate existing political/cultural arguments, especially if there are well-entrenched sides in conflict over the global issues raised by the science.

It is also worth considering whether the coverage of Spitzer's study would have veered so far into politicized sensationalism had objective scientific standards and fair media coverage been applied to his work. Words such as "explosive" and "controversial" in describing his study might have been replaced with terms such as "questionable," "problematic," "indeterminate," and "inconclusive." Inaccurate characterizations of Spitzer's study (mostly by antigay groups) as determining that homosexuality was "neither innate nor immutable" (as Reuters reported) might not have been considered for publication. And, for that matter, the considerable flaws in the study itself might have precluded its legitimization through mainstream media coverage at all.

This points to one of the fundamental problems with media coverage of scientific research: when the findings are as preliminary, as ambiguously stated, and as methodologically questionable as Spitzer's, the media do not have mechanisms in place to objectively evaluate the quality of the science. The media is consequently forced to rely on political filters to tell the story. Reuters allowing a quote about the innateness of homosexuality into an article about a study that has nothing to do with the "causes" of sexual orientation—only its ability to change—exemplifies how reporting that turns to political sources to provide scientific commentary misleads the audience and compromises the accuracy and quality of the journalism.

The other fundamental problem is the media's tendency to sensationalize—especially when the story escalates an existing conflict. When the AP's Malcolm Ritter published his original story before

Spitzer presented at the APA meeting, the lead sentence read: "An explosive new study says that some gays can go straight if they really want to." Two things stand out: (1) The use of the term "explosive" to describe the study. Technically, it was not the study that was explosive but rather the way the study was leaked to and exploited by certain political groups. The term "explosive" seemed a term more likely applied to an advertisement for a new movie than a news story about a scientific study of any kind. (2) No one in the media considered addressing the subject of bisexuality in the initial coverage (or frankly, in much of the follow-up) points to the other problem with media reliance on a short list of commentators: a lack of diversity that often results in obvious angles and criticisms going unheard.

CONCLUSIONS

In reviewing the extensive media coverage of the "ex-gay" ads and the release of the Spitzer study, several patterns can be discerned. First, media coverage routines dictate that coverage of scientific issues that intersect with political or cultural ones tend to minimize the science and focus instead on the political or cultural "conflict." Unfortunately, this tendency marginalizes legitimate scientific insights and promotes simplistic, misrepresentative interpretations of complex issues.

Second, the argument that conversion therapies aimed at gays and lesbians can be regarded as strictly a matter of science (and thus can be reported on in scientific terms only) is questionable at best. The historic and ongoing engagement between those who fight for and against cultural and legal equality for gays, lesbians, and bisexuals—combined with the opposition's insistence that any evidence that sexual orientation is mutable or a "choice" negates the validity of legal safeguards for gays and lesbians—suggests that the media's responsibility to cover related issues in a fair, accurate, and comprehensive manner is of vital importance.

NOTES

1. For a full account of those events, see Bayer, R. (1981), *Homosexuality and American Psychiatry: The Politics of Diagnosis*. New York: Basic Books.

2. See Drescher, J. (1998), I'm your handyman: A history of reparative therapies. *J. Homosexual.,* 36(1):19-42. Reprinted in: *Sexual Conversion Therapy: Ethical, Clinical and Research Perspectives,* eds. A. Shidlo, M. Schroeder & J. Drescher. Binghamton, NY: The Haworth Press, pp. 5-24.

3. The model for this approach can be found in the creation science movement, which argues in a pseudoscientific way against the theory of evolution. See Tiffen, L. (1994), *Creationism's Upside-Down Pyramid: How Science Refutes Fundamentalism.* Amherst, NY: Prometheus Books.

4. Johnston was also featured prominently in *It's Not Gay,* a video produced by the American Family Association that warns of the "health risks" associated with the gay and lesbian "lifestyle."

35

Political Science

Wayne Besen

THE SIGNIFICANCE OF SPITZER

When I was three years old, in 1973, all I cared about was collecting plastic dinosaurs and toy soldiers. Little did I know that I, similar to all gay people at the time, was considered mentally ill by the world's most respected psychiatric organizations. All that changed, however, in this year, in part to the open-mindedness of one researcher, Dr. Robert L. Spitzer.

Similar to many psychiatrists of this time period, Spitzer never questioned why lesbian and gay people were considered mentally ill. He simply assumed that homosexuality automatically disqualified a person from basic sanity and mental fitness. His schooling reinforced these ideas by presenting the biased work of antigay psychoanalysts Bergler, Socarides, and others as undisputed fact.[1]

Spitzer's view was unexpectedly turned upside down in the fall of 1972 while watching a presentation by the Association for the Advancement of Behavior Therapy, a group that specialized in electroshock "treatment" of gay people. Suddenly, the meeting was interrupted and overrun by screaming advocates from the Gay Activists Alliance (GAA) who stormed the presentation to protest the abuse of homosexuals by these psychiatrists. Aside from the activists in the room, nearly 100 protested outside the New York building, handing out fliers that asked, "Torture Anyone?"[2]

This chapter appeared originally in *Anything But Straight: Unmasking the Scandals and Lies Behind the Ex-Gay Myth,* by Wayne Besen (Binghamton, NY: Harrington Park Press, pp. 227-241), and was republished in the *Journal of Gay & Lesbian Psychotherapy* 7(3):69-82. Copyright 2003 The Haworth Press, Inc.

doi:10.1300/5503_35

Spitzer was livid and wanted the protesters removed from the building, but, in the heat of the moment, he and gay activist Ronald Gold began talking, and Spitzer for the first time listened to what the activists were saying. A married man with children and trained in the old school of psychiatry, it had never dawned on him that gays actually might be sane and grossly mistreated by the mental health establishment. According to the gay history book *Out for Good*, by Dudley Clendinen and Adam Nagourney, both reporters for *The New York Times*, the chance encounter between Gold and Spitzer proved to be of great significance. Spitzer was on the American Psychiatric Association's (APA) Committee of Nomenclature, the group responsible for revising the *Diagnostic and Statistical Manual*. As discussed in "Historic Injustice," only through revision of the DSM could homosexuality no longer be considered a mental illness.

For the next year, Spitzer intently listened to the heartfelt testimonies of lesbian and gay activists and educated himself on the issues and hardships facing these individuals. He was a sympathetic man who was willing to hear people who had previously been ignored. Through his willingness to listen to all sides of the issue, millions of homosexuals were declared sane in 1973. Because he challenged conventional wisdom and forced his counterparts to review science rather than stereotypes, the lesbian and gay community has long respected Dr. Spitzer.

"GET ME OUT OF THIS MESS!"

Fast-forward twenty-eight years later. "Wayne, help me get out of this mess," Spitzer begged me. "I'm being portrayed as a right wing zealot. I'm getting hate mail. Even members of my family are calling to say they can't believe I've joined the religious right and that I'm antigay."[3]

What could this respected Columbia University psychiatrist who helped remove homosexuality from the DSM have done to put him in such a pickle with the lesbian and gay community?

Spitzer's conundrum stemmed from a study he released on May 9, 2001, in New Orleans at the APA's annual meeting in which he claimed that *some*, "highly motivated" gay people could become straight through prayer, therapy, and "mentoring relationships."[4] This was obviously huge news, considering what Spitzer had done for lesbians and gay men in 1973.

What was eerie about Spitzer's new and controversial ex-gay study was how, in a twisted way, the circumstances that led to it mirrored his decision to embrace the pleas of gay activists in the early 1970s. At the 1999 APA convention in Washington, DC, Spitzer encountered a small throng of ex-gay protesters holding signs with slogans such as "Maybe the APA can't heal a homosexual, but god can!!"[5]

"He came up and said, 'You guys are out here again,'" antigay activist and admitted former homosexual Anthony Falzarano told the *Washington Times*. "I asked him if he would consider taking us more seriously and attend our press conference. I told him some prominent ex-gays would give their testimonies. To my surprise, he came."[6]

Spitzer was so mesmerized by these stories that after the press conference he asked the participants if they could provide him with a list of several hundred ex-gays so he could study whether they had actually changed sexual orientations, rather than simply their behavior. So the man who gave a sympathetic ear to a despised and misunderstood minority in 1973 was offering his sympathetic ear to another despised minority in 1999. However, although ex-gay activist groups may be despised, unlike the homosexuals of 1973, they are far from misunderstood. Anyone with a rudimentary knowledge of the political groups behind these misguided individuals understands that they exist, not to change gay people, but to change laws that protect gay and lesbian Americans from discrimination.

Spitzer, a neophyte in this political arena, did not understand whom he was embracing. He saw parallels between gay and ex-gay protests where there were none. Whereas one group's sole mission in 1973 was to get the mental health establishment to look objectively at the science, the mission of the ex-gays in 1999 was to deny gay people their basic civil rights. Unfortunately, Spitzer was unable or unwilling to differentiate between the aims of these two groups and, in my opinion, was duped into associating with strange bedfellows.

NO HALLUCINOGENIC HETEROS
OR SWITCH-HITTERS

I wrote Spitzer a letter expressing the Human Rights Campaign's concerns about his project. Although we welcomed new scientific research, we admonished him to steer clear of some very dubious characters and problems that might plague his study. The following are the main points emphasized in the letter and in subsequent communications.

Birds of a Feather. We made it abundantly clear that he should avoid coordinating with right-wing activists who held extremist antigay views. If these groups had anything to do with his study, it would be seen as biased and might affect the way it would be received by the scientific community, the media, and the public at large.

Ex-Gay for Pay? No Way. We warned Spitzer that in the current political environment his sample must be beyond reproach. This meant avoiding research subjects who were active members of right-wing organizations. Most important, none of the research subjects should make their living off of antigay lobbying or have a career as an ex-gay. In other words, no one who was "ex-gay for pay" should have been allowed to participate in Spitzer's study. This was common sense and a methodology any scientist should follow, we thought, when researching a controversial subject.

Truth or Dare. One indisputable fact about the ex-gay ministries and reparative therapy is that many of the people who claim "change" later recant and say they were always gay. Most of these individuals say they claimed they had changed only to find societal acceptance.

We told Spitzer that to do a study based solely on the testimonies of ex-gays is scientific suicide. Based on their history of double talk and double lives, any credible study on ex-gays must use objective data to see if the physical responses of subjects match their sworn testimonies. Two technologies would have enabled Spitzer to discern whether his subjects were truthful in their testimonies. The first is the polygraph, otherwise known as the lie detector test. Although this technology is not infallible, it is certainly more credible than relying on verbal testimony alone. The second technology is the penile plethysmograph, a test that checks sexual arousal by measuring blood flow into a subject's penis while he views erotic videos. University of Georgia psychologist Henry E. Adams used this technology in 1996 to show that men who were the most homophobic demonstrated significant sexual arousal to male erotic stimuli.[7] Taken together, the polygraph and the penile plethysmograph would have provided much needed physical data to supplement the ex-gay tales.

Seeing Is Believing. We urged Spitzer to get out of the ivory tower and visit, both as a guest and undercover, the ex-gay ministries. Only by visiting these places and meeting these people in their element could he understand that they are driven by fear and a desperate need to find acceptance in their churches and families. We also wanted Spitzer to talk to ex-gays who didn't know who he was, so he could get an honest portrayal of these ministries. We wanted him to see firsthand some of the bizarre techniques, such as exorcisms, touch therapy, and intrauterine memory recovery, that are a staple of the ex-gay ministries and reparative therapy. If he witnessed the insanity of these programs, we believed, he would see through the rhetoric and understand the reality of how these groups ruin lives.

Hallucinogenic Heteros. To achieve maximum credibility, it was essential that Spitzer interview his subjects at great length to see whether they were mentally competent to take part in his study. Although he did ask his subjects questions about their sexual orientation, perhaps the most important question Spitzer should have asked was, "Have you heard demonic voices or seen visions of holy figures in the past twelve months?" As discussed in "Undercover" [a chapter in *Anything but Straight*], a sizable portion of the people who claim to have changed appear to suffer from mental disorders or their judgment has been impaired from rampant drug abuse. In other words, if a person believes that Jesus lives in his or her television set or that Satan is stalking him or her, then it isn't far-fetched to assume that the person's heterosexuality may be a hallucination as well.

No Switch-Hitters. We told Spitzer that if he was going to study the possibility of gay people becoming straight, he must use people who are exclusively homosexual. If he used people who could be perceived as bisexual, critics would justifiably wonder whether a change in sexual orientation occurred or whether the subjects simply sublimated their homosexuality in favor of their heterosexual side.

The Crystal Ball. We vividly laid out his study's potential consequences if he did not follow our advice. First, he would be excoriated by gay political organizations for biased work. Second, the scientific community would publicly upbraid him for shoddy research and unprofessional sampling methods. Third, the religious right would enthusiastically embrace the study and use it as an opportunity to bash homosexuals and say they are unworthy of equal rights. Fourth, the media would sensationalize it, leading to distorted news coverage of the study. Finally, the results would lead to an increase in harassment against gays and be used to pressure young gay men and women into harmful ex-gay programs.

According to HRC's (Human Rights Campaign) letter to Spitzer, "What a shame it would be if countless individuals were subject to shame, indignity, and examination when the only thing that needed further examination was your research."[8]

CREATING A GIGANTIC SHADOW OF DOUBT

It became clear during my travels in researching this book *[Anything but Straight]* that Spitzer had not heeded our advice and was cavorting with right-wing extremists. No matter which ex-gay ministry I visited or reparative therapist I spoke to, Spitzer's name inevitably popped up—and never at my initiation. None other than Richard Cohen bubbled with excitement when he voluntarily brought up Spitzer's name. He told me that he was personally supplying Spitzer with research subjects and that he talked frequently with the Columbia University doctor. At the 2000 NARTH [National Association for Research and Therapy of Homosexuality] conference, Nicolosi[9] also spoke frequently and in great detail about his connections to Spitzer.

More astounding was discovering that Spitzer was using Dr. Laura Schlessinger to solicit for subjects at the same time that she was embroiled in an explosive spat with the lesbian and gay community. Gay civil rights groups were protesting Paramount Pictures for offering Schlessinger a TV show after she referred to homosexuals as "biological errors." Despite the controversy, Spitzer went on her show and espoused what can only be described as antigay views: "I agree that a homosexual who is not able to be aroused heterosexually . . . I think, implicitly, there is something not working," he told Schlessinger.[10] Spitzer tries to come across as "Mr. Nice Guy" when talking to the mainstream media or gay activists, but he was clearly singing an entirely different tune on Schlessinger's program.

In May 2000, the link between Spitzer and the extreme political right was outed in a very revealing way. At the APA's annual meeting in Chicago, Spitzer's seemingly objective panel discussion on the efficacy of reparative therapy was canceled after it was discovered that NARTH was surreptitiously working behind the scenes with Spitzer to organize the event. Nicolosi, in fact, had sent a clandestine letter to NARTH members claiming that Spitzer was "in close contact with NARTH officers about its implementation and the selection of speakers." The letter also said that Spitzer was "moved to rethink this issue," meaning he was reconsidering whether homosexuals should be labeled mentally ill in the DSM.

The pro-gay psychiatrists felt bamboozled with the uncovering of NARTH's secret involvement and wisely backed out of the ambush disguised as a scientific panel. Embarrassed by the revelation, Spitzer wrote a letter claiming that Nicolosi gave the "false impression" that NARTH had been instrumental in planning the debate, and that Nicolosi made "misleading statements" about Spitzer's position on the 1973 decision.[11]

One would think that once Spitzer had seen Nicolosi's underhanded methods in action he would have cut ties with the NARTH leader. Instead, he inexplicably joined forces with Nicolosi and appeared with him at a right-wing press conference to protest the cancellation of the debate. The press conference was orchestrated to show, according to Nicolosi, that "the gay and lesbian community does not tolerate discussion of scientific issues."[12]

In a breathtaking display of political naïveté, Spitzer sat alongside representatives from antigay organizations. Among those participating were Richard Cohen, [Focus on the Family's] John Paulk, the Family Research Council's Yvette Cantu Schneider, and Joseph Nicolosi. In a one-hour period of time, Spitzer squandered a lifetime of credibility and allowed his reputation to be sullied by teaming up with this bevy of antigay activists. After this publicity stunt, Spitzer's claim of working on an "objective" study was irreparably tarnished, and his stature in the scientific community greatly diminished.

Unfortunately, very few reporters at the time were paying attention—in either the mainstream or gay press. These disturbing facts would become meaningful only *after* Spitzer's study was unveiled a year later and it became necessary to show how Spitzer's work was predestined to find that gays could change. It is astonishing that he openly frolicked with antigay activists and believed that his study would still be taken seriously. It is almost as if Spitzer went out of his way to cast a gigantic shadow of doubt on his work. If that was his intention, this author congratulates him because that is exactly what he accomplished.

THE MEDIA MAELSTROM

When the story broke, it did so with an enormous bang. The first report from the Associated Press (AP) set the sensationalistic tone the rest of the media pack eagerly followed when it called Spitzer's work "an explosive new study [that] says some gay people can turn straight if they really want to."[13] This report set off a forty-eight-hour media frenzy with worldwide reverberations. The story was prominently featured in every major newspaper the next day, and television reporters and talking heads breathlessly regurgitated the incendiary AP report.

As the details of the study emerged, it was clear that Spitzer had ignored the vast majority of our suggestions. He had simply called up 200 ex-gays (143 men and 57 women) on the phone and interviewed them for a mere forty-five minutes. He asked these people—without ever meeting most of them in person—if they had changed, and most said "yes." What else would they say? After all, they were the religious right's handpicked sample, and many of them were professional antigay lobbyists.

"History has done some interesting twists," Spitzer said following the release of his study. "Some homosexuals can change, to varying degrees."[14]

The core of the study claimed that 65 percent of men and 44 percent of women attained what he called "good heterosexual functioning." A minority of subjects, 17 percent of the men and 54 percent of the women, claimed they had no gay attractions whatsoever, while 63 percent of the women and 29 percent of the men reported "no or only minimal" same-sex attractions. A staggeringly high 87 percent of the male and female respondents reported feeling more masculine (men) or feminine (women).

Lesbian and gay civil rights groups were quick to condemn the study. The National Gay and Lesbian Task Force called it "snake oil packaged as science."[15] The Human Rights Campaign assailed the research as "biased and unscientific."[16]

Meanwhile, right-wing organizations seized upon it as proof that homosexuals could convert to heterosexuals. Traditional Values Coalition Chairman Lou Sheldon said, "His research validates what we have been saying all along: That homosexuality is a behavior that can be changed."[17] Reverend Jerry Falwell said that "the results have suggested the unthinkable to homosexual-rights advocates who insist that they are born with a 'gay gene' or some uncontrollable element that leads to their homosexuality," and Nicolosi, who helped supply study subjects, trumpeted the report as "revolutionary."[18]

Many of Spitzer's colleagues distanced themselves from the study and made it clear that his work failed to meet basic scientific standards:

- "His sampling method was totally inadequate," said Dr. Lawrence Hartmann, a professor at Harvard and a respected researcher on homosexuality.[19]
- "For 30 years, Bob Spitzer may have been considered a careful researcher. But with this study, he no longer is. It is far from good science."[20]
- "There is no published scientific evidence supporting the efficacy of reparative therapy as a treatment to change one's sexual orientation," the APA's medical director, Dr. Steven Mirin, said in a statement designed to distance the venerated group from Spitzer.[21]

No one seemed surprised by the fallout except Spitzer, who appeared flummoxed over the hullabaloo. "I'm shocked at how my study is being used," he told me in a phone conversation. How could he have been shocked when HRC warned him more than a year in advance what would happen? At best, his feigning surprise was disingenuous, and, at worst, his reaction was a cynical maneuver designed to separate him from the damage he had done.

The only good thing the author can say about Spitzer's research was that it was so incompetently slapdash that even the average Joe or Jane on the street could see through it. For instance, I was in a cab the day the study came out and listening to a report about it on the radio. As the report ended, the driver said in broken English, "You've got to be kidding me. If a guy calls 200 people on the phone, that's more like a poll than a study. What a joke."

THE SPITZER STUDY:
ANATOMY OF A FAILURE

For society to move forward and evolve, we must embrace science and its conclusions, even if they are sometimes controversial. Spitzer had a great opportunity to use his study to examine the effects reparative therapy had on the individuals who took part in it. Thus, it is a shame that he did not conduct a rigorous study that embraced objective measures and included a control group of people who said that the therapy did not work.

The following examines where Spitzer's study failed to live up to accepted scientific standards and succeeded in drawing legitimate criticism from those critiquing his work. Interestingly, if he had followed HRC's original advice, he would have avoided the harsh reviews he received.

Birds of Prey. Although warned that his credibility would suffer if he allowed the right wing to participate in his study, Spitzer made antigay organizations an integral part of his work. An astonishing 43 percent of his sample came from the ex-gay ministries, and 23 percent were referred through the notoriously antigay NARTH. Religious pressure also figured prominently in attempts to change, with 93 percent of subjects saying that religion was extremely important in their lives. Clearly, the fear of religious rejection or persecution may have played a significant role in some subjects falsely claiming change had occurred. The bottom line: This study was essentially meaningless because it had the right wing's fingerprints all over it.

Ex-Gay or Propay? Antigay activists who get paid to lobby against gay rights were a large part of his sample. Exhibit A is Anthony Falzarano, Director of the Parents and Friends Ministries. As has been pointed out repeatedly, Falzarano has lobbied on behalf of antigay legislation in Louisiana, Maine, and Maryland and in numerous national media appearances. Falzarano also makes a substantial portion of his self-proclaimed $65,000 a year salary from antigay political organizations, including a large grant from the Family Research Council.

He once told CBS that Satan "uses homosexuals as pawns and then he kills them."[22] Most people would agree that it would be unethical to use a person with such biased views in a supposedly objective study, but Spitzer never took these concerns into consideration. He laced his study with homophobic lobbyists, some of whom made their livings from activities surrounding the ex-gay ministries, with no less than 78 percent of his sample of 200 men and women having spoken out publicly in favor of conversion therapy.

This raises serious conflict-of-interest questions. Can people be objective about their feelings toward conversion therapy when referred to Spitzer by antigay political groups who help pay their salaries? I think the answer is a resounding "no." Although his entire sample was not on the dole, for his study to be taken seriously, *none* of his sample should have been paid lobbyists. In this case, even one bad apple does spoil the whole barrel, and there were many rotten apples in this crop.

When I asked Spitzer why he had used outspoken activists who might taint his study, he said he had done so because he "had trouble" finding nonactivists for his research. He also mentioned in his study that he had "great difficulty" finding nonreligious therapists to refer subjects. But if tens of thousands of homosexuals have become straight, as the right often claims, then it should have been a relatively easy task to find at least 200 people nationwide who were not affiliated with far-right political groups. The "great difficulty" Spitzer encountered suggests that the number of ex-gays has been significantly inflated, and that there aren't many in existence who are not on the religious right's bulging payroll.

The Video Killed the Ex-Gay Star. Despite our insistence, Spitzer elected not to use physical evidence to corroborate the ex-gay testimonies. I asked him why he had refused to use either the polygraph or the penile plethysmograph on his subjects. According to Spitzer, "there was no way he could get his subjects to submit to such tests." It never seemed to dawn on Spitzer that these individuals were doggedly avoiding these truth-detecting instruments because they were not telling the truth.

"I'd love to see all the ex-gay types, who are often willing to talk about their conversions, submit to such a test—to basically relinquish their capacity to lie," said Dr. Larry Rudiger, a research psychologist from the University of Vermont. "Given the energy the Religious Right is willing to throw behind this subject, you'd think they'd be eager to cull such definitive proof."[23]

Spitzer said that some of his subjects felt these instruments were an "invasion of privacy." Hearing this, I countered, "Funny how some of your sample were not as concerned about 'privacy' when they spoke intimately about their sex lives on *The Jerry Springer Show*."

See No Evil, Hear No Evil. Spitzer did not do basic preliminary research by visiting the ex-gay ministries, either undercover or as himself. This deprived him of a firsthand understanding of the wacky activities that go on inside these places. For instance, Spitzer describes himself as an atheist Jew. Would it not have been good for him to watch the ex-gays debate whether the Jews killed Jesus? Might he be alarmed at watching a live exorcism? Finally, if he would have left his office and gone into the field, he would have heard the stories of people who are struggling to change but realize that these programs do not work. Unfortunately, he did none of this and relied solely on the well-rehearsed stories of ex-gay political activists.

Visions and Voices. Anecdotal evidence suggests that some of the people used in Spitzer's study were mentally fragile, yet there were no psychological tests administered to ensure they were competent to take part in this study. For instance, an alarmingly high 43 percent of the men and 47 percent of the women were "markedly" or "extremely" depressed before conversion therapy, and a disproportionate number (37 percent of males and 35 percent of females) of the individuals who took part in this study were suicidal before attempting conversion. Unlike many gay teens who sadly view suicide as an option, all of the participants in the study were adults with a mean age of forty-three. That many of these men and women were *still* contemplating suicide well into adulthood implies that they suffered from a higher rate of instability than the population at large. Psychological factors should have been given greater weight by Spitzer when picking research subjects.

Whose Team? Were all of the participants gay and was Spitzer cheating to pad his results? Of the sample, 47 percent of the men and 67 percent of the women admitted to having had heterosexual sex *before* they entered therapy, 21 percent of the men and 18 percent of the women were already married *before* therapy, and 54 percent of the men and 58 percent of the women acknowledged some attraction to the opposite sex *before* therapy. In addition, 15 percent of the male participants and 39 percent of the females had little or no sexual attraction to the same sex as teenagers, when sex drive is usually highest. Clearly, many of the "success" cases may have been bisexual or heterosexual prior to therapy.

THE STUDY'S CONCLUSION:
CHANGE IN SEXUAL ORIENTATION
IS HIGHLY UNLIKELY

The media reported the study as if Spitzer had shown that "highly motivated" individuals could, in some cases, change their sexual orientation. Upon closer examination, however, Spitzer's research shows quite the opposite. For more than a year the doctor solicited the majority of his subjects through right-wing political groups and media stars, such as Dr. Laura. Remember, these groups regularly boast in the media that they have helped hoards of homosexuals "escape the lifestyle." Yet, for all of their money, power, and braggadocio, the best these antigay behemoths could do was come up with 200 people, of which only 17 percent of the men and 54 percent of the women claimed to have changed sexual orientation *completely*. Moreover, 68 percent of the male subjects and 41 percent of the female subjects still had same-sex masturbatory fantasies after therapy! Most observers would not objectively define these people as "straight." As if these paltry numbers are not embarrassing enough, we must remember that the failure rate would be much higher if Spitzer had not chosen to lard his study with people who are arguably bisexual.

Activists and colleagues have blasted Spitzer's study, but it will be the subjects themselves who will, in the end, cause the study's eternal demise. Since his methodology was to rely exclusively on testimonies, if only one subject comes out of the closet, the entire study will be undermined, and the past shows us that several, if not a majority, of his subjects will come out or will be found out in the next decade. Spitzer may have briefly enjoyed his ephemeral moment of talking-head media glory, but I predict future stories will not be so kind. As sure as the sun rises and sets, this study will come back repeatedly to haunt him. It seems likely that one day headlines will read, "Spitzer Subjects Say They Lied, Validity of Entire Study Now in Question."

DAMAGE CONTROL

It was midafternoon and Spitzer's shaky voice on the other end of the line sounded a tad weary. He had taken a rhetorical beating and was beginning to have regrets about releasing such a profoundly unscientific study. He was also feeling guilty that his study might be used to coerce gay people into therapy. He called me because we had kept in contact while he was conducting the study and I had warned him repeatedly on its ramifications.

"Wayne, the right's using my work to attack gays, and the left is calling me a bigot," exclaimed an exasperated Spitzer. "How do we get out of this mess?"

My inclination was to say, "This is *your* mess and you can clean it up yourself," but, although history will judge him harshly for this study, he still had played a role in giving gay and lesbian people one of their biggest victories of all time. So, I swallowed my pride and worked with Spitzer to help him mitigate the damage he had already inflicted.

Spitzer's idea was to write an op-ed and place it in *The Wall Street Journal* to clarify what his study actually showed. The first point would be that his research should not be used to justify discrimination, and the second would be to note that the vast majority of gay people could not change even if they tried. Although this effort was clearly inadequate, it did help offset some of the damage. As another concession, I interviewed Spitzer, and he offered HRC the following statement via e-mail:

> I anticipated some misuse of the study results, but I did not anticipate that some of the media would say such ridiculous things as that the study raised the issue of homosexuality and choice. Of course, no one chooses to be homosexual and no one chooses to be heterosexual. I did anticipate, and in my presentation warn, that it would be a mistake to interpret the study as implying that any highly motivated homosexual could change if they really were motivated to do so. I suspect that the vast majority of gay people—even if they wanted to—would be unable to make substantial changes in sexual attraction and fantasy and enjoyment of heterosexual functioning that many of my subjects reported. I also warned against the study results being used to justify pressuring gay people to enter therapy when they had no interest in doing so and I have already heard of many incidents where this has happened.[24]

THE MOTIVATION BEHIND THE MADNESS

Despite Spitzer's efforts, some burning questions still bother me. Why did this respected scientist choose to ruin his reputation, undermine his credibility, and lower his status in the psychiatric community? Why did he elect to put his most unimpressive work under the biggest media magnifying glass he could find?

One theory is that Spitzer was reaching the twilight of his career and wanted his last hurrah. As the psychiatrist who said, "Gays aren't sick," he knew that releasing a study concluding that "some gays could become straight" was newsworthy. This was the classic "man bites dog" story. To Spitzer, this may have seemed a tantalizing proposition and an opportunity to go out with a bang. It had been a long time since Spitzer's name had appeared in bright, neon lights, and in this age of the great media circus, the temptation of achieving fame and recognition can be a powerful narcotic. It is alluring enough for some individuals to throw away a reputation that took decades to earn. "I'm willing to admit that I like controversy and to be in the center of burning debates," Spitzer told *The Advocate*'s Chris Bull.[25]

Perhaps Spitzer should have blazed a different career path and put his energies toward becoming a host on CNN's *Crossfire*. Although in many professions creating publicity is an advantage, Spitzer should be well aware that in the scientific arena it is best not to create "controversy." Legions of people in turmoil about their sexuality should not have to endure unnecessary trauma because of Spitzer's ego trip and desire to see his face on the little screen.

Another theory is that cunning members of the religious right manipulated Spitzer, using sympathetic ex-gay stories to dupe him into conducting a politically loaded study.

Most likely, Spitzer's foray into *political* science was a combination of the two theories. It is a fact that people such as Paulk, Falzarano, and Nicolosi recruited the scientist, who was known for his sympathetic ear, but in the process of this seduction, I believe, Spitzer realized that he could leverage a controversial study to line up media appearances and speaking gigs.

Unfortunately, Spitzer's attempts to minimize the damage came up far short of what was needed. Although I believe he never intended to hurt lesbian and gay people, there is no doubt that his sloppy work—whatever his true motivation—has caused unnecessary suffering. In fact, the day after his study was released, I received a call from a college professor who said an openly gay student was harassed and told by fellow students that she should seek change because Spitzer's study proved she could. I also got a call from a young man whose previously accepting parents had a change of heart and told him he could be straight if he would only "try harder."

In the end, however, the real loser is Dr. Spitzer. Whether he was an over-the-hill stage horse galloping toward the limelight or a court jester hoodwinked by a scheming religious right is unimportant. What matters is that Spitzer's embarrassing travesty of scholarship will surely go down as his defining work, a professional pockmark that will indelibly taint his once splendid career.

NOTES

1. See Bergler, E. (1956), *Homosexuality: Disease or Way of Life*. New York: Hill and Wang and Socarides, C. (1968), *The Overt Homosexual*. New York: Grune and Stratton.

2. Clendinen, Dudley and Adam Nagourney (1999), *Out for Good: The Struggle to Build a Gay Rights Movement in America*. New York: Simon and Schuster, p. 209.

3. Phone conversations with Robert Spitzer, no dates recorded. All quotes are from these conversations unless otherwise noted.

4. Spitzer, Robert (2001), Can some gay men and lesbians change their sexual orientation? 200 participants reporting a change from homosexual to heterosexual orientation.

5. Duin, Julia (2001), New psychiatric study says gays can alter orientation. *The Washington Times*, May 9.

6. Ibid.

7. Adams, Henry E. (1996), Is homophobia associated with homosexual arousal? *Journal of Abnormal Psychology*, 105(3):440-445.

8. Besen, Wayne (1999), HRC letter to Dr. Spitzer.

9. Joseph Nicolosi, PhD, is author of *Reparative Therapy of Male Homosexuality: A New Clinical Approach*. Northvale, NJ: Aronson, 1991, and a founding member of NARTH.

10. See www.narth.com.

11. Spitzer, Robert L. (2000), Letter to Dr. Joseph Nicolosi, March 15. A copy of this letter was mailed to this author by Spitzer.

12. Barlow, Gary (2000), Ex-gay flap at APA meeting orchestrated by antigay activists. *Dallas Voice*, May.

13. Ritter, Malcolm (2001), Study: Some gays can go straight. Associated Press, May 9.

14. Duin, New psychiatric study.

15. McFeeley, Tim (2001), NGLTF responds to flawed Spitzer study on so-called reparative therapy. National Gay and Lesbian Task Force press release, May 8.

16. Human Rights Campaign (2001), New conversion study is biased and unscientific. Press release, May 10.

17. Sheldon, Louis (2001), Noted psychiatrist says homosexuals can change! Traditional Values Coalition press release, May 9.

18. Falwell, Jerry (2001), Can "gays" really change? *Falwell Confidential,* May 10; Nicolosi, Joseph (2001), New research shows homosexuals can change. *Family Research Council Culture Facts,* May 11.

19. Talan, Jamie (2001), Study of gays flawed? Researcher: Therapy helps change orientation. *Newsday,* May 10.

20. Ibid.

21. APA statement in response to media articles regarding alleged changes in sexual orientation reported at APA annual meeting (2001). U.S. Newswire, May 9.

22. CBS (1995), Faith and politics: The Christian Right. *CBS Reports,* with Dan Rather, September 7; Hausman, Ken (2001), Furor erupts over study on sexual orientation. *Psychiatric News,* July 6.

23. Gay.com (2001), May 10.

24. E-mail interview with Robert Spitzer, May 16, 2001.

25. Bull, Chris (2001), Much ado about changing. *The Advocate,* June 19.

36

The Spitzer Study
and the Finnish Parliament

Olli Stålström
Jussi Nissinen

HISTORY OF THE FINNISH
PARTNERSHIP BILL

Historically, the first suggestions for complete social and legal sexual equality could be traced to an emancipation movement in connection with the French revolution (de Villette, 1790)[1] and, more directly, to the German gay rights pioneer Karl Heinrich Ulrichs (1864).[2] In Finland, legal recognition of same-gender partnerships was first proposed in 1974 in the charter of the Finnish Organization for Sexual Equality (SETA).[3] Initially, demands for partnership laws in Finland were tentative as SETA had partial roots in both Stonewall radicalism and the London Gay Liberation Manifesto of the early 1970s. These movements cited religion, psychiatry, and the family as the three main sources of gay and lesbian oppression. From that perspective, the "family" was defined as one dominated by a heterosexual male. In later years, however, the Australian sociologist Dennis Altman (1981)—an influential figure in the birth of the Finnish gay and lesbian movement—suggested a redefinition of marriage to include same-gender couples.

As the civil rights struggle against more blatant forms of discrimination (such as criminalization of homosexual acts and censorship laws limiting the dissemination of factual information about homo-

This chapter appeared originally under the same title in the *Journal of Gay & Lesbian Psychotherapy* 7(3):83-95. Copyright 2003 The Haworth Press, Inc.

sexuality) advanced, the demands for legal recognition for same-gender couples became stronger. A major figure in shepherding this process over the years was Tarja Halonen, a prominent, heterosexual human rights lawyer. In 1980, she became the chair of SETA and was later to become the Finnish Minister of Justice and eventually the President of Finland in 2000.

In 1993, an initial bill which originated from SETA and a formal Private Member's Bill proposing civil unions was introduced in the Finnish Parliament by Outi Ojala, an MEP[4] belonging to the Left Alliance. Simultaneously, Tarja Halonen appointed a committee to study the legal position of families in general (Committee on Families, 1992). Although Ojala's bill did not pass in 1993, it was reintroduced in 1996 and gradually gained the support of Finland's ruling parties of that time (Left Alliance, Social Democrats, Swedish People's Party, Greens). Eventually, the Social Democratic Prime Minister Paavo Lipponen indicated his cabinet's support for the bill as well.

The proposed civil unions bill had evoked strong opposition since its first introduction in Parliament, but by 2001 the margin between supporters and opponents had diminished. Having discussed Ojala's Private Member's Bill for five years, the members of the Finnish Parliament requested an official proposal from the cabinet on such an important matter. Although the overwhelming majority of the parties in power supported the bill, the majority of members in parties on the right, the former agrarian party, the Christian Democrats, and various populist and ultra-religious groups opposed any partnership laws for same-gender people.[5] Opponents argued that the approval of same-gender partnerships would threaten the basic fabric of Finnish society. Arguing in support of their position, however, they offered discredited psychoanalytic theories that pathologized homosexuality. Jorma Hentilä, former secretary general of the Left Alliance and chairperson of SETA, described the background in the debate:[6]

> In comparison with the earlier debates, the present discussion in Parliament and the media, the new aspect is that religious and moralistic condemnation is now couched in a form resembling scientific discourse. The articles have the appearance of scientific abstracts with their percentages and references, and they refer to various research results.

The sources [of this research] are primarily from the so-called reparative therapy research institutions from the United States and Europe. Common to them is the fact that they challenge Freud's original view of the polymorphous nature of sexuality. On an ideological level, they limit the purpose of sexuality to procreation, which makes non-reproductive sexuality a disturbance. These researchers and institutions have close ties with the American religious right and the political goals of its European supporters.

An important background organization is the National Association for the Research and Therapy of Homosexuality (NARTH), led by psychologist Joseph Nicolosi. This organization founded by psychoanalysts and psychiatrists still holds to a view of homosexuality as a personality disturbance, which was discarded by the scientific community in the U.S. in the 1970s. NARTH considers lesbians and gays "broken," but that they can be "repaired" with the help of therapy. Joseph Nicolosi (1991) has sketched "reparative therapy" in his book *Reparative Therapy of Male Homosexuality* (Hentilä, 2001a).

THE SPITZER STUDY

In the 2001 parliamentary debates, the most powerful scientifically framed argument against the partnership bill was the citation of an unpublished study of so-called ex-gays. The study had been conducted by Robert L. Spitzer, MD, and had been presented with much publicity on May 9, 2001 at the Annual Meeting of the American Psychiatric Association (APA) in New Orleans. The methodology of the study—a 45-minute telephone interview of subjects primarily recruited through NARTH and ex-gay groups—raised questions about its major finding that some people can change their sexual orientation through sexual conversion therapy. However because of his historic role in removing the diagnosis of homosexuality from the APA classification of mental disorders, the *Diagnostic and Statistical Manual of Mental Disorders,* in 1973 (Bayer, 1987), Dr. Spitzer's reputation and opinions on this subject carried much weight. Consequently, the results of the Spitzer study were trumpeted by antigay religious organizations opposed to civil unions and reported widely by the popular and tabloid press (Lund and Renna, 2003).

News about the Spitzer study spread quickly around the world, particularly in countries such as Germany and Finland which were preparing to debate gay and lesbian civil unions during the summer of 2001. Opponents of civil unions saw the Spitzer study as supporting their belief that gay men and lesbians should not be granted legal protections for their relationships. Scientific supporters of civil unions fired back with criticisms of Spitzer's study. For example, on May 15, 2001, a leading German newspaper, *Süddeutsche Zeitung,* interviewed Hartmut Bosinski, the Head of the Department of Sexual Medicine of the University of Kiel,[7] about the Spitzer study, as Bosinski had just published a paper on the civil union bill in Germany (Bosinski et al., 2001).

Despite the sensation created by the Spitzer study, Germany nevertheless passed its civil union law on July 17, 2002.[8] In Finland, the civil union bill was to be debated in September, 2001. Starting in May, reactions to the Spitzer study generated a "science-by-headlines" mentality in the Nordic press and "politics-by-headlines" in the Finnish Parliament as well. Many Nordic tabloid newspapers published Spitzer's findings on their front pages in a sensationalistic and misleading form. Their reporting style and headlines compounded the original inaccuracies of the Spitzer study. For example, one Norwegian tabloid, *Aftenposten,* had a May 17 headline that read, "Homophiles can become heteros" *("Homofile kan bli hetero"),* and another paper, *Dagbladet,* carried banner headlines declaring "Gays can become straight" *("Homser kan bli streite").*

The headlines trumpeted Spitzer's findings with the claim that 66 percent of gay men and 44 percent of lesbians had achieved "a good heterosexual life." The tabloid press, which tends to be antigay, also praised Spitzer's courage in publishing his findings, emphasizing his role in the 1973 declassification of homosexuality in the DSM. Spitzer's definition of "a good heterosexual life," however, was found in the small print, operationalized as one satisfactory heterosexual intercourse per month. Also in the small print, at the end of the tabloid Norwegian articles, following the headlines and accompanied by photos of semi-nude gay men in leather gear, was the fact that Spitzer himself was not sure how many gay men could change their orientation.[9] Finally, again in very small print, some papers noted that Douglas Haldeman of the American Psychological Association had criticized Spitzer's findings for their biased sampling, inaccurate analysis, and lack of follow-up studies.[10]

THE FINNISH PARLIAMENTARY DEBATE— VOICES OF OPPOSITION

Minister of Justice Johannes Koskinen opened the debate and appealed to the Finnish MPs [members of Parliament] to keep the debate calm and matter-of-fact. He noted that civil unions had recently been passed in the Netherlands, Germany, and other Nordic countries (Sweden, Norway, Denmark, Iceland). Minister Koskinen stated that the Finnish Government wished only to increase equality in the country by granting same-sex couples the right to register their unions. The proposed bill did not include the possibility of adopting children or of having church weddings.

Opposition to the civil union bill primarily consisted of MPs from the Christian Democratic Party, especially Päivi Räsänen, MP, who has constantly warned against "homosexuals." Räsänen argued that the proposed bill would threaten the foundations of the institution of marriage as well as pose a threat to the children of Finland. Another very vocal opponent was Raimo Vistbacka, MP, of the populist, right wing Basic Finns party *(Perussuomalaiset)*. He warned that the civil union bill was a Trojan horse intended to undermine the basic Finnish Judeo-Christian values of "Home, God, and Country." Vistbacka tried to link the presumed threat of homosexual civil unions to other social issues, claiming that if homosexuality were openly permitted, the population of Finland would diminish and the Finns would have to import gypsies "who are too lazy to work."[11]

A Christian Democrat MP, Kari Kärkkäinen, introduced psychiatric and mental health issues into the Parliamentary debate. He made the false claim that leading members of the APA, among whom he cited Spitzer as just one example, believe that "homosexuals" can change their sexual orientation through reparative therapies. An attempt was made to create the impression that Spitzer, who had played a key role in removing homosexuality from the DSM, had changed his mind about that decision. This presumed reversal by Spitzer was then used to argue that since "homosexuals" can change, they do not deserve civil rights protections or the privileges society grants married couples. Kärkkäinen strongly warned that the proposed law was against the official doctrine of the Finnish Evangelical-Lutheran State Church which had decreed homosexuality a sin from which one has to refrain (Finnish Bishops' Statement, 1984). Kärkkäinen warned that the Members of Parliament must not offend the State Church of Finland by passing the bill. Kärkkäinen also praised a Finnish ex-gay group, Aslan, as trying to help and defend the right of those "homosexuals" who want "relief from their affliction."[12]

Kärkkäinen strongly praised Professor Spitzer for his courage to come out with "scientific truth," despite his having given into appeals from "radical homosexual activists in the 1973 APA decision." Of Spitzer's study, Kärkkäinen said:

> New data about the possibilities to change homosexuality were published in the annual meeting of APA in May this year. This is one of the most thorough studies on this subject . . . this is a very revolutionary study, published by, as we all know, by Robert L. Spitzer, a professor of Columbia University, who participated in 1973 in the deletion of the diagnostic label.[13]

Religious opponents of the bill, mainly members of various Pentecostal movements, staged high-profile demonstrations against its passage.[14] One of the main parliamentary religious opponents was Lauri Oinonen, MP (Center), an Evangelical-Lutheran State Church priest. He came out of Helsinki's Parliament House to formally greet a self-proclaimed American prophet, Shirley Arnold, who then preached on Parliament's steps. Standing in front of the cross, the national flag, bibles, and large signs warning of the threat of the civil union bill to the children of Finland, she reminded Finns about the fate of Sodom and Gomorrah. Oinonen said he regretted that some MP's were now defending the registration of homosexuals when registration should have been enacted over ten years earlier to prevent the spread of HIV/AIDS.[15]

The heated Parliamentary debate continued for several days with many MPs warning against the deleterious effects of civil unions. Even an MP from the traditionally tolerant Swedish People's Party, Nils-Anders Granvik, warned that tolerance is being carried "too far" and that "The civil unions would be a step toward the disintegration of Finnish society and a blatant violation of the Order of Creation."[16]

THE FINNISH PARLIAMENTARY DEBATE—
SUPPORTING VOICES

Susanna Rahkonen, a Social Democratic MP, noted that the American Psychiatric Association warned that Parliamentarians should not treat gays and lesbians as if they were strange monsters or laboratory animals. She called comparisons of homosexuality with pedophilia and of civil unions with incest or zoophilia "degrading and insulting." She noted the APA has repeatedly been critical of so-called reparative therapy. Rahkonen warned that "reparative therapy may increase depression, anxiety, and self-destructive behavior."[17] Rahkonen further cited Finnish attitude studies, noting that although homosexuality had previously been perceived as a deviation and threat, this was due to its criminalization and illness label. She likened the situation to the historically imagined threat of marriages between members of different ethnic groups. She added that attitudes had changed considerably since homosexuality's decriminalization in 1971, revision of the Finnish classification of disorders in 1981, and the revision of the Finnish Constitution in 1995, which extended protection against discrimination also to sexual orientation (see Stålström and Nissinen, 2003).

Rahkonen cited a Finnish female psychiatrist, Tytti Solantaus, who noted that homosexuality has been stable and constant throughout the ages and that it is not spread by example. She also cited a leading theological ethicist, Martti Lindqvist, who has defended the equality of gays, lesbians, transsexual, and people with HIV/AIDS for decades. According to Lindqvist, homosexuality cannot be erased by controls, discrimination and sanctions, which only tend to push it underground. Rahkonen further noted that the vice rector of Helsinki University, Raija Sollamo, a Biblical researcher, had publicly defended the right of sexual minorities to live in lasting and safe civil unions.

MENTAL HEALTH PROFESSIONALS WEIGH IN

Both sides in the Finnish Parliament debate appealed to professional organizations in their fields, both in Sweden and the United States. The opposition to the partnership law appealed to reparative therapy organizations such as NARTH and Living Waters and conservative political organization such as Paul Cameron's Family Research Institute. Arguments for the opposition were imported by the ex-gay organization Aslan. They argued the position of Puonti (1995), who claimed that homosexuality was declassified by the APA because of political pressure. It was further asserted that lesbians and gay men form a negligible fraction (around one-half of a percent) of the total population (Kontula and Haavio-Mannila, 1993, p. 250). Buttressed by their interpretation of Spitzer's data, the Finnish religious right concluded that legal recognition of same-gender partnerships would grant only "special rights" demanded by small but vocal and aggressive groups of gay activists (see Turunen, 2002).

Proponents of the bill received support from the American Psychological Association, the American Psychiatric Association,[18] and the American Psychoanalytical Association. A professional organization, Finnish Association of Lesbian and Gay Professionals within Social Work and Health Care (STEAM) and a Web magazine (FinnQueer), cooperating with the lesbian and gay movement SETA, imported and transmitted via the Internet the arguments supporting the partnership bill.[19]

SPITZER PERSONALLY CLARIFIES
WHAT HIS STUDY MEANS

The heated debate continued in the Finnish Parliament with opponents and supporters being of roughly equal strength. The outcome of the final vote scheduled for September 28, 2001, was very uncertain. As the final vote approached, with the Christian Democrats using the Spitzer argument as their trump card, it became possible that civil union opponents might win. Therefore, the Web magazine FinnQueer contacted Spitzer and asked him to clarify his own position and intentions. Spitzer reacted very quickly and sent the following open e-mail letter to Kari Kärkkäinen, MP, on September 24, 2001, just days before the final vote:

> I am disturbed to hear (although not surprised) that the results of my study are being misused by those who are against anti-discrimination laws and civil union laws for gays and lesbians.

My study, based on a very unique sample, indicated that—contrary to the current view of most mental health professionals—some homosexuals can change their sexual orientation to a significant degree. However, I also indicated in the discussion section of my presentation, that such results are probably quite rare, even for highly motivated homosexuals. I also said that it would be a serious mistake to conclude from my study that any highly motivated homosexual can change his or her sexual orientation, or that my study shows that homosexuality is a "choice."

Whether or not some homosexuals can change their sexual orientation is a scientific issue that to me, is totally irrelevant to the ethical issue of whether homosexuals are entitled to anti-discrimination laws and civil unions laws. As a citizen (not as a scientist), I personally favor anti-discrimination laws and civil union laws for homosexuals.[20]

This public letter was read in the plenary session of the Finnish Parliament by Kirsi Ojansuu, MP (Greens). It was also published in the major Finnish daily newspaper *Helsingin Sanomat*'s domestic front page on September 26, 2001. On September 28, 2001, Finland's Parliament voted 99 to 84 to pass the same-sex partnership bill.[21]

CODA

In Hentilä's (2001b) analysis, most Finnish MPs had decided their position on same-sex civil unions long before the final debate in September 2001. The final battle was for the minds of those MP's who had either not yet made up their minds, those who had not indicated their stand, and those who were vacillating between accepting or rejecting the law. The number of undecided was around thirty, however, considering the closeness of the vote, these few became the decisive group.[22] Spitzer's open letter of protest to Kärkkäinen, read in Parliament two days before the vote, may well have tipped the scales in persuading a number of uncertain members of Parliament who had difficulties reaching a decision in the atmosphere of conflicting scientific claims from various sides.

NOTES

1. A polemical pamphlet, *Les Enfan[t]s de Sodome* [The Children of Sodom], dated 1790, by the Marquis de Vilette, a friend of the Enlightenment philosopher Voltaire, demanded full legal and social equality for gays and lesbians; although the text did not yet explicitly specify legalization of same-gender partnerships. In the 19th century, the French Academy decided that the word for "children" be spelled with a "t" ("Enfants").

2. Ulrichs (1864) may be the first writer in history to explicitly introduce the idea of an institution of marriage *(Institut der Ehe)* for men who love men (*Urninge*, in Ulrichs' terminology). Although Ulrichs defended explicitly only the legal equality of men-loving men *(Urninge)* he acknowledged that there are both men and women who love members of the same gender, and therefore constitute, in his theory, a third gender *(drittes Geschlecht)*.

3. The authors of this article were active in SETA as a founding member (Jussi Nissinen) and an author of the charter (Olli Stålström). The 1974 SETA founding document set forth the principle of complete social equality. However, some controversial points, such as same-gender partnerships, could not be agreed upon before the final Action Program of 1976.

4. Member of European Parliament. The European Union requires complete legal equality, regardless of sexual orientation, of its member states.

5. A notable exception were the many women on the political right who openly supported the bill. In general, the most active and visible supporters of the bill were women MPs from various parties. Not all left-wing politicians supported the bill, however. Some openly religious left-wing politicians opposed it quite vehemently.

6. These remarks were first published in an article transmitted by FinnQueer Web magazine on April 17, 2001, to Finnish Parliament members, http://www.finnqueer.net/juttu.cgi?s=68_47_2.

7. Bosinski criticized Spitzer's methodology of 60 questions over the telephone in 45 minutes to members of religious ex-gay groups and the absence of any follow-up interviews or control groups. Bosinski further noted that sexuality cannot be seen as a dichotomous black-and-white phenomenon, that the dimensions of sexuality are changing and multifaceted.

8. This was after the German Constitutional Court decided, in response to an appeal by the opposition, that the civil union law passed by the *Bundestag* did not violate the German Constitution.

9. In Spitzer's published study, he speculates that "the marked change in sexual orientation reported by almost all of the study subjects may be a rare or uncommon outcome of reparative therapy" (Spitzer, 2003, p. 413).

10. See Lund and Renna's "An analysis of the media response to the Spitzer study" in this issue for an example of how such public relations phenomena operate.

11. Traditionally, Roma people have been oppressed in Finland perhaps even more strongly than gays and lesbians.

12. The ex-gay ideology imported to Finland by Aslan is mainly derived from the American organization NARTH (http://www.narth.com/) and the ex-gay movement Living Waters. Both conversion programs and the associated literature have been directly translated into Finnish. Living Waters' Web site summarizes the ex-gay ideol-

ogy prevailing in Finland: "The numbers estimating the percentage of homosexuals in the population are often drastically exaggerated. However, we've had more than thirty years of increasingly strident propaganda promoting homosexual acts as normal and beyond reproach in the public media and popular entertainment. The evidence and symptoms that once defined homosexuality as a damaging disorder in psychology textbooks didn't change, it was simply discarded and the diagnosis and treatment rejected. Nevertheless, homosexuality is still dangerous and self-destructive, spiritually, physically, and psychologically. It is still wrong, and should be resisted by all who are attracted to it. Homosexuality still keeps company with numerous health, behavior, and attitude problems" (Living Waters, http://www.livwat.com/past/homolove.html).

13. Parliamentary Record PTK, 96/2001, September 19, 2001, p. 13.

14. Parliamentary Record PTK, 96/2001, September 19, 2001, 16. The Finnish ex-gay movement Aslan (http://www.aslan.fi/showpage.php), associated with NARTH and Living Waters, had lobbied Finnish Parliamentarians. Aslan had translated information and arguments from its American model, NARTH, and submitted them to the Law Committee. Their basic message was expressed by the psychiatric spokesman of Aslan, Ari Puonti (1995), whose article was sent to all MPs. Puonti claims that homosexuality is a form of a broken or damaged psychological state and a deviation.

15. Parliamentary Record PTK 96/2001, September 19, 2001, p. 37.

16. Parliamentary Record PTK 96/2001, September 19, 2001, p. 30.

17. Parliamentary Record PTK 96/2001, September 19, 2001, p. 17.

18. FinnQueer Web magazine asked Ralph Roughton of the American Psychoanalytic Association (http://www.finnqueer.net/juttu.cgi?s=108_5_1) and Jack Drescher, MD, chair of the American Psychiatric Association's Committee on Gay, Lesbian and Bisexual Concerns to clarify the history of how homosexuality was declassified, the meaning of having Spitzer's study presented at an APA meeting, and to elucidate how American psychoanalysts understand homosexuality today. Drescher wrote:

> For the record, a presentation of any study at a meeting of the APA does not mean that the APA endorses the study. The APA meeting provides a forum for the exchange of ideas, even those whose scientific validity have yet to be proven. In other words, the presentation of a study at one of APA's meetings does not carry the same scientific weight as having the study published in a peer-reviewed journal. To date, the study has not been published in a peer-reviewed journal.
>
> As for the scientific merits of [Spitzer's] study, I believe it is significantly flawed. One flaw is that the majority of subjects in the study had one 45-minute telephone interview with Dr. Spitzer and no follow-ups. Other than Dr. Spitzer, I can find no reputable researcher who will agree that this is an accurate way to assess whether a person has changed their sexuality.
>
> That point was underscored in another study presented at the same symposium. Schroeder and Shidlo's study [2001; also see Schroeder and Shidlo, 2002] found that many individuals who claimed to have changed sexual orientation during a first telephone interview changed their story at a second, follow-up interview (FinnQueer, September 9, 2001, http://www.finnqueer.net/juttu.cgi?s=116_47_2).

19. These groups educated Finnish Members of Parliament via the scientific Web magazine FinnQueer, which carried the statements on homosexuality and civil unions by the American Psychiatric, Psychological, and Psychoanalytic Associations (see http://www.finnqueer.net/juttu.cgi?s=68_47_2).

20. In an interview with *Psychiatric News* (Hausman, 2001), Spitzer described as "nonsense" the argument that the decision to remove homosexuality as a DSM diagnosis was a political decision due to the APA succumbing to pressure from gay groups and their allies in the profession. According to Spitzer "both sides of the controversy were convinced that science was on their side" when they made their decision.

21. The margin of victory of 15 votes was extremely close considering that there were 17 abstentions.

22. In part, the intense lobbying by extreme opponents of the law backfired and reduced their credibility. As one fundamentalist opponent himself later wrote (Turunen, 2002), many of their actions were counterproductive. For instance, the fundamentalists brought a coffin to a demonstration draped with the Finnish flag, to mournfully symbolize the death of traditional morality. Because the police warned them this might constitute defamation of the flag, they instead painted the blue cross of the Finnish flag on the coffin. In an anti–civil union prayer demonstration on the steps of the Parliament house, the demonstrators tried to crawl up the stairs of the Parliament House in a kneeling position. These activities were reported as being in bad taste by many newspapers. Many straight people were so distressed by the fundamentalist attacks that they volunteered to support gays and lesbians. One of these was author Marja-Leena Parkkinen (2003), who published a book of interviews of gay men and lesbians to counter the fundamentalist campaign. It became a best seller in March 2003.

REFERENCES

Altman, D. (1981), *Coming Out in the Seventies*. Boston: Alyson Publications.

Bayer, R. (1987), *Homosexuality and American Psychiatry: The Politics of Diagnosis*, Second Edition, New York: Basic Books.

Bosinski, H.A.G., Kirchhof, P., Nave-Herz, R., Robbers, G., & Rotter, H. (2001), *Eingetragene Lebenspartnerschaft. Rechtsicherheit für homosexuelle Paare— Angriff auf Ehe und Familie* [Registered Domestic Partnership: Offense Against Family and Marriage or Legal Certainty?]. Regensburg: Verlag Friedrich Pustet.

Committee on Families (1992), *Perheet ja laki. Perhetoimikunnan mietintö.* [Families and the Law. Report of the Committee on Families] KM 1992:12. Helsinki: Ministry of Justice.

de Vilette, C. J. (1790), *Les Enfan[t]s de Sodome*. Paris: Chez le Marquis de Vilette.

Finnish Bishops' Statement (1984), *Kasvamaan yhdessä* [To Grow Together]. Helsinki: The Evangelical-Lutheran Church of Finland.

Hausman, K. (2001), Finland's Parliament assesses U.S. reparative-therapy study. *Psychiatric News*, December 21, 36(24):11.

Hentilä, J. (2001a), Memorandum to the Finnish Parliament, April 17, 2001: Claims of the ex-gay movement lack scientific foundation. *FinnQueer Web Magazine,* http://www.finnqueer.net/juttu.cgi?s=68_47_2.

Hentilä, J. (2001b), *Uhattuna pyhä sukupuolijärjestys?* [The holy gender order under threat?]. *Z Magazine,* 201:4.

Kontula, O. & Haavio-Mannila, E., eds. (1993), *Suomalainen seksi* [Finnish Sex]. Juva: WSOY.

Lund, S. & Renna, C. (2003), An analysis of the media response to the Spitzer study. *J. Gay & Lesb. Psychother.,* 7(3):55-67.

Nicolosi, J. (1991), *Reparative Therapy of Male Homosexuality: A New Clinical Approach.* Northvale, NJ: Aronson.

Parkkinen, M-L. (2003), *Ulos kaapista* [Out of the Closet]. Helsinki: Like Kustannus.

Puonti, T. (1995), *Seksuaalinen suuntautuminen on altis muutoksille* [Sexual orientation is malleable]. In: *Syntyjä syviä: Erilaisen homoseksuaalisuuden näkökulma* [Deep Truths: The Perspective of Different Homosexuality]. Vantaa: Painomeklari.

Schroeder, M. & Shidlo, A. (2001), Ethical issues in sexual orientation conversion therapies: An empirical study of consumers. *J. Gay & Lesb. Psychother.,* 5(3/4): 131:166. Reprinted in: *Sexual Conversion Therapy: Ethical, Clinical and Research Perspectives,* eds. A. Shidlo, M. Schroeder & J. Drescher. Binghamton, NY: The Haworth Press, pp. 131-166.

Shidlo, A. & Schroeder, M. (2002), Changing sexual orientation: A consumers' report. *Professional Psychology: Research & Practice,* 33(3):249-259.

Spitzer, R. L. (2003), Can some gay men and lesbians change their sexual orientation? 200 participants reporting a change from homosexual to heterosexual orientation. *Arch. Sexual Behavior,* 32(5):403-417.

Stålström, O. and Nissinen, J. (2003), Homosexuality in Finland: The decline of psychoanalysis' illness model of homosexuality. *J. Gay & Lesbian Psychotherapy,* 7(1/2):75-91.

Turunen, P. (2002), *Homoseksualismi—Rakkautta ja rajoja* [Homosexualism—Love and Limits]. Saarijärvi: Kuva ja Sana.

Ulrichs, K. (1864), *The Riddle of "Man-Manly" Love,* trans. M. Lombardi-Nash. Buffalo, NY: Prometheus Books, 1994.

37

An Interview
with Robert L. Spitzer, MD

Jack Drescher

The *Journal of Gay & Lesbian Psychotherapy* has been publishing a series of biographical interviews of psychiatrists and other mental health professionals who have made important contributions to psychiatric attitudes about gay and lesbian patients and toward enhancing the lives of gay and lesbian therapists. Robert L. Spitzer, MD, has had a profound impact on both groups. As a junior member of the American Psychiatric Association's (APA) Committee on Nomenclature, Dr. Spitzer helped shepherd a process that led to the 1973 removal of the diagnosis of homosexuality from the *Diagnostic and Statistical Manual of Mental Disorders* (DSM).

This chapter appeared originally under the same title in the *Journal of Gay & Lesbian Psychotherapy* 7(3):97-111. Copyright 2003 The Haworth Press, Inc.

Published by The Haworth Press, Inc., 2006. All rights reserved.
doi:10.1300/5503_37

Dr. Spitzer is a professor of psychiatry at Columbia University and chief of the Biometrics Research Department at the New York State Psychiatric Institute. He has achieved national and international recognition as an authority in psychiatric assessment and the classification of mental disorders. He is the author of over two hundred and eighty articles on psychiatric assessment and diagnosis.

In 1974, the American Psychiatric Association appointed Dr. Spitzer to chair its Task Force on Nomenclature and Statistics, and in this capacity he assumed the leadership role in the development of DSM-III,[1] published in 1980, which became the authoritative classification of mental disorders for the mental health professions, not only in this country, but internationally.

In 1983, Dr. Spitzer was appointed to chair the American Psychiatric Association's Work Group to Revise DSM-III and coordinated that effort, resulting in the publication of DSM-III-R[2] in the spring of 1987. He was active in the development of DSM-IV,[3] as a special advisor to the American Psychiatric Association's Task Force on DSM-IV.

Dr. Spitzer has received numerous honors from his professional colleagues. Among these are the American Psychiatric Association's 1987 Adolf Meyer Award for "outstanding contributions to the science and practice of psychiatry." In 1994, he received the American Psychiatric Association's Award for Psychiatric Research for his contributions to psychiatric assessment and diagnosis. In 2000, he was the Thomas William Salmon Medal recipient from the New York Academy of Medicine for "outstanding contributions to psychiatry."

Dr. Spitzer has pioneered in the development of several widely used diagnostic assessment procedures, including the Research Diagnostic Criteria, the Schedule for Affective Disorders and Schizophrenia (SADS) and the Structured Clinical Interview for DSM-IV (SCID). His most recent research efforts have been in the development of the PRIME-MD, a widely used instrument designed to assist physicians and researchers in the recognition and diagnosis of mental disorders in the primary care setting.

JGLP: Where are you from and how did you decide to become a psychiatrist?

DR. SPITZER: I grew up in Manhattan. Actually I was born in White Plains, lived in Scarsdale till I was two, then lived in Manhattan until I went to college at Cornell. I grew up in the 1930s and 1940s and my mother was a big fan of psychoanalysis. She was kind of a chronic outpatient in psychoanalysis. In fact, one of her therapists was Judd Marmor before he moved from New York to Los Angeles.[4] In fact, when I used to meet Judd Marmor every now and then at the APA annual meetings he used to ask "How is your mom doing?"

So the idea of becoming a psychoanalyst seemed naturally what I wanted to do. I went to medical school for that reason. There was a very brief period when I was thinking of internal medicine, but I pretty much always wanted to be a psychiatrist, and specifically a psychoanalyst. I was a psychology major at Cornell and then went to NYU School of Medicine. I did an internship at Montefiore Hospital where they allowed you to take a four to six week elective elsewhere, and I took one at the Psychiatric Institute (PI). I think because of that, and because I had published some articles as a medical student I was accepted into PI as a resident in 1958 and I've really been there ever since. No one's offered me a good job so I've stayed there *(laughs)*. So that's how I got into psychiatry.

JGLP: When you decided you were going to be a psychiatrist and were getting your psychiatric training, who were the people most influential in the development of your own thinking as a psychiatrist and a psychoanalyst?

DR. SPITZER: I was in my second year of residency at Columbia when I became a student at the Columbia Psychoanalytic Center— they've changed the name since then.[5] I started off with Abraham Kardiner as my analyst.[6] I chose him because I felt I needed somebody really experienced if I was going to make any fundamental change. That didn't work out, so I switched to Arnold Cooper, who was, at the time, very influential in my thinking. He had been a supervisor of mine and I saw that he had a very different approach to treating patients than all of my other analytic teachers. Another person who was influential was Will Gaylin. Those were the big teachers for me at the time. Rado had just about finished when I came there. Rado was no longer the Director of the center when I came there.[7]

JGLP: You didn't have any contact with him.

DR. SPITZER: I didn't. I think he gave one or two lectures, but he was pretty much finished.

JGLP: Did you finish your analytic training?

DR. SPITZER: I actually graduated—barely—from the Columbia Psychoanalytic Center.

JGLP: How is that you came to pursue research rather than a career in psychoanalysis?

DR. SPITZER: When I started my residency, my thought was I would do both clinical work and research. The research that interested me was evaluation of treatment. That was what really turned me on. The nice thing about Psychiatric Institute in those days was that they had a lunch room where the staff and the residents ate with the senior research people. They even had nice tables with linen and silverware. There, I became friendly with Joe Zubin, who was head of the Biometrics Research department. When I finished my residency, I started a fellowship with him, and that got me into rating scales, and standardized interview schedules.

But at that time I wasn't that interested in diagnosis, so I got into diagnosis—again by who I met at lunch. One of the people who had lunch at PI was Ernie Gruenberg, a well known psychiatric epidemiologist. This was 1968 and I had been a research fellow Joe Zubin's Biometric Research Department for a few years. One day at lunch Gruenberg said, "I'm chairing a committee that's developing DSM-II.[8] We're almost done. I could use somebody who could take notes and maybe do a little editing. Would you be interested?" I said, "Is there any money involved?" He said, "No." I made a quick decision. I said, "Well, that's not important." As a result of that, I joined his committee and helped edit DSM-II. There's a little introduction to DSM-II that I wrote. So that's how I got into the APA, DSM business.

DR. SPITZER: Then, when DSM-II was finished, the Task Force on Nomenclature kept meeting. They have not been meeting between editions since DSM-III. But in those days, between the first and second editions, there was always a Task Force on Nomenclature that would meet once or twice a year. They wouldn't have very much to do, but they would meet. What they mainly did was answer letters from record room librarians asking things like, "How do I code mental retardation with psychosis?" So I joined the Task Force after DSM-II was completed in 1968. A few years later, I became involved in the homosexuality controversy and that's how I became known to people like Judd Marmor. As a result, in 1974, I was appointed to chair the committee that developed DSM-III.

JGLP: What happened around the homosexuality controversy?

DR. SPITZER: Well, first off, pretty much everybody who was trained in those years took it for granted that homosexuality was not only an illness, but it was a very severe illness. It was considered not just an illness of sexual functioning, but really a widespread personality disturbance. The psychoanalysts at Columbia had a special interest in this area because of Rado, I guess, and some of the people there had written several articles on the treatment of homosexuality. Lionel Ovesey had written about the treatment of homosexuality and also taught that homosexuality had to be distinguished from pseudohomosexuality—the fear that a passive heterosexual might have of being homosexual.[9] So that was the way I saw things as well.

Then, I guess it was around 1972, I was becoming disenchanted with psychoanalysis. I did some clinical work as an analyst, but I never really felt very comfortable doing it. I became interested in a lot of different kinds of nonanalytic psychotherapy. At that time, I was very interested in behavior therapy. There was a meeting of the Association for the Advancement of Behavior Therapy, and they had a symposium on the treatment of homosexuality. They had invited some poor guy from London to come all the way to New York to give a talk. So I'm at this symposium and about ten minutes into it, a group of gay activists[10] started standing up. I don't remember exactly what they said, but essentially what they said was, "This meeting has got to stop! We can't take this anymore. You're pathologizing us!" The chair of the symposium tried to get them to stop, but eventually said, "Okay the meeting is over." The poor guy from London never got to present his stuff (chuckles).

I felt this was pretty awful, breaking up a meeting. I went over to one of the guys demonstrating, Ron Gold, and I introduced myself. It turned out we actually had a friend in common, but I didn't know it at the time. I told him I really thought that it was pretty awful, breaking up the meeting. We got to talking and somehow it came out that I was on this APA Task Force on Nomenclature and Statistics. He said, "Gee, could my group talk to your group?" So I thought, "Gee, that's an interesting idea." So I went back to the committee. The chairman of that committee was Henry Brill, a state hospital administrator. I said there's this group that would like to meet with us. Of course, at this time there was a lot of furor in psychiatry. Gays were saying how terrible things were being done to them by psychiatry pathologizing homosexuality. It was not a new idea that there was some controversy.[11] Brill said, "Okay, let's meet with them and see what happens." We arranged for this meeting, I'm not sure how many of them came. I was talking to Charles Silverstein who remembers it better than I do, since he was at the meeting.[12]

So this group came and gave their presentation, where they essentially said there's no scientific basis for this diagnosis; that terrible things are done to homosexuals. I'm not sure if they said it explicitly, but implicit was the idea that the only way gays could overcome civil rights discrimination was if psychiatry would acknowledge that homosexuality was not a mental illness. So they left the meeting. I don't know how they felt their presentation went over, but when they left Brill turned to me and he said, "Okay Bob, you've gotten us into this mess. Now what do we do?" So I came up with the idea of, "Let's have a symposium." I organized a symposium at that year's APA 1973 annual meeting which was held in Hawaii. If I remember correctly who was on the symposium, it was Robert Stoller, Richard Green, Judd Marmor, Ron Gold, Irving Bieber, and Charles Socarides.[13]

During the several months before this symposium, I started having more contact with Ron Gold and other colleagues of his. It was really the first time that I had any personal contact with people—although I'm sure I had had contact without knowing it—that were openly homosexual. It was quite a different experience for me because they became human people. I started to think what could be done with this? I guess my own feelings were of compassion, wanting to be helpful. At the same time, wanting to do what made sense scientifically. So my own view started to change in terms of basic assumptions. Now, how much of that was a result of true scientific logic? I would like to think that part of it was that. But certainly a large part of it was just feeling that they were right! That if they were going to be successful in overcoming discrimination, this clearly was something that had to change.

I started to think, "Was there some way to resolve what seemed like totally incompatible viewpoints?" On the one hand, there was the traditional view that homosexuality was an illness, a serious illness, which should be treated.[14] On the other hand, there was the argument that it was just normal variation. I like to think that later, when I was working on DSM-III, that I was very good at a kind of nosological diplomacy, in other words, thinking of compromises that could move and resolve a controversy. I started to think, "Okay, psychiatry has never defined mental disorder," and that was now clearly the issue. Of course, in general medicine, there is no accepted definition, but general medicine doesn't really feel a need to have one. But clearly if you're going to have some people saying homosexuality is not a mental disorder, well, then what is a mental disorder?

To answer that question, I said to myself, "Well, why don't you look through DSM-II, look at all the different disorders and ask yourself, is there something that intuitively stands out—something that all these diagnoses share?" As I did that, of course, I'm thinking in the back of my mind, "Is there something that they all share that I can argue does not apply to homosexuality?" Well, what they seemed to by and large all share was that people who had these conditions were usually not very happy about it. They had distress, or if they didn't have distress, in some way the condition interfered with their overall functioning. What was clear was that, where it used to be thought that every homosexual must be dissatisfied with their condition, if you accepted what the activists said, clearly there were homosexuals who were not distressed by being homosexual. Instead, they might be distressed by how people reacted to their being gay.

I concluded that the solution was to argue that a mental disorder must be associated with either distress or general impairment. The reason I said "general" was that you could certainly argue that homosexuals can't function heterosexually. Of course the gays say, "Well, heterosexuals can't function homosexually." So I said "Well, it's not just functioning, it's generalized functioning," and that was around the time when there were several studies showing that if you compared general psychopathology among nonpatient gays in the community and nongays, there weren't many differences. There was also Hooker's study showing no difference in terms of at least obvious psychopathology.[15]

So based on that, one could argue, "Yes, there was some new scientific findings about homosexuals and here's a definition of mental disorder that makes some sense; and based on that, homosexuality should not be in the DSM-II."

When DSM-II came out in 1968, there was no talk of DSM-III. In 1973. what we were actually talking about was successive printings of DSM-II. Every time they would run out of copies, they would print enough to last another six months or so. The issue really was, "Should the next printing of DSM-II have homosexuality in it?" As I assessed the political situation, there was no way that the membership or the APA was going to stand for totally removing the category.

There was also the whole issue of "Can you treat homosexuality? Should you? Is it effective?" I believed in my own mind, that although homosexuality might not be an illness or a mental disorder, if somebody with homosexuality wanted to be treated, there ought to be a way of giving that person some kind of a diagnostic label. I came up with the idea of "sexual orientation disturbance."[16] Part of that was political; I knew that there was no way that homosexuality was going to be removed entirely from DSM-II, but if you had a category where you could say, "Okay, for the homosexual who's dissatisfied, you can still treat it and that's the disorder—sexual orientation disturbance." With that proposal, the Committee on Nomenclature, this small little group, approved removing homosexuality and replacing it with sexual orientation disturbance. The proposal[17] went through several other steps: the Council on Research and Development, to whom our committee answered, the APA Assembly of District Branches, and finally the Reference Committee. That committee[18] sent it along to the Board of Trustees and they voted on it.[19] I don't recall whether it was unanimous, but I think it may have been.[20]

In any case it was approved. Then, as many people know, the group that opposed this included Socarides, Bieber, and colleagues. They organized a petition, because at that time, the constitution of the APA had a provision where if they could get 200 members to sign this petition, you could vote on anything you wanted. They subsequently changed that bylaw (laughs); they don't want that to happen again. So this group initiated a referendum to undo the decision of the Board of Trustees. There was a several month period during which there was heated debate and letters going out, and I became kind of the ring leader of the group, arguing not to allow this referendum to overturn the decision. I worked with the gay group and at one point we had a mailing that went out which they helped fund. The membership voted, and I think it was something like 60 percent in support to 40 percent opposed.[21] Now I'm sure that had the vote been homosexuality in or out, with no compromise category, there was no way that would have passed. So in retrospect, I think that my strategy was very successful.

Now, what I think I have to say is how do I now feel about two things: there's both the decision and the logic of the definition of mental disorder. First of all, as far as the definition of mental disorder, I've given that a lot of thought over the last thirty years. A lot of other people have given it thought, and I would certainly not defend my 1973 definition now because I think it's quite inadequate. Its inadequacies were actually pointed out at the time by the group opposed to removing homosexuality from DSM-II. Bieber said, "Well, what does that mean, you're going to throw out all the paraphilias?" Because certainly some of them are not necessarily associated with distress or impairment. At the time, I really had no answer to that. In fact there was a debate that I had with Bieber that was published in *The New York Times*.[22] It came out just a few days after the 1973 decision. We debated the definition. I must say in retrospect, I think that I would have difficulty with some of his arguments at the present time. Because, for example, recently there's been a move to change the criteria for pedophilia on the grounds that if it does not cause distress or general impairment in functioning, it's not a disorder. Well, I think pedophilia is a disorder whether it distresses you or not. So in terms of the 1973 definition I wouldn't defend it, but I think there's nothing wrong with thinking, thirty years later, that things are a little more complicated than you had originally thought. As far as the 1973 decision itself, I certainly think more people have been helped than have been hurt. I'm proud that I had something to do with it.

JGLP: Fast forward to recent events where you find yourself once again in a controversy surrounding homosexuality.

DR. SPITZER: *(Laughs)* What recent events?

JGLP: How did you get interested in the issue of sexual conversion or as you call it "sexual reorientation" therapy?

DR. SPITZER: It's funny, because in some ways there are interesting parallels. I got into the original 1973 controversy because I was at this meeting where I started to talk to the people breaking up a meeting. In 1999, there was a protest at the APA annual meeting by some ex-gay groups. I don't know exactly which groups, but essentially the religious ex-gay groups. They may have had about thirty or forty people marching in front of the Convention center with signs saying things like, "Homosexuality can be changed. APA is doing terrible things by declassifying it." I started to talk to one of these guys, and he tried to tell me about how he had changed. And, I admit, there is something in me that is always looking for trouble or something to challenge the orthodoxy. After talking to him—and he just talked about himself, I don't remember exactly what he said—I got the idea, "Gee, could it really be that maybe there are some gays that can change?" Now what did I think thirty years ago about treating homosexuality? I'm trying to recall, what was my attitude about the possibility of change? There's one actual fact that says something about my attitude back then. It was probably in the late 1970s or early 1980s. Geraldo Rivera did a television show on whether gays can go straight. I remember Socarides was there. The television producer had called up the American Psychiatric Association. He asked, who could they suggest that would answer Socarides? I was the natural choice. I remember being on this program. Socarides brought a few of his former patients, and there were also some religious ex-gays. I gave the American Psychiatric line, which was that there were only anecdotal reports of change, no real case studies, and it was probably very unlikely that anybody could change.

Anyway, back to 1999. I got the idea, "Gee, well maybe it's not so open and shut about changing sexual orientation." Certainly, the conventional wisdom for many years was that gays could change their behavior, but they're not going to actually change their feelings. That all the gays who claim to change, what they've really changed is how they see themselves. Well, this guy and others claimed that real change of feelings was possible. So I got the idea, "How about having a debate on this?" So I proposed a symposium with myself as Chair and with two people on either side.

About six weeks before the symposium was to happen, the gay side withdrew. Marshall Forstein,[23] who was going to be in the debate, wrote me that he decided not to participate. A few months before the symposium started, it occurred to me that what everybody was going to say was that we don't really have the data to answer the question about the possibility of changing sexual orientation. So I got the idea "Maybe I could actually do a study." So Forstein wrote, "I'm not participating, both because NARTH[24] is using it politically, and also because you clearly cannot be an impartial moderator." So I wrote him back and I said "No problem about me being a moderator, we can find somebody else. The scientific program committee can find somebody else. I don't recall if he answered me, I think he did. So I spoke to the chairperson of the Scientific Program Committee, Rodrigo Muñoz, and I said "Listen, these guys have withdrawn from the debate. That's not fair, you should let the other side present." And he essentially said, "Bob, how can you do this to your career? You must be crazy to do this." He wasn't going to help me, so the debate never happened. NARTH, of course, picketed. They had a press conference at which I appeared. For them I was the big cheese there.

JGLP: They ran a full page ad in *USA Today* attacking the APA.

DR. SPITZER: Yes, and Dr. Laura[25] mentioned "the debate that never was" and she said, "Who do you think withdrew from the debate?" So that's that. So I decided to do this study. I've done it and that's all history.

JGLP: There was not only the issue of the canceled 2000 debate, but also what happened when you presented your preliminary findings in New Orleans the following year at the 2001 APA annual meeting. That drew a lot of media attention.[26] How do you feel doing this study has affected your professional career? How have you been personally affected by the experience?

DR. SPITZER: That's a tough question. I'm glad I did the study. I'm not entirely satisfied with the way I wrote it up and, as you know, I'm now deciding on how to respond to the twenty-five commentators on the study that will appear in the *Archives of Sexual Behavior*. I think the study had value. I try to think, "Why wasn't I able to take a more measured approach?" I think part of it was the study so quickly became politicized. When I first started the study, without really having any data, there was such rage at me from gay colleagues that I think it stiffened my back, which was unfortunate. I got a lot of hate mail. But my career? You know, I'm seventy. I've had a distinguished career *(laughs)*. I mean, people still talk to me. You talk to me, we have lunch together. I regret that I didn't write it up in a more measured way.

JGLP: Is there anything you would say, in a calm moment, without your back up against the wall, to those who would say you have given aid and comfort to the enemy?

DR. SPITZER: Well, there is no doubt about that. I think there's an interesting, what is it, ethical, philosophical issue? I have given aid and comfort to the enemy. I suppose more people were hurt than might be helped, but I believe the study had some scientific value. What do you do in such a case? I think the study does provide some information that is of value which was not there before the study. I think that as a scientist you are entitled to study what you decide is of scientific interest. Also, you never know how many people you're going to hurt or not.

Now one of the main concerns was that the Christian Right is going to use the study to argue, "Okay, this shows that gays can change. Therefore, homosexuality is really a choice. Therefore, they're not entitled to 'special rights.'" I've been interested in how the Christian Right has used this study, and you and I have had this discussion before. In the case of Finland,[27] there was clearly the use of the study to directly say, "We should not legitimize gay civil unions." So there I did the best I could to not let my study be used in that way, and you helped with that. I appreciate that. As far as I can see, I don't see evidence of the same thing happening in America. In other words, in legal issues like the sodomy laws, I don't think the Christian Right, to my knowledge, and I think I would know about it, have used the study to support their political agenda. Now have they used it in a general sense to support their viewpoint? Have they said, "Spitzer, who has some credibility, has shown that gays can change?" Sure they have! There's no doubt about that. But in the more specific use of saying "Okay, this shows a direct connection, gays can change so therefore they should not be given the rights they are asking for," I don't think they've done that.

JGLP: And on the other side, what would you say to people on the conservative religious right?

DR. SPITZER: Well, it's kind of funny. They take pleasure in saying "Spitzer is for gay marriage, he's for gays in the military, so he can't be accused of bias." I mean they kind of take pleasure in that.

JGLP: So what would your response to them be?

DR. SPITZER: As far as I can see, except for the Finland, I don't see how they have used my study. I'm not going to say "You should never mention Spitzer's study."

JGLP: What would you say to them in reference to fighting gay and lesbian civil rights protection?

DR. SPITZER: I've made it very clear to them that I support all those things, gays in the military, and civil unions. You know, in my article my study, one of the things I've been accused of is dismissing the issue of harm. I don't think that's fair. I think in the article it acknowledges there is concern about harm. But that's not what my study is about.

JGLP: What are you working on now?

DR. SPITZER: *(Laughs)* I suppose I'm working on overcoming my block on writing my response to the twenty-five commentaries on my study. *(Laughs)* Of those, the majority are very critical and about ten say, "Unethical, should not be published." "Spitzer has given up scientific objectivity," you know. This is painful. One of the contributors, Milton Wainberg, his article has, I don't know, twenty co-authors.[28] I guess his point is well, what is his point? It's like a petition to denounce me. That's okay.

JGLP: Are you working on any other research projects?

DR. SPITZER: Other research? There is life after this? I'm doing a study of dimensional systems for personality assessment because there's a lot of dissatisfaction with the traditional categorical approach to personality diagnosis. Psychologists for years have been saying that dimensional systems make more sense, but no one has actually done a study to see whether clinicians using dimensional find it more useful. I'm in the middle of that study, and that's kind of fun There's a DSM casebook that has come out for each edition: DSM-III, DSM-R, DSM-IV. There's now going to be a companion casebook where we have big shot clinicians who will write on how they would approach the treatment of thirty-five different diagnoses.

JGLP: And you're going to be a discussant on a panel at the 2003 APA in San Francisco where the presenters argue to remove some other DSM diagnoses.

DR. SPITZER: *(Chuckles)* Paraphilias and GID. It's interesting because the argument about homosexuality is the opening wedge. Their argument is that if homosexuality is not a disorder, why should anything connected with sex be a disorder? I have to come up with some good reasons for retaining these diagnoses. The issue is social constructionism versus essentialism. There's the appeal. These people—transgender, transsexual—all these people who have been treated terribly, just the way the gays have. So if you have any sympathy for these people, "Let's get these diagnoses out of this bloody book." This argument has some intuitive appeal. I was thinking of starting off my discussion by asking the audience to vote on how many of them agree, before they heard me, with the previous speakers. I think that most of the people in that audience will be sympathetic to those speakers arguing for removing these diagnoses from the DSM.

NOTES

1. American Psychiatric Association (1980), *Diagnostic and Statistical Manual of Mental Disorders,* Third edition. Washington, DC: American Psychiatric Press.

2. American Psychiatric Association (1987), *Diagnostic and Statistical Manual of Mental Disorders,* Third edition—*Revised.* Washington, DC: American Psychiatric Press.

3. American Psychiatric Association (1994), *Diagnostic and Statistical Manual of Mental Disorders,* Fourth edition. Washington, DC: American Psychiatric Press.

4. Judd Marmor, MD, a member of the *JGLP*'s Editorial Board, is a Past President of the American Psychiatric Association. In addition to his early scholarly work on nonpathological psychiatric theorizing about homosexuality (see Marmor, J., ed. [1965], *Sexual Inversion: The Multiple Roots of Homosexuality.* New York: Basic Books), Dr. Marmor was also a key figure in the removal of homosexuality from the DSM (see Bayer, R. [1981], *Homosexuality and American Psychiatry: The Politics of Diagnosis.* New York: Basic Books).

5. It is now known as the Columbia University Center for Psychoanalytic Training and Research.

6. Kardiner, A. (1955), *Sex and Morality.* London: Routledge and Kegan Paul LTD.

7. Sandor Rado was the founder of the Columbia Institute (see Roazen, P. & Swerdloff, B. [1995], *Heresy: Sandor Rado and the Psychoanalytic Movement.* Northvale, NJ: Aronson) and a major figure in post-Freudian theorizing about ho-

mosexuality and its characterization as psychopathology (see Rado, S. [1940], A critical examination of the concept of bisexuality. *Psychosomatic Med.*, 2:459-467. Reprinted in *Sexual Inversion: The Multiple Roots of Homosexuality*, ed. J. Marmor. New York: Basic Books, 1965, pp. 175-189 and Rado, S. [1969], *Adaptational Psychodynamics: Motivation and Control*. New York: Science House).

8. American Psychiatric Association (1968), *Diagnostic and Statistical Manual of Mental Disorders*, Second edition. Washington, DC: American Psychiatric Press.

9. Ovesey, L. (1969), *Homosexuality and Pseudohomosexuality*. New York: Science House.

10. The Gay Activists Alliance; see Bayer, *Homosexuality and American Psychiatry*, p. 115.

11. Scasta, D. (2002), John E. Fryer, MD, and the Dr. H. Anonymous episode. *J. Gay & Lesbian Psychotherapy*, 6(4):73-84.

12. Charles Silverstein, PhD, is a member of the editorial board of the *Journal of Gay & Lesbian Psychotherapy*. His account of that meeting, *Are You Saying That Homosexuality Is Normal?*, excerpted from his forthcoming book, *For the Ferryman*, will appear in a future issue of the *JGLP*. Also see, Bayer, *Homosexuality and American Psychiatry*, pp. 117-121.

13. Bayer, *Homosexuality and American Psychiatry*, p. 125.

14. Bieber, I., Dain, H., Dince, P., Drellich, M., Grand, H., Gundlach, R., Kremer, M., Rifkin, A., Wilbur, C., & Bieber, T. (1962), *Homosexuality: A Psychoanalytic Study*. New York: Basic Books, Hatterer, L. (1970), *Changing Homosexuality in the Male*. New York: McGraw-Hill, and Socarides, C. (1968), *The Overt Homosexual*. New York: Grune & Stratton.

15. Hooker, E. (1957), The adjustment of the male overt homosexual. *J. Proj. Tech*, 21:18-31.

16. According to sexual orientation disturbance (SOD) criteria, only those who were "bothered by," "in conflict with," or "wished to change" their homosexuality had a mental disorder. SOD, however, had two significant conceptual problems. First, the diagnosis could also apply to heterosexuals, a solution to APA's internal debate that did not quite concur with clinical reality. There were no reported cases of unhappy heterosexual individuals seeking psychiatric treatment to become gay or lesbian. This overinclusiveness was resolved in the DSM-III where SOD was in turn replaced by *ego-dystonic homosexuality* (EDH). The name change, however, did not resolve a thornier conceptual issue, which was that of making patients' subjective experiences of their own homosexuality *the determining factor* of their illness. To rely upon patient subjectivity alone was now incongruous with the new evidence-based approach that psychiatry was embracing. This ultimately led, in 1987, to EDH being removed from the DSM-III-R.

17. Spitzer R. L. (1973), A proposal about homosexuality and the APA nomenclature: Homosexuality as an irregular form of sexual behavior and sexual orientation disturbance as a psychiatric disorder. A symposium: Should homosexuality be in the APA nomenclature? *Amer. J. Psychiatry*, 130:1207-1216.

18. The Reference Committee was comprised of the chairs of the various APA councils and the president-elect of the APA (Bayer, *Homosexuality and American Psychiatry*, p. 134).

19. December 15, 1973 (Bayer, *Homosexuality and American Psychiatry*, p. 135).

20. There were eighteen APA trustees at the time, three of whom were absent for the vote. At the final vote, thirteen voted to remove homosexuality and replace it with sexual orientation disturbance; none opposed, and two abstained (Bayer, *Homosexuality and American Psychiatry,* p. 137).

21. Of 10,091 psychiatrists voting, 58 percent voted in support of the Board of Trustees, 37 percent opposed the Board's decision, and 3 percent abstained (Bayer, *Homosexuality and American Psychiatry,* p. 148).

22. *The New York Times,* Sunday, December 23, 1973.

23. Marshall Forstein, MD, is a past President of the Association of Gay and Lesbian Psychiatrists and a member of the editorial board of the *Journal of Gay & Lesbian Psychotherapy.*

24. The National Association for Research and Therapy of Homosexuality (NARTH), whose founders include, Charles Socarides and Joseph Nicolosi. "NARTH's primary goal is to make effective psychological therapy available to all homosexual men and women who seek change" (http://narth.com/menus/goals. html).

25. Conservative commentator, Dr. Laura Schlesinger.

26. Lund, S. & Renna, C. (2003), An analysis of the media response to the Spitzer study. *J. Gay & Lesbian Psychotherapy,* 7(3):55-67.

27. Stålström, O. & Nissinen, J. (2003), The Spitzer study and the Finnish parliament. *J. Gay & Lesbian Psychotherapy,* 7(3):83-95.

28. Wainberg, M.L, Bux, D., Carballo-Dieguez, A., Dowsett, G.W., Dugan, T., Forstein, M., Goodkin, K., Hunter, J., Irwin, T., Mattos, P., McKinnon, K., O'Leary, A., Parson, J., & Stein, E. (2003, in press), Science and the Nuremberg Code: A question of ethics and harm. *Arch. Sexual Behavior,* 32(5):455-457.

SELECTED PUBLICATIONS
OF ROBERT L. SPITZER, MD

Spitzer, R.L., Cohen, J., Fleiss, J.L. & Endicott, J. (1967), Quantification of agreement in psychiatric diagnosis: A new approach. *Arch. Gen. Psychiatry,* 17:83-87.

Spitzer, R.L. & Fleiss, J.L. (1974), A re-analysis of the reliability of psychiatric diagnosis. *British J. Psychiatry,* 125:341-347.

Spitzer, R.L. (1976), More on pseudoscience in science and the case for psychiatric diagnosis: A critique of D.L. Rosenhan's "On Being Sane in Insane Places" and "The Contextural Nature of Psychiatric Diagnosis." *Arch. Gen. Psychiatry,* 33:459-470.

Spitzer, R.L., Endicott, J. & Robins, E. (1978), Research diagnostic criteria: Rationale and reliability. *Arch. Gen. Psychiatry,* 35:773-782.

Spitzer, R.L. & Williams, J.B.W. (1987), Introduction. In: *Diagnostic and Statistical Manual of Mental Disorders,* Third Edition, Revised (DSM-III-R). American Psychiatric Association: Washington, DC.

Spitzer, R.L., Gibbon, M., Skodol, A.E., Williams, J.B.W., & First, M.B. (1988), *DSM-III-R Case Book.* American Psychiatric Press: Washington, DC.

Spitzer, R.L. & Williams, J.B.W. (1988), Having a dream: A research strategy for DSM-IV. *Arch. Gen. Psychiatry,* 45:871-875. Reprinted in: *The Validity of Psychiatric Diagnosis,* ed. L. Robins. New York: Raven Press, 1989.

Spitzer, R.L., Severino, S.K., Williams, J.B.W., & Parry, B.L. (1989), Late luteal phase dysphoric disorder and DSM-III-R. *American J. Psychiatry,* 146(7):892-897.

Spitzer, R.L., Williams, J.B.W., First, M.B., & Kendler, K.S. (1989), A proposal for DSM-IV: Solving the "organic/nonorganic problem." Editorial in *J. Neuropsychiatry,* 1(2):126-127.

Spitzer, R.L., Williams, J.B.W., Gibbon, M., & First, M.B. (1992), The Structured Clinical Interview for DSM-III-R (SCID) 1: History, rationale and description. *Arch. Gen. Psychiatry,* 49:624-629.

Spitzer, R.L., First, M.B., Kendler, K.S., & Stein, D. (1993), The reliability of three definitions of bizarre delusions. *American J. Psychiatry,* 150:880-884.

Spitzer, R.L., Yanovski, S., Wadden, T., Wing, R., Marcus, M.D., Stunkard, A., Devlin, M.J., Mitchell, J., Hasin, D., & Horne, R. (1993), Binge eating disorder: Its further validation in a multisite study. *Intl. J. Eating Disorders,* 13:137-153.

Spitzer, R.L., Williams, J.B.W., Kroenke, K., Linzer, M., deGruy, F.V., Hahn, S.R., Brody, D., & Johnson, J.G. (1994), Utility of a new procedure for diagnosing mental disorders in primary care: The PRIME-MD 1000 Study. *JAMA,* 272: 1749-1756.

Spitzer, R.L., Kroenke, K., & Williams, J.B.W. & the Patient Health Questionnaire Primary Care Study Group (1999), Validation and utility of a self-report version of PRIME-MD: The PHQ Primary Care Study. *JAMA,* 282:1737-1744.

Spitzer, R.L. (2001), Values and assumptions in the development of DSM-III and DSM-III-R: An insider's perspective and a belated response to Sadler, Hulgus, and Agich's "On Values in Recent American Psychiatric Classification." *J. Nerv. & Ment. Disease,* 189:351-359.

Index

Page numbers followed by the letter "f" indicate figures; those followed by the letter "t" indicate tables.

Adams, Henry E., 294-295
Adolf Meyer Award, 324
Aftenposten, on Spitzer's study, 312
Age, sexual behavior, 156
Altman, Dennis, 309
Amendment Two, 108
American Academy of Pediatrics, 29, 36
American Counseling Association, 29
American Family Association, 278, 279
American Medical Association, 29, 37
American Psychiatric Association
   Finnish civil unions, 316
   on homosexuality, 3, 4, 14, 23n.5, 30,
      68, 190, 251-252, 277, 311, 323
   New Orleans symposium, 13
   on sexual conversion therapies,
      23n.3, 29-31, 37, 39, 59, 110,
      252, 262
   on sexual orientation change, 134, 148
   Task Force on Nomenclature and
      Statistics, 18-19, 23n.4, 107,
      323, 324
American Psychological Association
   Finnish civil unions, 316
   informed consent, 90
   on recent scientific research, 263
   on reparative/conversion therapies,
      29, 252, 262
   on sexual orientation change, 134
American Psychologist, 84
"Americanize," 121
"An Analysis of the Media Response to
   the Spitzer Study," 21-22,
   277-290

Androgen replacement, 253, 271n.7
"Anti-complaining therapy," 38
Anxiety, behavioral therapy, 156
*Anything But Straight: Unmasking the
   Scandals and Lies Behind the
   Ex-Gay Myth,* 22
Archives of Sexual Behavior, 6
Arnold, Shirley, 314
Aslan, Finland, 314, 316, 318-319n.12
Assessment, Beckstead's study, 75
Associated Press, Spitzer's study, 278,
   286, 288-289, 298
Association for the Advancement of
   Behavior Therapy
   conversion opposition, 266
   electroshock therapy, 291
   treatment symposium, 327
Attraction, 103
Augustine, 167
Aversion therapy
   antihomosexual techniques, 253,
      271n.8
   behavioral technique, 67
   and sexual responses, 154-155, 156

Bayer, Ronald, 15, 16
Beckstead's studies
   sexual reorientation change, 225
   sexual reorientation therapy, 75-80
Spitzer's critique, 56-57
Behavioral activation, 148-149
Besen, Wayne, 22